The Presenter's Fieldbook:
A Practical Guide
Second Edition

The Presenter's Fieldbook: A Practical Guide

Second Edition

By Robert J. Garmston

with Illustrations by
Michael Buckley

Christopher-Gordon Publishers, Inc.
Norwood, Massachusetts

Credits

Every effort has been made to contact copyright holders for permission to reproduce borrowed material where necessary. We apologize for any oversights and would be happy to rectify them in future printings.

Excerpts from

"As training grows shorter, follow-up plays a bigger role," by Robert Garmston,"*JSD* Fall 2003 (Vol. 24, No. 4)

"Triple track presenting," by Robert Garmston, *JSD*, Spring 1996 (Vol. 17, No. 2)

"Anticipating change: Designing a transition meeting," by Robert Garmston,"*JSD*, Fall 2004 (Vol. 25, No. 4)

"Getting to Know You," by Robert Garmston,"*JSD*, Spring 2001 (Vol. 22, No. 2)

"Why Cats Have Clean Paws," by Robert Garmston,"*JSD*, Fall 2003 (Vol. 24, No. 4) reprinted or excerpted with permission of the National Staff Development Council, www.nsdc.org, 2005. All rights reserved.

The Pathways Learning Cycle, pp. 11–12, from Lipton & Wellman (2003), Pathways to Understanding, Sherman, CT. copyright © MiraViaLLC. Used with permission.

Cognitive Coaching is a registered trademark.

Christopher-Gordon Publishers, Inc.
Bridging Theory and Practice
1420 Providence Highway, Suite 120
Norwood, MA 02062
800-934-8322
781-762-5577
www.Christopher-Gordon.com

Printed in the United States of America

10 9 8 7 6 5 4   14 13 12 11

ISBN: 978-1-929024-88-9

Library of Congress Catalogue Number: 2005922993

For
Anika,
Ethan,
Nicole,
Sean,
and the
next
bright and happy
grandchild!

Contents

Preface to the Second Edition

This book is written for any person who has occasion to present to others. This includes the novice and the expert presenter, the teacher sharing expertise with colleagues, the professional developer refining the craft, and the administrator speaking to parents, fellow educators, or a board. Each in his or her own way serves as a guide for transformational learning. Here are some tidbits, tips, and treasures to add to one's presentation repertoire.

A decade has passed since the first edition of this book. The world, even then, was rapidly changing. In 1991, just 3 years before the publication of the first edition, the World Wide Web was created. Now we take it for granted that we can shop at Amazon.com (1994), do searches on Yahoo (1995), or buy on E-Bay (1995). By 1998 Napster had been invented by Boston college student Sean Fanning, and by 1999 the first online university was opened in cyberspace. Technological changes are also finding their way into schools, as are emerging sociological realities.

Today Americans are more security conscious and less naive about global affairs. Many are redirecting their energies to core values. As a people and as educators we yearn to make a greater difference in our lives and positively affect our students, our families, and ourselves. We have more and richer tools with which to do this.

Educational reforms in North America influence and have counterparts in the rest of the world. Educators here and abroad are better informed and more challenged. I have been fortunate to work with schools in 16 countries since writing the first edition. Many of these new experiences are reflected in this book.

Readers of the first edition will find many new topics as well as the elaboration of earlier ideas. Among the fresh topics are speaking to groups with languages and cultures different from your own, tips and traps for PowerPoint, "stealable" examples of presentation strategies, and speaking globally. Also new is a guest chapter by Kendall Zoller, who brings state-of-the-art information on how to use nonverbal skills to lift energy, enhance memory, and improve focus and information flow. Another topic addresses the fact that everyone has a racial identity, and it gives tips for presenters on this topic. Michael Buckley has returned as illustrator and gives practical tips for developing graphics with ease and confidence.

Some of the ideas in this book were first reported elsewhere. They have been published by the National Staff Development Council, the Association for Curriculum and Supervision Development, the Association for Training and Development, or by the Education Department at California State University at Sacramento. Here they appear together—refined, updated, integrated into new material, and organized cohesively by a set of values and assumptions about adult learners and the school organizations in which educators work.

Because many of these writings found their first expression in a personal journal format, the word *I* appears many times. Viewed together in this collection, the frequency of the personal pronoun may seem overdone and self-centered. I hope that readers will overlook this impression, should it surface for them, and interpret the personalization as originally intended: as the candid report of the struggles of one person's continuing journey in learning effective presenting.

This book takes the view that a presentation's greatest importance lies not in the skills and knowledge that participants might gain from a particular session, but in the contribution that those skills, knowledge, and attitudes make to participants' work and the broader dynamics of the work culture. Teachers' thoughts, feelings, decisions, and behaviors are influenced more by the culture of the workplace than by their skills, knowledge, and prior or current training. As the work culture of schools change, so do the schools themselves.

Schools are indeed changing. In communities throughout North America and other parts of the world, schools are adopting new programs, changing assessment protocols, reorganizing schedules, revising curriculum, reinventing instruction, or changing personnel. Faculties are becoming assessment literate, developing professional communities, and learning to work together in high-performance communities to achieve standards, solve problems, and improve learning for all students.

This collection of writings describes how to structure and deliver presentations intended to support such change. Effective presentations honor participants as responsible, growing, autonomous, and interdependent adults. Presentations are a special type of intervention in an interactive and dynamic sea of school change. The presentation ideas described here presume good schools and the best audiences and discuss how to artfully achieve the best for and with them. Such an orientation to presentations helps to put people in touch with their own genius and groups with their own power.

Acknowledgments

In many ways I am like the boy who never grew up and the student who could learn only experientially. Many people have permitted me access to their expertise, been models of premier presenting and gracious staff developers, and given me opportunities to teach, to travel, and to write, as writing is an essential contributor to my learning. To them I am grateful. I am also thankful to the thousands of audience members who continue to help me refine my craft.

Valerie Von Frank and Joan Richardson at the National Staff Development Council (NSDC) have both encouraged and pressed me in the process of refining my writing. Jane Ellison and Carolee Hayes, co-directors at the Center for Cognitive Coaching, remain constant inspirations and models. Bruce Wellman and Laura Lipton of MiraVia write well, think brilliantly, and are premier presenters. Every moment with them is another leg on my journey of learning. Art Costa, partner, colleague, and mentor, continues to amaze and offer new intellectual vistas.

Abroad, directors of overseas schools operations David Chojnacki at the Near East South Asia Council of Overseas Schools (NESA) and Dick Krajczar at the East Asia Regional Council of Overseas Schools (EARCOS) have extended my perspectives at international school conferences and provided opportunities for learning through travel and interaction with remarkable educators. In Kuala Lumpur and earlier in Africa, Bill and Ochan Powell challenged my thinking as we engaged in deep work culture reform in their schools.

I pay tribute to others I have mentioned in this book: Suzanne Bailey, Michael Buckley, Michael Dolcemascolo, John Dyer, Carolyn McKanders, and Kendall Zoller. To Michael Grinder I owe a deep debt of gratitude for opening my eyes to the world of nonverbal communications. There are so many others, and I regret not having the space to list them all.

Closer to home, a special thank you goes to Robin Basten, my administrative assistant, who oversaw the completion of this manuscript, skillfully guided me through edits and revisions, put up with numerous changes, and put up with me. In that department, I also want to recognize Margaret O'Sullivan, whom many remember as my administrative assistant in my office these past 10 years. More than that, she was friend, left brain, right brain, and best brain, cheerfully representing me to others around the globe. She is now supporting her NFL son, J.T., being at as many games as she can manage. Go, Packers!

My deepest appreciation goes to my wife, Sue, who endures my absences, continues to support me, and provides ultimate meaning in my life.

CHAPTER 1

Make a Difference: Present to Transform

*You can change people and organizations
for the better—sometimes immediately.*

Presentations can have deep and lasting transformational significance. They can create, shape, and contribute to personal and group development long after the presentation is over. The ideas in this chapter address this bigger picture, the transforming nature of significant presentations and their defining attributes.

Transformational change can occur in an instant or be the result of reflection on experiences. The most profound learning changes who we are, what we believe are our capabilities, and to what we aspire.

I experienced a transformation during the writing of the first edition of this book. My wife, Sue, and I spent a month in East Africa, most of it in Tanzania. We began in Dar Esalam on the Indian Ocean, working with educators at the International School. From Dar we sailed to Zanzibar, where we were delightfully lost in the ancient sensations, sights, and sounds of a Muslim world of architecture, language, prayer calls, food, and history. Then we flew back to the mainland and this century, where we began an incredible 11-day photographic safari in the Serengeti. We were guests in a Masai village, visited the archaeological site at Olduvai Gorge, which marks the beginning of human life nearly 3 million years ago, and climbed to 15,500 feet on Mt. Kilimanjaro with a guide and four porters. Now I tell my friends that the experience was transforming. What do I mean?

I cannot view the world in the same way again or take life for granted. Now I vividly see what was previously unnoticed. In my own country I am conscious of bird cousins to the flamboyant flamingo, the cory buzzard, the secretary bird, and the lilac-breasted roller, all of which still strut, fly, and preen in my mind's eye. I am filled with awe that lions and gazelles, leopards and wildebeests, predators and prey, should live in such easy distance of one another and that predators, unlike the human animal, are to be feared only when they are hungry. The modern rural Tanzanian knows a way of life so different from ours that it causes me to question mine. The Masai, great keepers of cattle with homes made of brambles and cow dung, whose patterns of living are as unchanged as the migratory movements of the wildebeests following the short-grass plains during the rains, have me wondering who we are in the scope of things. I come from a "taker culture," which ravages the earth's resources for expansion and progress; they live on the land with the rhythms of the seasons, leaving the land as they find it.

Since my trip to Africa, my work has taken me to other settings on 5 continents and 16 countries. I've been privileged to trek in the Himalayas, journey by elephant in Thailand, stay in the homes of hill tribe members in Laos, sail the Yangtze in China, navigate by compass in the Arabian desert, tramp the Amazon jungles, and be silenced in the presence of the temples in Burma. I've witnessed courageous educators in Singapore, Kuala Lumpur, Jerusalem, Bangkok, Cairo, and other cities who work creatively with challenges common to all schools and challenges unique to their settings. Like a character in *Alice Through the Looking Glass*, my perceptions of what is and what can be keep expanding. Also like Alice, I feel increasingly miniaturized in my own importance.

Humans live in a world of their own making, constructed by collective and individual mental models. As the Zander wife-husband team write in *The Art of Possibility* (Zander & Zander, 2000) "It's all invented." Perhaps the greatest gift we can give to one another is the opportunity to look beyond our mindscapes, for any model fixes ways of viewing and imposes constraints and limitations. Our best work with one another is work that transcends current perceptions and self-imposed realities. Michele Pierce, director of the Harriet Tubman Charter School in the Bronx, tells me, "I believe in the exceptional." The exceptional is manifest in her work and in the work of those around her.

Juma was our guide in the Serengeti. I use my experiences with him to introduce and frame a number of ideas in this book. As you first meet Juma, you might think of how important it is for you to know your participants well.

REMEMBER

1. Humans live in a world of our own making—it's all invented.
2. One of the greatest gifts we can give one another is a look beyond our own mindscapes.

Be a Guide

To be an effective guide, teach people to fish.

A guide must be familiar with the territory. Our territory is the culture of learning, in which two goals dominate: modify the workplace culture, and enhance educators' capacites to modify themselves. Adult relationships influence student learning, and teachers working together produce more than teachers working alone (Bryk & Schneider, 2000; Fullan, 2001). The transformational educator is a guide who delivers more than expected. What you do as a presenter influences how people talk and work together.

> ### Notes From a Safari Journal
>
> We met our guide Juma at the Mt. Kilimanjaro International Airport near Arusha. When I commented on how long we would be with him, he said, "We'll get to know each other very well."
>
> Today's professional developer is truly a guide. His or her territory is the culture of learning. Guides and travelers become intimately acquainted, as did Juma and I.

Take trust, for instance. Schools with a high degree of relational trust are more likely to make changes that improve student achievement. Bryk and Schneider (2000) consider relational trust as having four dimensions: respect, competence, personal regard, and integrity. In studies of Chicago schools, they found that schools measuring high on relational trust had a 50% chance of making gains in student learning in reading and mathematics.

In contrast, schools with a low trust index had only a one in seven chance. Tellingly, the few low-trust schools that did improve also improved in relational trust. However, trust by itself is not enough.

As I write this I am working with a school that would rate high on Bryk and Schneider's scale for trust. The leader is loved. People come first. Teachers care for one another. Students are showered with affection and respect and bloom socially and interpersonally in this setting. However, the work culture remains one of solo teaching and relative isolation in professional interactions, which cripple staff and students in terms of higher performance. For this school, creating an island of safety and respect was seen as a necessary first step to learning. Only now are they working to deprivatize teaching and focus together on common goals.

Learning-focused presenters know that the culture of the workplace influences how teachers think about their work and what they do far more than does personal training, prior experience, or degrees. Some time ago a superintendent confided in me that although he supported and encouraged many workshops, study groups, and presentations for his staff, he did not do this so that people would gain more skills and knowledge. Puzzled, I asked why. He replied that these were settings in which people could work with "the best of who they were." Given experiences like this, he said, when the pressure was on, they could work effectively with the "worst of who they are." In other words, they could overcome issues of territoriality, perceptions of scarcity and competition for resources, psychological tensions about change, reality wars about being right, and other disruptive dispositions that might surface during times of challenge. Intuitively, his goal was to modify the workplace culture for cooperation, innovation, and adaptivity.

The various studies about the positive effect of teacher collaboration on student learning are astounding in the common nature of their findings. At each level—elementary, middle, and high school—when teachers regard students as "our kids," not "your students" and "my students," dramatic and systemwide improvements in student learning occur. This is the territory toward which presenters can guide, regardless of the specific topic of instruction. Reflective dialogue, deprivatization of teaching, clear values and norms, collaboration, and a central focus on student learning are contributing factors (Louis, Marks, & Kruse, 1996). Because the medium is the message, how presenters teach can strengthen these factors.

Presenters as guides work toward intangible yet essential attributes, such as what it means to collaborate. Collaboration means working as equals with people of different resources (e.g., role, cognitive style, culture, ethnicity, gender, or age) toward common goals and results.

Dispositions for teamwork cannot be taught, only mediated. There are learnable and teachable skills involved, but the inclination for collaboration is "an inside job" created only by the self. I use the word *taught* here in a narrow sense: to tell, demonstrate, set standards, give lessons, provide feedback, advocate, or preach. To *mediate* means to be in the middle—like a median strip on a highway. By mediate, I mean taking a position between a learner and the learner's experience and with nonjudgmental questions, bringing more of that experience to the learner's awareness. Such awareness, either about events or the learner's reaction to events, is necessary in order for new meanings to be constructed. This is presenter as midwife—between mother and birthing, or between learner and meaning. Midwives are careful to say they "catch" the baby rather than deliver the baby. Theirs is a process of responding in the moment. This is the foundation of teaching thinking skills in classrooms and many mentoring, coaching, and supervising programs, particularly those informed by Cognitive Coaching[SM] (Costa & Garmston, 2002). It also foreshadows a new era in professional development.

REMEMBER

1. A guide must be familiar with the territory—ours is the culture of learning.
2. Transformative presenters know that the culture of the workplace influences teacher thoughts and behaviors far more than personal training, prior experience, or degrees.
3. Trust in schools is essential but not sufficient for student learning.
4. High-trust schools are more likely to make changes that improve student achievement.
5. Transformative presenters enhance teachers' capacity to modify themselves.
6. Dispositions for collaboration cannot be taught, only mediated.

You and the New Professional Development

You make the greatest difference when you
influence groups, not individual teachers.

Anton Chekhov, the Russian playwright, said that any idiot can deal with a crisis; it's the day-to-day living that gets most people down.

What is it that's tough about providing effective professional development? What might you like to see stopped, continued, or started?

In the "good old days" (Don't you love that term? It implies things were simpler and better.) Staff development, especially presentations, were treated like an event. A presenter could work hard, plan carefully, rehearse, and provide exquisite presentations. These presentations would either motivate (Remember the back-to-school teacher institutes with a speaker?) or instruct. Many were quite good; they drew design principles from specific models of teaching and were presented congruently with the best that was known about adult learners.

For all their brilliance (for many presentations were), they were mostly episodic. As Chekhov infers, the challenge is what happens after the presentation. Today, implementing, monitoring, and follow-through are recognized as legitimate concerns for professional developers and leaders, and the context of learning has become important as well—improve the workplace culture and the capacity of teachers to modify themselves.

Teacher-needs assessments were used to determine what would be offered. The primary aim of staff development was to develop individual teachers. Project mentality drove decisions. (Project mentality means that when funding stops, professional development ends.) Teachers were seen as independent cogs in an instructional delivery system. Improve the units, and better learning would result, was the reasoning.

We must not lose focus on the individual teacher, for the most important factor affecting student learning is the teacher (Marzano, 2003). However, the workplace culture exerts the dominant influence on what teachers do (Wright, Horn, & Sanders, 1997), so how can professional development affect the group and the teacher simultaneously? For you as professional developers, the question becomes how do we affect the behavior of groups of teachers toward collaborative quests for improvement, common goals, common curriculum, and pedagogy? The challenge for professional development has always been how to affect individual teacher performance. Today we know that it is through collaborative efforts in schools that teachers' behaviors change.

District-coordinated efforts in professional development have value. The trend focuses on interpreting and using data, building teacher knowledge and skills, aligning curriculum and instruction, and directing interventions to low-performing students and schools. Much of this work is organized and delivered at the school level (Massell, 2000).

Gone—or at least going—are the days when professional development programs were composed of a menu of topics garnered from teacher needs or interest assessments.

Pritchard and Marshall (2002) find that the most effective focuses for learning are first on district purposes and only second on individual selection. However, the most important dimension of the new professional development is an expectation that professional development is a responsibility for every employee.

Although dispositions can only be midwifed, skills and structures for professional collaboration can be taught. The best news is not that student learning improves in collaborative work cultures more than in schools in which the work culture is one of solo teaching; the best news is that teacher development is greater in collaborative systems, leading to even greater efforts for students. Studies in the cognitive sciences assure us that adults can continue to develop, not just in gaining knowledge or skills but also in the capacity for problem solving, moral reasoning, ego states, and self-directed learning. In some schools this is more evident than in others.

Four leadership functions, operating in orchestration, help groups to make impressive gains toward these goals.

REMEMBER

1. Teacher-needs assessments used to determine what professional development opportunities would be offered.
2. The old "staff development" focused on individual teachers rather than the group.
3. The new "professional development" asks how to affect the group and the teacher within the group.
4. The new professional development is the responsibility of every employee.
5. Although dispositions for professional collaboration can only be mediated, the skills and structures can be taught.
6. Adults continue to grow cognitively in collaborative cultures, but not as much (if at all) in school cultures of teacher isolation.

Wear Four Professional Hats

Define the hat you wear to get the response you intend.

Four professional development "hats" are used to support teachers and schools moving toward self-directed learning, the thrust of the new professional development. As I was learning from Juma, a guide must sometimes give directions, sometimes inquire, at other times advise, and sometimes move to create safety. In our work, professional developers perform four primary functions: presenting, coaching, facilitating and consulting (Garmston & Wellman, 1999). Most people who present also perform several of these functions. I describe them here for two reasons. First, it is useful to have common terminology for what we do and therefore for what others expect of us. Often today, for example, the terms *facilitate* and *present* are used interchangeably, which is incorrect. Second, although there is a unique knowledge and skills-set to each role, there is also a large domain of concepts and skills common to all. Become a better presenter, and much of your confidence and competence will transfer to the other roles.

The four functions, or "hats" are described below.

Notes From a Safari Journal

More on being a guide:
Juma does things for us at the beginning of the trip—raising and lowering the viewing roof and the stepping plate to enter and exit the Land Rover. Then either I do it or he asks if I would. Later I volunteer: "Juma, if you stop the car, I'll pull the top down." When what I do is incomplete, he advises, "Lift up a little and pull down hard." He inspects to see that it is right.

He spots a cheetah and takes us to it. Later we head toward a moving figure. "What do you think it is?" asks Juma. "A big cat," I offer. "Is movement off the rocks," he clarifies. "Cheetah went from rock into grass." I get about three 200 mm pictures of the cheetah then nearly a roll of 500 mm as it lay in the grass, got up, and walked away.

Later, we see a cheetah hunting a wildebeest. Juma got the Land Rover in between the two for best positioning in case there was an attack. The cheetah circled; the wildebeest watched and kept distance; the herd to the right and down the slope saw the cheetah and ran.

Later, we see a male lion alone, lying in a field near zebras. It is panting hard, and there are lots of flies. Juma is silent.

Later, on the Kopjes, we see four or five lions on the rocks in the grass.

Presenting

To present is to teach. A presenter's goals are to extend and enrich knowledge, skills, or attitudes and to have these applied in people's work. A presenter may adopt many stances—expert, colleague, novice, or friend—and use many strategies of presentation—facilitation, lecture, cooperative learning, study groups, and many more. Premier presenters are guided by clarity of instructional outcomes and continual assessment of goal achievement.

Coaching

Since the turn of the century, the term *coach* has taken on many meanings. At the time of this writing, Barnes and Noble lists 5,001 books with *coach* in the title. Categories include athletics, motivation, personal growth, business executives, work performance, mentoring, parenting, spirituality, anxiety and depression, facilitation, and childbirth, to name a few. Some models are informed by behaviorist psychology, some by a humanist orientation, some by constructivist theory and cognitive psychology, and some by an amalgamation of these.

I use the term *coach* to describe a person who serves as a midwife to another's perceptions, decisions, and cognitive development. In this model, a coach helps another person to take action toward his or her goals while also helping to develop expertise in planning, reflecting, problem solving, and decision making. A coach is nonjudgmental and uses the tools of open-ended questions, pausing, paraphrasing, and probing for specificity. These same tools are also used in presentations. A skillful coach focuses on the perceptions, thinking, and decision-making process of the other person to mediate resources for self-directed learning (Costa & Garmston, 2002).

Facilitating

To facilitate means to make easier. A facilitator is one who conducts meetings in which the purpose may be dialogue, shared decision making, planning, or problem solving. A facilitator helps the group to get its work done but, unlike a presenter, maintains neutrality toward the content. A facilitator directs the procedures to be used in the meeting, choreographs the energy within the group, and maintains a focus on one content and one process at a time. A facilitator should not usually be the person in the group with the greatest role or knowledge authority. A presenter might use facilitation concepts and skills in the delivery of instruction—which potentially could lead to confusion between the two roles (Garmston & Wellman, 1999). Facilitators are servants of the group, whereas presenters are teachers.

Consulting

Juma tells me to lift up and pull down hard, allowing his expertise to be used by me. A consultant can be an information specialist or an advocate for content or process. As an information specialist, a consultant delivers technical knowledge to another person or group. As a content advocate, a consultant encourages the other party to use a certain strategy, adopt a particular program, or purchase a specific brand of equipment or materials. As a process advocate, a consultant attempts to influence the client's methodology. Like a presenter, a consultant brings expertise to the table. As we shall see later in this chapter, it is often important for a presenter to be a consultant first, before providing presentation services.

All "hats" play parts in supporting faculties as they work together for improvement in student learning. In the best schools, each of these hats is worn by many people who share leadership and responsibility for school success. These schools are transformative, having the essential resources to change themselves.

In the next section we will define transformation and examine how presentations can stimulate it.

REMEMBER

1. Professional developers perform four primary functions: presenting, coaching, consulting, and facilitating.
2. Presentation and facilitation are different functions with different goals and should be called by different names.
3. To present is to teach.
4. To coach is to midwife thinking and internal resources for excellence.
5. To facilitate is to make a group's work easier.
6. To consult is to allow your expertise to be used by others.
7. In transformational schools, all the players wear all the hats.

Transform by Presenting

Think how hard it is to change yourself.
Imagine how hard it is to change others.

What do you envision for an audience with which you work? What strategic approaches might make it more likely that your groups can achieve exceptional heights?

Notes From a Safari Journal

Yesterday, from the rim of Ngorongoro Crater, Juma pointed out elephants some 3,000 feet below. We could barely make out dark shapes against the green fields. Later, we too can see elephants from a distance—not from quite as far away, but farther than we'd ever imagined possible or useful. Now Juma adds distinctions and details: These are male, those are female; those trees have the bark rubbed off by the elephants; and he tells us their more common name—Elly.

Like Juma, guides become more explicit and detailed as a journey develops. Their presentations are tuned to broad, long-range perspectives as well as immediate and detailed goals. Transformational presentations modify the perspective

or capacities of audience members. I've come to think that transformational presenters operate much like Juma did, intuitively or consciously utilizing certain
macromaps as starting points. Three macromaps will be explored here: four audiences, nested levels of learning, and audience empowerment.

A macromap looks at the long view, the large picture, in order to understand
the entire territory and plot reasonable destinations and routes. It is also a way of
looking at the territory through certain lenses. On a backpacking trip, for example, the macroview allows the hiking planner to see the boundaries of the
wilderness region, the two or three major established trails that may exist in the
area, the distance in miles (but not in perspiration or fatigue) between two points,
and the valleys, rivers, meadows, and mountains that make up the area. It is only
from this comprehensive picture of the terrain that the hiker can set overall goals
for the trip. This is so because once one is on the forest trail, visibility is reduced
to the bend ahead, and aspirations can be diverted by emotional and physical
fatigue. Unexpected events like a blistered foot or temptations like an idyllic
stream encountered near high noon can take the hiker off course. It is knowing
the whole map that allows the traveler to flexibly engage with these distractions
yet still achieve intended outcomes.

Like the hiker, presenters with conscious access to their macromaps can make
decisions during the presentation that are congruently related to the large picture. They can seize opportunities, which would go unrecognized without the
maps, to move a group toward envisioned destinations. Three macromaps that
guide the work of premier presenters will be discussed here: (a) Each audience
contains four sub-audiences, (b) learning accelerates at higher levels on an intervention taxonomy, and (c) efficacy facilitates personalized learning, transfer, and
application (Figure 1-1).

Presenters apply knowledge of these maps by speaking to four audiences to
get their message heard and learned, leveraging presentation time to transform
the power of their work, and empowering audiences as the ongoing subtext of
their message.

Figure 1-1. The Three Macromaps

Guides Carry These Maps
☑ Four audience species: habits and marking
☑ Nested levels of learning
☑ Efficacy is a road to learning, transfer, and application

Four Audiences

I once watched a performer in a Beirut nightclub present to an audience whose
members spoke Arabic, French, or English. Like the carnival performer who spins
a series of plates on sticks, this trilingual performer balanced his time in the three

languages, being careful not to spend too much time in, for example, French, because the English and Arabic speakers might feel left out and grow bored.

In a similar manner, because of audience learning-style preferences and variations in the ways in which people take in and process information, premier presenters target four different audiences in each presentation.

The presenter designs each session, and each segment within a session, to attend to four audience types: the "professors," the "friends," the "inventors," and the "scientists." As shown in Figure 1-2, these groups are primarily concerned with answering different questions. These are, respectively, what, so what, what if, and why.

What? The "professors" value data and expect the presenter to be an authority. They appreciate handouts, bibliographies, a sequentially arranged agenda, and structure. Seating arrangements that signal a lecture are pleasing.

So What? The "friends" might enjoy entering a room with round tables or seating in a circle because these signal that interaction will occur in the session. They will appreciate an opening mixer that allows them to meet others and will probably value wearing name tags.

What If? The "inventors" may appreciate an agenda displayed as a mind map (this may drive the "professors" crazy). They enjoy colorful charts and synectic exercises, particularly as openings. Synectics is an approach to solving problems based on the creative experience of people from different areas of experience or knowledge. Synectic exercises often involve a small group using metaphor or analogy to describe something or solve a problem. For example, a small group might answer this question: "Teaching to standards is like what sporting event, and why?"

Why? The "scientists" will value agendas that are organized around questions central to the topic and handouts that provide space for reflection and inquiry.

Skilled presenters warm the stage for each of these audiences prior to a presentation and attend to these four styles within the opening minutes and throughout the presentation. They may do this at first by informally saying hello to participants before the presentation begins and by including in the opening a brief self-introduction that establishes the presenter's credentials on this topic, a relevant story, a few figures or facts, and an opportunity for participants to talk with one another. Within the space of a few minutes, the presenter has connected with each of the audience styles. Unless one is presenting to a highly specific subset of the profession, such as technology experts or drama teachers, most audiences will be mixed, and a skilled presenter will watch carefully to maintain a balance throughout the rest of the presentation. After a session, they read the evaluations to learn which groups they served well and which felt unattended. Not surprisingly, presenters tend to do best with audience members most like themselves and are least effective with the group least like themselves. Taken in this light, the participant evaluations become a valuable self-coaching tool. Scan for comments from a group you might be missing. Make corrections in your next presentation.

Figure 1-2. The Four Audiences

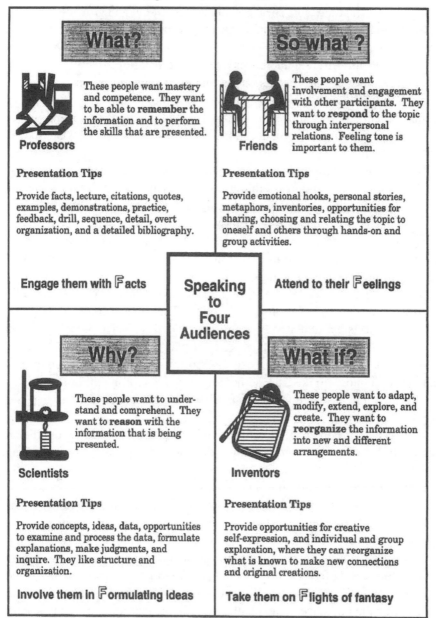

What?

Professors

These people want mastery and competence. They want to be able to **remember** the information and to perform the skills that are presented.

Presentation Tips

Provide facts, lecture, citations, quotes, examples, demonstrations, practice, feedback, drill, sequence, detail, overt organization, and a detailed bibliography.

Engage them with 𝔽acts

So what ?

Friends

These people want involvement and engagement with other participants. They want to **respond** to the topic through interpersonal relations. Feeling tone is important to them.

Presentation Tips

Provide emotional hooks, personal stories, metaphors, inventories, opportunities for sharing, choosing and relating the topic to oneself and others through hands-on and group activities.

Attend to their 𝔽eelings

Speaking to Four Audiences

Why?

Scientists

These people want to understand and comprehend. They want to **reason** with the information that is being presented.

Presentation Tips

Provide concepts, ideas, data, opportunities to examine and process the data, formulate explanations, make judgments, and inquire. They like structure and organization.

Involve them in 𝔽ormulating Ideas

What if?

Inventors

These people want to adapt, modify, extend, explore, and create. They want to **reorganize** the information into new and different arrangements.

Presentation Tips

Provide opportunities for creative self-expression, and individual and group exploration, where they can reorganize what is known to make new connections and original creations.

Take them on 𝔽lights of fantasy

Adapted from the "Thoughtful Education Model" developed by Hanson, Silver Strong Associates, Morristown, NJ.

Nested Levels of Learning

Given the recognition that you most usually work with several audience types, what else might you consider to get maximum results? Regardless of your topic, you can deliver more than expected by directing your presentation energies where they will produce the most growth.

Anthropologist Gregory Bateson first formulated the notion of relating systems of learning to human growth. Later Robert Dilts (1994) applied this form of systems thinking to seminars and presentations. The major concepts are as follows:

1. Any system of activity is a subsystem embedded inside another system. This system is also embedded in an even larger system, and so on.
2. Learning in one subsystem produces a type of learning relative to the system in which you are operating.
3. The effect of each level of learning is to organize and control the information on the level below it.
4. Learning something on an upper level will change things on lower levels, but learning something on a lower level does not necessarily inform and influence the levels above it.

The last two points offer great promise in presenting. Once we know the arrangement of systems and subsystems related to learning, we can strategically design our presentations and processing questions to intensify seminar benefits.

Bateson identified four basic levels of learning and change. As shown in Figure 1-3, each level is more abstract than the one below and has a greater degree of impact on the individual.

Figure 1-3. Nested Levels of Learning

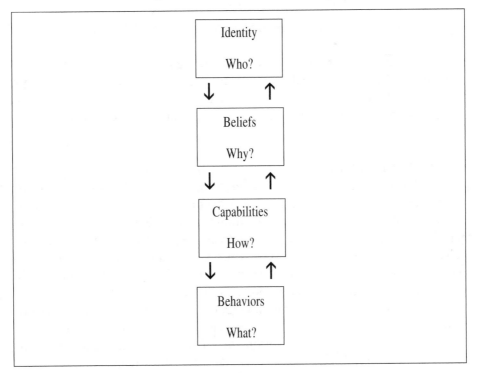

Identity

On the day my son Kevin became a father, everything changed for him and for those around him. Perhaps the transformation was in process just before Sean's birth, but we could all see it when Sean was born. Kevin set aside those activities that would interfere with time for Sean. After-school coaching went—not reluctantly but with satisfaction. With a shift in identity to father, Kevin's values shifted, his beliefs reshaped, and his mental capabilities strengthened to take on behaviors he now wanted to do. Such is the power of changes in identity. Behavior patterns can be instantly redirected. Kevin's discretionary attention turned full-time to his new son.

The level of identity is about who I sense myself to be. Who I am relates to what mission I perceive is mine and how I go about achieving it. All our perceptions of ourselves, others, and the environment flow from this sense of identity. This is true for groups and individuals. To observe how this works, consider anyone you know who has transitioned into a new role—professional developer, principal, teacher association leader—and notice some of the corresponding values and behavioral shifts that accompanied that transition almost immediately.

Teachers might view themselves as artists, technicians, dispensers, or facilitators of student learning. How they think, what they believe, and what they do will be congruent with whatever identity they hold.

Presentation approaches that affect identity are often associated with repeated experiences over time. A central goal of Cognitive Coaching[SM] seminars, which are organized in 8 days of training over several months, is to develop the skills and identity of a mediator. A mediator is one who is a midwife to another's cognitive development. We often hear participants say that the experience has been life changing.

Other presentation approaches involve writing prompts. "Who are you in *X* situation?" "Who do you need to be for maximum effectiveness?" "If your life were a story, how would you as the main character be described?" Have groups ask themselves the following: "Who are we?" "About what do we care?" "How much do we dare?"

Beliefs and Values

The level of beliefs is about values and belief systems. Values are our internal guidelines for what is good, bad, worthy, or unworthy. Beliefs are ideas or concepts that we hold to be true. In addition to developing behavioral skills and capabilities, a training program must address the presuppositions, beliefs, and values of the participants. The way in which some learning fits (or does not fit) into the personal or cultural value systems of individuals within the group will determine how it will be received and incorporated.

Beliefs have to do with permission. Participants grant themselves permission to engage in new behaviors. For example, when a teacher begins to believe that students can learn more by working together than working alone, he or she will be motivated to learn and apply the ideas and skills related to cooperative learning. When presenters engage participants in exploring their beliefs related to a topic, when they use metaphors to indirectly suggest a topic-appropriate useful belief structure, when they offer data that support a belief in a practice—such as cooperative learning—when they ask questions that cause beliefs to be challenged, and when they invite participants to examine situations from the perspectives of others, they are intervening at the level of beliefs. Interventions at this level provoke greater changes than training directed at the levels of capabilities or behaviors.

Presenters also intervene at the level of beliefs when they offer opportunities for participants to challenge their assumptions and their understanding of a topic. All learners come to the learning situation with preconceived beliefs. My friend and colleague Laura Lipton tells about a kindergarten child who reported that red leaves are heavier than green ones because they fall first from the tree! Because humans absorb new information in ways that reinforce their current understanding, some of their prior understanding will enhance learning and some will interfere. Activating prior knowledge and examining misconceptions can surface and resolve such impediments to learning.

A classic film that demonstrates this phenomenon is *Project Star: A Private Universe* (Scheps & Saldler, 1992). Harvard graduates were asked on their graduation day, "What causes the seasons?" Of about 24 people interviewed (including a science major), only one was able to answer the question correctly. For these bright and educated people, early misunderstanding about the tilt of the earth as it orbits the sun, the varying distances between the earth and the sun, and other ideas had dominated and shaped all new information they had learned on this topic. Interventions at the level of values and beliefs provoke greater changes than training directed at either the levels of capabilities or behaviors. For more information on how misconceptions inform learning, see the *Private Universe Project: What Are Your Ideas?* (Annenberg, 2004).

Capabilities

Capabilities are about mental strategies and maps used to guide behaviors. Behaviors without some form of mental map to guide them are like kneejerk reactions or rituals. The richer the mental maps, the more understanding there will be about under what condition to use a behavior, ways of assessing the behavior's effectiveness, and the processes for self-monitoring. The more understanding there is, the richer the choice points will be. To elegantly perform an activity or a behavior requires learning at the level of capability. It is at this level, I believe, that we can teach for transfer. Transfer, says David Perkins (1995),+ is stimulated by helping people to reflect and process abstractions and connection making.

Behaviors

Identifying characteristics of at-risk children, distributing student response opportunities more equitably, using a credible voice to get class attention, becoming a better listener, identifying a dependent clause, and learning to wait after asking students a question are all examples of behavioral-level training objectives. Presentation goals at this level are low on Bloom's taxonomy (Bloom, Englehart, Furst, Hill, & Krathwahl, 1956) of the cognitive domain and are expressed as the attainment of knowledge or skills. They contribute least to transformational growth yet are necessary building blocks for effective performance.

Ask Taxonomy Questions

Charles Shultz's cartoon character Charlie Brown once said that he taught his dog to do tricks but the dog didn't learn. We've discovered some truth in that when working with Cognitive Coaching[SM] and Adaptive Schools seminars—if we want participants to achieve behavior change, we must teach, simultaneously, at levels above behaviors. To do this, we focus participants' attention on higher levels than the behavior being taught. Thus, when we teach a skill like getting the attention of a class, we have the participants review capabilities—the decisions they will make—such as where and how to stand, what voice tone to use, and what to say, before the actual practice. The questions in Table 1-1 focus participants at various levels of the map. They each presume that paraphrasing is the skill being learned. Persist with this type of processing to intensify learning.

Table 1-1. Processing Questions

The Skill (Behavior) Being Taught	Sample Processing Questions
Paraphrase	What strategies did you employ to set aside your own autobiographical listening? (capability)
Paraphrase	How did you know your responses were useful? (capability)
Paraphrase	Why did you choose to paraphrase? (beliefs)
Paraphrase	Why does paraphrasing seem to be important to you? (values)
Paraphrase	How does paraphrasing relate to your image of yourself as a professional educator? (identity)

The literature is full of behavioral prescriptions to help teachers engage in complex endeavors like getting students to compare and contrast, use wait time, or organize cooperative learning lessons. Educators always have a list of skills to be mastered: focusing on key ideas, maintaining rapport, planning with the end in sight, collecting success indicators, and managing the classroom. If, like me, you worry that we inservice each other on the least important parts of these endeavors (behaviors) without sufficient attention to the catalytic glue that makes the parts come together for the whole, I invite you to experiment with strategically working with nested levels of learning.

The good news is that we do know how to teach behaviors. The challenge and the promise is to strategically offer processing questions at levels of abstraction above the level we are teaching in order to accelerate and deepen learning.

Transformational presentations regard these levels of intervention as "nested"; that is, influencing one level will automatically modify the levels below. Transformational presenters ask themselves, "How can I teach behaviors in ways that can affect capabilities, beliefs, and identity?"

As a postscript to this discussion of intervention levels, Dilts (1994) points out that there is a level of influence higher than identity. This is a sense of mission, not in the organizational sense, but in the spiritual sense. You may notice for yourself, and with those around you, that when there is a sense of connection to that which is larger than you, you are in touch with an ultimate guidance system.

Empower Audiences

Arnold Schwarzenegger, Hollywood actor and body builder, was swept into the California governor's office after a recall vote for the previous governor, Gray Davis. Interviewed early in his occupancy of that office, Schwarzenegger was asked to assess his strengths and weaknesses as governor. He said that there is a lot to learn, it's complicated, and it's a huge learning process for him. Then he added, "But my determination and will and my positive attitude and knowing that things can be fixed is so big that it overshadows by far the lack of the details of the knowledge I still need" (Weintraub, 2004).

The "governator" was referring to efficacy—our third macromap, related to people feeling empowered. Efficacious people work harder than those who are less efficacious, and they are more successful. I will have more to say on this important concept later.

The best presenters consistently aim to assist audiences in reaching a realization of empowerment, and central to this is a sense of efficacy. This state of mind contributes to a sense of personal identity that is capable of taking charge and producing results. Appendix A describes five states of mind that constitute a powerful macromap.

Efficacy is knowing that one can make a difference. Efficacious teachers know that if they apply their professional knowledge they can overcome almost any obstacle. To be efficacious is to regard oneself as the driver rather than the passenger in life (Bandura, 2001; Enderlin-Lampe, 2002). Efficacious teachers persevere through difficulties. They seek to understand multiple causes for instructional problems, come up with alternative solutions, and find the resources necessary to take action. It is interesting to note that efficacious teachers also experience less stress than more externally controlled teachers (Figure 1-4).

Presenters encourage efficacy with a number of subtle moves. They provide choice: where to sit, how long the break should be, what personal goals to work on, whom to pick as a partner, how to approach a small-group task, and which homework suggestions to pursue. In most settings they do not repeat a group member's question or comment so that others can hear. Rather, they establish at the beginning that when one cannot hear, participants should say, "Louder, please." When you sense that a contribution is not being heard, you look toward the back of the room and ask if people can hear the speaker. If the answer is no, you say, "What do you say when you can't hear?", placing the responsibility for taking care of oneself in the hands of the participants.

Figure 1-4. Benefits of Efficacy

When teachers are efficacious, they . . .

◆   are more successful

◆   experience less stress

◆   are optimistic

◆   display more common sense

◆   are more flexible

◆   have students who learn more and are more cooperative

Presenters also consistently use language that presupposes the existence of a state of efficacy: "As you decide what's most important to you . . ."; "As experienced educators . . ."; "As you tell others what you have learned from this day . . ." "As you recall previous successes . . ."; "Knowing that you are busy people and that you intend to produce as much value for yourself as possible today . . ."; "As you examine your strengths . . ."; and so on.

Presenters avoid giving directions with the following language: "What I want you to do next . . ."; "I'd like you to . . ."; "I have designed this activity so that . . . ." Instead they use phrases like "The benefit to you in this activity is . . ." or "For you, the major value in this idea is . . . ." Put the focus on the learner, not on what you want the learner to do for you! I learned this from Claudette Landry, an associate trainer for Adaptive Schools.

Efficacy is enhanced when participants shape agendas, teach others, control their own learning goals and environment, and look at their own behavior from the perspective of choice. Presenters promote this viewpoint when they respond to statements such as "There's just too much to cover, and not enough time" with language that reminds the participants that despite existing environmental constraints, they always maintain choice—for example, "So you're in the process of deciding which portions of the curriculum are most important for your students."

Because educational goals are achieved through groups of people, it makes sense to speak to each person in the way that allows him or her to learn best; to promote awareness of personal identities that are caring, collaborative, and successful; and to continually shape efficacy in ourselves, our audiences, and our students. It is the hiker who knows that he or she can complete the journey who does so; it is the traveler who knows the territory who attains the outcome and enjoys the trip.

The next section will explore ways to give gifts to empower groups.

REMEMBER

1. Like a hiker, presenters with conscious access to three macromaps can make decisions during the presentation related to long-range and overarching goals.
2. Because of variations in learning style preferences, presenters assume—and teach to—four different audience types.
3. Regardless of your topic, you can deliver more than expected.
4. Learning something on a higher level in the taxonomy of nested learning will automatically influence learning on lower levels.
5. All perceptions of ourselves, others, and the environment flow from our sense of identity.
6. An ultimate goal is to help audiences realize they are empowered—provide access to efficacy, consciousness, and interdependence.
7. Efficacious teachers work harder, persevere longer, and are more successful and less stressed.

Make Your Presentation a Gift

In presenting, it is better to give than to receive,
for the receivers give back to you.

I first met Lucy in Shanghai. She was to be our guide while we were in China. Her first gift to us was telling us to be careful about the "one dollar people" who would greet us each time we disembarked from the bus, wave goods at us and shout, "One dollar! One dollar!" Anything they were selling for a dollar, she told us, we could get for half that amount. Her second gift was teaching us some Chinese phrases. I watched her throughout the trip, learning a great deal about presenting from this frenetic and unlikely teacher.

Presentations can be gifts. This is an important achievement in presentations that seek to transform, because gifts bring an audience and a presenter together in special ways. A relationship emerges in which personalization and caring prevail. The audience is signaled, "I know who you are, I care for you, and I have selected something specifically for you."

I learned this concept first from working with John Grinder of Grinder, DeLozier Associates, and later from watching and working with presentation virtuoso Suzanne Bailey. I've learned to apply this concept in practical ways during a presentation or workshop.

In the verb *to present* lives the inference that three entities exist: (a) a presenter (one who presents), (b) a present (an action, or that which is being presented), and (c) a presentee (the receiver). A presenter, then, is one who brings a present.

Consider the attributes of an exemplary presentation. It is personal, selected specifically for you; it is communicated about and perhaps received within an aura of suspense; it is attractively wrapped; and it is useful.

The Best Gifts Are Personal

Consider the best gifts you have received. It's likely that in each case, regardless of cost, it was special because it was something picked exclusively with you in mind; not just any blouse or shirt, cologne, or card, but one that's "you," specially suited to your interests and tastes. This first attribute is related to the three rules for effective presenting, as espoused by so many authorities: (a) Know your audience! (b) Know your audience! (c) Know your audience! Presenters who apply this first attribute customize presentations for the specific audience they are addressing. To customize requires knowledge about the group. With just a little effort, you can do the research necessary to personalize your presentation through customizing your comments about the time, the place, the circumstances, or yourself.

Figure 1-5 shows four examples of customizing comments that don't take a lot of preparation. Of course, anything you say to personalize your presentation must convey respect for the audience. An attorney once opened a presentation to teachers by saying, "I always wanted to be a teacher." That seems like a good start in making a connection with the audience, doesn't it? "But," the speaker went on to say, "when I found out how much money teachers make and how much attorneys make, I changed my mind." That comment also changed the rapport that was beginning to build with the audience—for the worse. This is not the kind of personal reference you want to use.

Make a presentation personal by learning who the group is and what they are about before you present. Request copies of newsletters, staff memos, mission statements, or statements of practice or policy to give you a deeper understanding of the values, events, and issues important to the group. Search for phrases that appear several times and use them. I often have a phone conversation with several of the participants to learn about their expectations and concerns.

Kendall Zoller, an expert in nonverbal skills whom you will meet in chapter 4, and I are designing a course for police officer instructors. Our charge is to improve the quality and effectiveness of instruction given to both novice and experienced officers. In this case, to learn about another work culture, we will spend several days "on the job" with police officers to better understand the norms, values, challenges, and practices of their work.

For any presentation, coming early and getting to know representative members of the group allows you to refer to them in your presentation. "As Shanita would probably tell you . . ." or "When I was talking with several members of the science department earlier, I learned that . . . ." Statements of acknowledgment, when sincere, are also appreciated and help to connect you with the audience: "In this district where you enjoy such an excellent reputation for leadership . . . ."

Figure 1-5. Customize Your Presentation

Quick-Prep Steps to Customize Your Presentation

1. The time. During your opening comments, refer to the time, date, holiday, or significance of this time for this topic. *"It's appropriate that we be gathered here for this topic on the eve of celebrating Martin Luther King Day."*

2. The place. Mention the location in which you are working to establish a common reference with the group. *"Today we meet in this room called a Learning Center, surrounded by books and technology. But if this is the Learning Center of the school, then what are the classrooms? You and I know that the learning that occurs in your classroom each day through your interaction with students is the learning that counts most. That is the learning we will address today."*

3. The circumstances. Comment about a current item in the news. Make reference to the setting: it's hot, cold, crowded, or snowing, or report cards have just been issued. For example, when in Chicago you can say, *"What about those Bulls in last night's game!?"*

4. Yourself. Use something unique about yourself as a point of reference. *"I like to hike and whenever I can I will go into the mountains for a few days with a friend, a backpack, and a good map. On my last trip something happened that comes to mind when I think of today's topic."*

Stir in Some Suspense

A second characteristic of a great gift is that it's cloaked with suspense. Remember birthdays as a child—the waiting, the curiosity, the urge to peek? Presenters create some of this same anticipation in opening remarks—"Later I will describe a special gift that I think you'll find useful"—or in the overview: "We'll conclude by reporting the findings on topic X, some of which you may find surprising." This foreshadowing can activate some of the curious child in audience members.

Wrap It in Beautiful Paper

A third characteristic of an appreciated gift is that it is attractively wrapped. Carefully designed handouts send a signal that you care enough to send the very best. Arranging the room for comfort and easy visibility and hearing wraps you and your message nicely. The way you dress is important. For an excellent source on choosing the right clothes for presentation, see Elizabeth Urech's (2002) *Speaking Globally* or Iain Ewing's (1994) *The Best Presentation Skills*. A guideline I use is to dress just a shade more formally than the audience. This communicates respect. If I have estimated incorrectly and I am too dressed up, I can "dress down" during the presentation by removing a coat or tie or by rolling up my sleeves.

Presentation wrapping might also include artful phrasing, a surprising sequence, a public agenda posted on chart paper, food (in the section on openings in chapter 3, I'll report on research linking food to audience approval of ideas!), or even a bit of drama. Compose sentences to have a surprise meaning revealed in the last word or phrase, as in the following example:

> The passenger next to me was an off-duty pilot. I thought about the stereotype we have of pilots: tall, good-looking, bronzed face, easy grin. This one was no exception. "Cockpit management and an emphasis on the interpersonal skills of leading a crew is now the rage in pilot inservice training," she said.

Make It Useful

Finally, and perhaps most important, an appreciated gift is more than aesthetic, it is something that you will want to use right away. Lucy taught us how to say the Chinese phrases for thank you (*shei shei*) and very good (*ding ding how*). She also taught another phrase that my wife believes applies to me—*mamma ha ha*, which means absent-minded.

I've found it helpful to suggest uses for ideas that I am teaching in several other contexts. In chapter 2, I will offer some specific strategies to help participants transfer what they've learned into a variety of activities. Again, the adage "know your audience" prevails and guides a presenter in a careful balance between theory and practice. This leads some presenters to be called "amphibians": They are easily at home with the theory of things and can also explain the day-to-day details of implementation.

Knowing an audience includes knowing with what initiatives or stresses they may be working. The next section addresses dealing with groups who are experiencing change.

REMEMBER

1. Presentations can be gifts and, as such, forge a special relationship between audience and presenter.
2. Gifts signal that I know who you are, I care for you, and I have something specifically for you.
3. The best gifts are personal and communicate your understanding of the group.
4. Use suspense as foreshadowing that the best idea will come after the break.
5. Wrap your gifts attractively, with graceful words, relevant images, and personal stories.

Present to Groups Experiencing Change

Use these ideas to help yourself through changes,
and to effectively support others.

> ### Notes from a Safari Journal
>
> Change happens, even for elephants. The African elephant is an impressive creature, as big as a truck and with a nose as long as its legs. The trunk serves as siphon, snorkel, squirt gun, trumpet, and a feeding tool powerful enough to rip branches from trees but delicate enough, with fingerlike projections at the tip, to pick up a pea.
>
> For centuries the elephants conducted an annual migration from the Serengeti—which in the language of the Masai means "endless plain"—to the Ngorongoro Crater, a water- and vegetation-rich haven. Less than 100 years ago, however, farmers planted corn and potatoes in the sweeping hills between the plains and the crater, and the migrations stopped. Today, of the elephant family, only a few resident bull elephants remain, grazing at the bottom of the crater.

Movement stops in schools in which change is experienced as overwhelming. Some people will cling to old ways, some will work harder with no better results, some will experience immobilizing sadness, and some will become either apathetic or angry. Others, however, will process the psychological demands of change and reinvent themselves and their work to accomplish the goals.

Coping With Change

Schools face daunting shifts: They adopt programs, change assessment protocols, reorganize schedules, revise curriculum, reinvigorate instruction, or change personnel. Some schools encounter multifaceted change, others singular change. Regardless, the challenges are similar.

In a seminal and timeless work, William Bridges (1980) found that it is never the change itself that is difficult; rather, it is the psychological adjustments, the natural processes of disorientation and reorientation that accompany challenging changes. He describes three phases: endings, neutral zones, and new beginnings. For schools and individuals to cope effectively with these stages, it's useful to know what they are and to have some idea of how to deal with them. Information on transitions should often be one of the professional developer's gifts.

People make new beginnings, says Bridges, only if they have first made an ending and spent some time in a neutral zone. Most presentations, however, focus on the beginnings. Presenters can give a valuable gift to an audience when they learn enough about the organization to know in what stage of transition it is, and then organize their messages and learning experiences congruently with that transition zone.

I once worked with members of an organization in which catastrophic changes were occurring. Many had lost their jobs as a result of declining resources, and more positions were sure to go, but nobody knew which ones. The management team was struggling to implement a new strategic plan and introduce team building and participatory decision making into this formerly compartmentalized and top-down organization. Uncertainty and suspicion abounded, and many employees felt like turkeys being asked to vote on Thanksgiving.

At this time two gifts were given to me. First was a realization that whatever the nature of the organization's agenda, the people were undergoing extreme stress and uncertainty. For the organization's goals to be achieved, personal anxieties had to be addressed. Second, colleague and change-consultant extraordinaire Suzanne Bailey placed two books in my hands by William Bridges (1980, 1991) that spoke specifically to helping ourselves and others deal with transitions. I began to ponder how a presenter, either internal or external to an organization, might make use of this knowledge to support people and organizations in high states of transition. The following are some thoughts on this matter.

Endings

Every transition, even from a joyous event, starts with an ending. For the young couple welcoming a new baby in the house, there are still the endings: of a full night's sleep, of private time for the couple, of extra money. In schools, a new program or curriculum, no matter how positively anticipated, brings an ending to the old familiar ways of doing things: texts and exercises, instructional strategies, patterns of relationships with other adults, and perhaps even changes in status.

During this period it is normal to feel a sense of loss, even grieving, for the old. It is sometimes a slow process, for we may have identified some portion of who we are with what is past. It is a time in which people might feel disoriented, disenchanted, angry, or depressed. Because the biggest task each person faces during an ending is to let go of what is passing, perhaps the most important service that professional developers can give is to let others react to the ending. Endings are, after all, experiences of dying, says Bridges, and in some sense we might feel that the changes mean the end of us. Yet our logical minds know that an ending marks the beginning of a new life.

Tips for presenters working with groups at endings. Bridges advises us to expect and accept some signs of grieving. People may be sad, angry, depressed, nonrational, frightened, or confused. Take these as signs of coping with loss, not as bad morale. What you can offer participants at this stage is a nonjudgmental atmosphere and a process through which feelings can be expressed. For example, have people in pairs list all the losses involved in a change, or have small groups list the worst things, the best things, and the most probable things that might happen in relation to a new program. Have people talk about their feelings. Have groups respond to prompts such as, "Working with the new program is like what household object? Why?"

The trick in endings is to let go. Prepare yourself for presentations by thinking about who in the organization will be losing what in the change. Think and feel from their perspective. The loss of comfort, confidence, routines, security, relationships, status, and years of "being effective doing it this way" might be involved. Is there something that's over for everyone? Perhaps a chapter is over in the school's history. Perhaps the school is experiencing a loss of significant personnel or declining enrollment or changes in demographics. Tell stories that legitimize participants' uncomfortable feelings with endings as well as stories that signal the transitions to follow.

To help people let go, include in your presentation information about transitions. Put more energy into explaining the circumstances that led to the change and less energy into the solutions. We typically try to "sell" the solutions, says Bridges, before the problems that necessitated the changes are fully understood and accepted. Identify the specific behaviors that participants will need to be able to accomplish the change. Be explicit about them and teach them. Give people information about the change. Update the data. You cannot communicate too much. My friend Michael Buckley, whose illustrations you see in this book, says we must "overcommunicate." Finally, treat the past with respect. Frame whatever is passing as useful to what you are moving toward. Remember that people may identify with past practices.

The Neutral Zone

Bridges (1991) calls this state the neutral zone because it is a "nowhere between two somewheres." In organizations, anxiety rises and motivation falls. Performance declines, and the number of missed workdays increases. People get overloaded, signals are mixed, systems are in flux, and more things go wrong. In significant life transitions, people often intuitively seek solitude to sort things out. The critical task at this stage is to give in to the emptiness that one is experiencing and trust that a death-and-rebirth process is in progress. It is this very process of disintegration and reintegration that becomes the source of renewal.

Tips for presenters working with groups in the neutral zone. The first order of business is to take care of yourself. To get in touch with what it's like to be in the neutral zone during your own transition, and to get maximum benefit, try these ideas. Find a regular time to be alone, even if it is as simple as rising half an hour earlier each day to have a cup of coffee and reflect. Develop a journal of your own journey through the neutral zone. What are you thinking and feeling? What new awareness about yourself are you developing? This can be a rich period of personal discovery and creativity. Take advantage of it. Arrange a few days' "passage journey" for yourself in which you are alone in a new setting without distractions. Provide a holiday for the mind and soul, as it were, and a chance for the processes of reintegration to take place.

In your presentations, normalize the neutral zone. Forecast its occurrence, processes, and benefits. Select metaphors with positive attributes to describe the changes that people are experiencing. Instead of a "sinking ship," speak of the ship's new route. (This presumes a destination, a new port, possibly a retrofitting.) Use metaphors of life cycles, seasons, and growing things to talk about the changes.

Stimulate ideas. Frame problems as entryways to new solutions. Get people brainstorming, sharing, and envisioning. Because the neutral zone is the place of new growth, work to get as many ideas out in the open as possible. Let people know that the neutral zone is the best place in which to generate and test new ideas and that innovation will take place naturally if they seed the ground with many thoughts. A team of three fifth-grade teachers deep in the neutral zone were dismayed that they would no longer work together when the school moved from a 9-month to a 12-month calendar. Nevertheless, because there was an opportunity to explore ideas, they came up with the idea of being a vertical team in the new schedule—one each at fourth, fifth, and sixth grades.

Work to strengthen each person's sense of interdependence. Use presentation strategies that involve group problem finding and solution sharing. Interdependence is an essential state of mind for schools in transition. Susan Rosenholtz (1989), in her study of elementary schools in Tennessee, found that the single most important characteristic of successful schools was goal consensus. Saphier and Gower (1987) report that the definition of a good school is so simple that it's embarrassing: People have common goals and work together toward those goals.

People who are interdependent seek collegiality and give of themselves to group goals and needs. They feel a sense of community. They ask for help and they give help. Just as they contribute to a common good, they also draw on the resources of others. Anything that presenters do to enhance the skills and attitudes of interdependence supports a group in moving healthily through the neutral zone and is a potent resource for dealing with the beginning. Appendix A describes interdependence as one of five desirable states of mind.

Beginnings

Genuine beginnings start within us. They are psychological phenomena that we come to, paradoxically, only at the end of something else. This is the time for action and the pursuance, step by step, of a plan to take us to the new place.

School leaders will want to identify specific behaviors that participants need to accomplish the change. They need be explicit about and teach skills, then plan for implementation, mutation monitoring, and redesigning.

In all changes, everyone is urged to treat the past with respect. Frame whatever is passing as useful to what you are moving toward. Remember that people may identify with past practices in a positive way. Never, never, never demean the old way of doing things.

Tips for presenters working with groups at beginnings. Focus participants on the processes that will lead to outcomes, not on the outcomes themselves. Foreshadow for people the normal brief decline in effectiveness when working with any new strategy. As learners move through the stages of unconscious incompetence (I don't know that I don't know) to conscious incompetence (I know that I don't know) to conscious competence (I know that I know), they often expect the effortlessness that comes only at the later stage of unconscious competence (I know it so well that I don't think about it). By alerting people to the effort required in the conscious competence stage, you encourage them to not abandon ship during the rough seas, so they can stay on board for the smooth sailing that will come.

Be clear with people about the purpose of the beginning and support them in identifying themselves with the result. Offer precise pictures of what staff and students will be saying, doing, and feeling once the change is complete. Invite them to help construct images of the desired state. Do not, however, build a picture of the future so complicated and far removed from existing realities that people feel overwhelmed and intimidated by the task.

Finally, monitor yourself for what Bridges calls the marathon effect. Speakers on change have often already gone through the three stages of transition themselves before they make presentations to others. They are like professional athletes in a public marathon. Hundreds of people are lined up at the starting line. The race begins, but the occasional runners, those at the very end of the pack, don't actually cross the starting line until the ones in the lead have already settled into their stride. After a while, the front-runners are thinking about the end of the race and the next challenge. In that moving mass of runners, however, there are still many who are dealing with just starting.

Once, in a race that my wife and I experienced, friends would periodically join a runner, run alongside to pace that individual, and offer encouragement. The best presentations will do that verbally for each member of the audience, regardless of which stage of the "race" he or she is in at the moment.

Can presentations be transformational even in the midst of change? The very fact that the system has been disturbed may provide special opportunities for transformational learning, especially if this has been considered during the contracting phase.

REMEMBER

1. It's not change that is difficult; what is hard is the psychological adjustment to change.
2. Movement in schools stops when change is experienced as overwhelming. Help faculties cope by teaching about transitions.
3. Schools face daunting shifts: They adopt programs, measure growth against standards, reorganize schedules, revitalize curriculum, and reinvent instruction.
4. People make beginnings only if they have dealt with the feelings associated with endings.
5. The trick in endings is to let go.

cont.

6. Disorientation and creativity are conditions of the neutral zone.
7. Strengthen each person's sense of interdependence.
8. Expect and accept signs of grieving.
9. Because transitions are right-brain work, use ceremonies.
10. Never, never, never demean the old way of doing things.

Consult Before You Present

Talk in order to ensure you do the right work
for the group and work that can be done.

A consultant in Texas had a phone conversation with a school representative who said the following:

> I'm calling to arrange for some staff development. We have six days and would like you to do one day on assessment, one day on differentiated instruction, one day on thinking skills, one day on classroom management, one day on teaming, and one day on interdisciplinary curriculum.

There was a lo-o-ong silence while the consultant collected her thoughts. Finally she said:

> I'm pleased for you that your school has been able to make such a significant commitment to staff development, and I'd be delighted to work with you. However, it is not possible to do justice to so many topics in six days. What I can do is to spend a day giving snapshots of these six areas and helping the staff choose one area that has the greatest relevance to their campus goals. Then we can design five days in depth on that one topic.

This incident illustrates a problem that is all too common to those of us who are asked to make presentations. Sometimes the request has not been well thought out, and if we do what we are initially asked, we may waste valuable resources. I say resources, not just time, because the most valuable resources are relationships and attitudes. Should these be damaged by inappropriately designed presentations, we have lost ground in the journey toward continuing school renewal. This problem is magnified when the presenter's orientation is toward engaging participants in transformational work.

I am fortunate to work frequently with many accomplished presenters, including Art Costa, John Dyer, Carolee Hayes, Jane Ellison, Laura Lipton, Sue Pressler, Suzanne Riley, Bruce Wellman, and others. From these people I have learned the following about contracting for a presentation: (a) You are a consultant before you are a presenter, (b) arrange a group contracting conversation, (c) work from a standard set of design questions, and (d) work from a standard set of logistics questions.

You Are a Consultant Before You Are a Presenter

As we will explore in chapter 2, "who am I" is one of most important design questions and is especially relevant at this stage in your relationship with a client. Far from being just a hired mouth or an intelligent-looking face (I should be so lucky) to fill an hour of time, you bring values and an expertise to the relationship that goes beyond your content knowledge. Once you are asked to present, you serve first as a consultant, a person whose expertise is used by others. Your role in the contracting dialogue is to be proactive, probing for the motivation behind the presentation request, pressing for precision in the description of outcomes, and being politely prescriptive (if your client hasn't considered it) about assessment and follow-up. Regardless of your work role—you are a teacher and the principal has asked you to present, or you are a staff developer and the superintendent wants a presentation to the board—remembering that you are first a consultant in this relationship will support you and the requesting party in creating the best possible presentation.

Arrange a Group Contracting Conversation

The person who contacts you for a presentation has one set of perceptions about what is needed. Several people will add dimensionality and richness and will increase the odds for a successful experience. I've learned to ask for either a face-to-face meeting or a group telephone call with four to eight persons representing different roles, levels, and perspectives within the group with which I'm being asked to work. Not only does this provide me with higher quality data about the existing and desired conditions, it also provides local ownership for the presentation event. A 45-minute phone call is usually sufficient as long as I'm consciously working from the lists below. Some tips for group phone calls: Have a roster of names and ask people to name themselves before speaking. If you notice that someone is silent, you can ask for his or her reflections on what has been said so far. Have at least a verbal agenda so that you and the group can keep track of where you are. Reserve the right to limit decisions during the phone call to areas like outcome, audience, and logistics. Reserve final design rights to your deeper reflection.

Work From a Standard Set of Design Questions

I find it useful to work from the following questions. By "work from," I do not mean that I use this as a sequential checklist; rather, I use it as a reference document to remind me of particular areas that are useful to explore in this conversation.

Is there a problem this event is intended to solve? If so, is training the best solution? Are there other solutions?

Who is the audience? Are they volunteers? What are their roles? What are their attitudes about this topic, this presentation, or the work environment in general? What experiences, knowledge, skills, and potential contributions do they bring to this event?

What are the outcomes? What will be seen, heard, or felt by the end of the presentation? What will be measurably different 6 weeks after the event? What is the connection between these outcomes and the long-term goals of the organization? What values will this event express and reinforce? In what ways will this event contribute to the states of mind of efficacy, interdependence, and consciousness?

What is the mood of the group? How do they feel about the presentation being planned? Are there issues at work that may influence their mental states—and receptivity—either positively or negatively? If the group is not looking forward to the event, it's best to know it now so that you can prepare some appropriate openings (see chapter 4 on acknowledging resistance by choreographing openings).

What is most important? Of all the possible outcomes, which are most critical? What types of outcomes are most desired—knowledge, skills, or attitudes?

What follow-up support will be provided? What can be done to troubleshoot during implementation? What can be done to monitor for mutations—changes made during the application of learned skills that could either reduce or enhance their effectiveness? What can be done to personalize (individualize) follow-up? What data can be gathered with which to assess effects and design the next steps? For thoughts about follow-up, see the end of this chapter.

What resources will we have to use? How much time will there be? Will there be a pre-event reading or dialogue? What syllabuses or readings should be provided at the event? What should be communicated, and to whom, prior to the event?

Gather Information About Logistics

Might there be any surprises in the amount of actual presentation time? Can people really get back from lunch that soon? Will there be any business to conduct before this presentation starts?

What are the physical characteristics of the presentation site?

What will be required in regard to name tags, audiovisual equipment, room arrangement, and materials? On this item, I am supplying information and working out details with the client. See Appendix B for a form on which you can identify the logistics requirements for your session.

What travel and transportation details should we check? How do I get to the place, and how long will it take me? Can I get in the room an hour before the event? Can someone help me to transport materials and equipment?

In summary, presenters are consultants first, sharing their expertise and asking both design and logistics questions that are useful to the client. I encourage you to make your own set of contracting questions, tailored to your style and situation. Finally, here are two concluding tips. To paraphrase the advice of Publilius Syrus in 42 B.C.E., never promise more than you can perform. To extend that advice from the perspective of staff development as we now envision it, never do only what is asked for, do what might be hoped for if it could be imagined.

With transformation in mind, much of your effectiveness stems from how you design your sessions. In the next chapter we will explore design ideas, some of which will save you preparation time, and all of which will contribute to valuable experiences for your participants.

REMEMBER

1. Sometimes the request for your services has not been well thought out. It's up to you help the client think through what will be best.
2. Consider arranging a group contracting conversation to get several perspectives.
3. Work from a standard set of design and logistical questions.
4. Your role in a contracting conversation is to be proactive, probing for reasons behind the request and precision in the description of outcomes and being politely prescriptive (if the client hasn't considered it) about assessment and follow-through.
5. Ask about the mood of the audience. Are there issues at stake, perhaps unrelated to this presentation, that might influence their mental states?
6. Ascertain, of all the outcomes, which are most important.

Summary

Transformational change can occur in an instant. Presentations can create such change and provide participants new lenses through which to interact with colleagues and their work. The most profound changes are those that alter our sense of who we are or of what we are capable. Today's staff developer is a guide in the territory of the culture of learning, and through intention and actions creates opportunities for transformational learning. His or her overarching goals are to modify the culture of the workplace and enhance educators' capacity to modify themselves.

Professional development is shifting from a focus on the individual teacher, menus of courses based on teacher needs or interest surveys, and one stop–one shop learning seminars. Instead, implementing, monitoring, and follow-through are recognized as legitimate concerns for professional developers and leaders. Emphasis on the needs of the group related to student learning is the organizing feature within which individual teacher needs are addressed.

Professional developers wear three hats in addition to the presentation hat— as coaches, consultants, and facilitators. Each of these distinct functions calls on similar and different skills for professional developers.

Three macromaps were presented in this chapter: working with four audiences, ways to address nested levels of learning for greater impact, and deliberate attention to such empowerment outcomes as teacher efficacy. Presenters stimulate efficacy when they have participants shape agendas, teach others, and control their own learning goals and environment, as well as when presenters provide choice. Teacher efficacy is directly related to student achievement.

Today schools face daunting shifts: They adopt programs, change assessment protocols, reorganize schedules, revise curriculum, reinvigorate instruction, and change personnel. Some schools encounter multifaceted change, others singular change. Informed presenters, in their roles as consultants and presenters, assist groups through these tumultuous waters.

In-house professional developers, in particular, find themselves occasionally trapped by impossible assignments. Ways to overcome this were presented. You are a consultant before you are a presenter. Suggestions for group contracting conversations and a set of design questions were made.

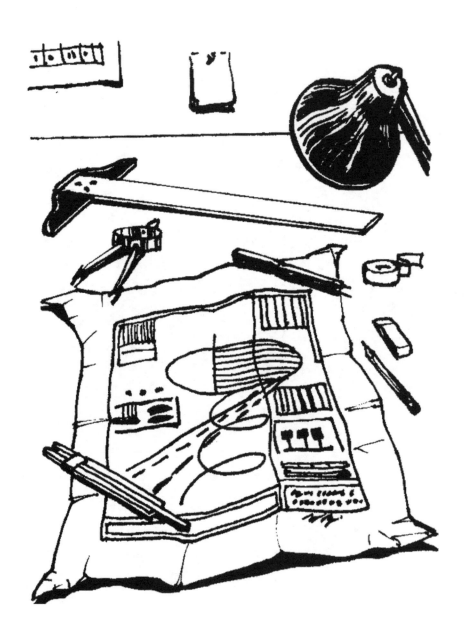

CHAPTER 2

How to Design Persuasive Presentations

Use planning ideas that enhance your effectiveness and ease your load.

Aristotle was wrong. He said there were three types of speeches: informative, persuasive, and "decorative"—speeches of praise and the like. But there is really only one kind: the persuasive.

—Nick Morgan (2003, p. 4)

In chapter 1 we explored the notion that presentations can have a transformational effect. We examined several macromaps related to this: Speak to four audiences, teach to multiple levels of learning, and teach for efficacy—the "I can do" sense that fuels high performance.

The presenter as guide uses these maps and also, like our guide in the Serengeti, uses navigational aids of greater detail and specificity. Among these are a model of how participants construct learning, steps to take before a presentation, contracting your work, deciding which content is most important, and getting the right mix of content and process. This chapter introduces new organizers to save planning time, how to give a 2-minute speech, and ideas for designing follow-up.

A presentation or speech is never about you; it is about the audience. Morgan's assertion that all speeches are persuasive should make us think about the group with which we will work. Who are these people, what are their needs, and how can material be organized so that it is most effectively received?

Notes From a Safari Journal

I notice that Juma has a stack of books in the space between the driver's seat and the passenger's seat. Occasionally he will stop the Land Rover, reach for his binoculars, and then refer to one of his reference books. "That's a reichenow weaver," he says, pointing to a yellow-eyed bird with a black ear patch encircled with yellow and a bright yellow forecrown. "It's a small

cont.

> *finchlike bird with a pointed beak that is good for eating seeds of grasses, buds, and insects. Look, there might be its nest!" Amazed, we follow his direction to see dozens of round yellow straw-bag nests hanging from branches like ornaments on a Christmas tree.*

Develop a Designer's Mind

Measure twice, cut once, goes the carpenter's mantra. You cannot have two many lenses through which to design your work. Each lens views aspects not visible through other lenses. Ultimately, it is the aggregate of all that makes you effective in whatever you do—present, consult, facilitate, or coach.

To present is to learn. Like Juma, I surround myself with books, I have access to other educators, and slowly (I am a technopeasant) I am learning to access the Internet as well. Five people have been especially instrumental in my learning about design: Jane Ellison and Carolee Hayes from the Center for Cognitive Coaching; Laura Lipton and Bruce Wellman of MiraVia: Pathways to Learning; Jay McTighe of Understanding by Design; and my good friend, colleague, and mentor, Art Costa.

Fundamental to design thinking are four questions: What do I want participants to learn? How will I know they are learning it? What strategies or approaches will I use? What can I learn by designing and delivering the content and how can that inform refinements? Whenever I feel stuck at the design stage in a presentation, I go back to the first two questions. The answers to these focus my thinking.

Also fundamental to good design is a rudimentary knowledge of how meaning is constructed in educational settings. I rely on a model for teaching and learning developed by Lipton and Wellman (2003), which posits three phases of learning, illustrated in Figure 2-1 and described below.

Figure 2-1. The Pathways to Learning Model

Organizing and Integrating

Synthesize and represent information

Develop and index new understandings

Managing
Modeling
Mediating
Monitoring

Activating and Engaging

Engage prior knowledge, skills, and understandings

Expand the knowledge base for individuals and groups

Surface and articulate frames of reference

Exploring and Discovering

Examine and differentiate information in light of current schema

Investigage hypotheses, concepts, and principles

Reconsider and tentatively refine schema

Phase 1: Activate and Engage

Adults have much information, but it is not organized in alphabetical order, says Lipton. An initial step in teaching is to activate the prior knowledge of the learner related to the topic being introduced. Using interactive strategies to activate prior knowledge at the beginning of a session brings three benefits: It sets the norm for interactive, not passive, learning; it levels the playing field of knowledge; and it provides the psychological safety necessary for the social construction of meaning.

Activation alone produces little conceptual change; participants must talk about what they know and debate positions to produce conceptual change reports (Guzzetti, Snyder, & Glass, 2003). Activation does get relevant information into working memory, which creates "velcro bristles" in the brain so that new information has some organizers on which to "stick." Purposes at this phase include articulating frames of reference about the topic and expanding the knowledge base. Many activities can do this. These include paired verbal fluency, visual synectics, stating hopes and fears, and brainstorming and categorizing.

Learning at this stage calls for generative and associative thinking. Tasks that have participants recall, brainstorm, identify, forecast, estimate, or speculate serve these purposes. Starting a session on presentation skills, for example, I might begin by having partners fill out a list of hopes and fears about presenting. Such an activity has the added benefit of normalizing the fears.

Phase 2: Explore and Discover

At this phase new content is introduced. Content is provided in a variety of ways—a lecturette, a case study, a demonstration, paired reading activities, or inventories. For learners to explore the new content, which is related to what they have previously activated, they must use the skills of cognitive processing. How much and what kind of processing leads to a perennial presenter dilemma that I will address later in this chapter.

Exploring and discovering requires that content be processed by learners. Useful skills include comparing, storytelling, analyzing, inferring, relating, and seeking causality or effects. The purposes are to investigate concepts, a hypothesis, and principles; examine information in light of the current schema; and reconsider and tentatively refine new ways of understanding.

Phase 3: Organize and Integrate

Finally, in the third phase of this model, participants organize and integrate their learning to make it uniquely their own. I was hugely disappointed when I first learned that I could not do this for groups. I like to create organizational schemata to show the relationships of concepts. Eventually I learned that this is the work of the learner, not the presenter. It is the stage, in fact, in which learners crystallize meaning for themselves. Useful activities for this phase are to catalogue and index new understandings, develop frameworks and models, and synthesize and represent learning. Synthesis and evaluative thought are required at this phase.

The learning and teaching cycle can be used to plan a unit of instruction, a topic during a seminar, or a full day or more of work. The learning-focused presenter constantly monitors for participant success and instructional effectiveness. Some examples of activities for each phase follow.

Examples

Activate and Engage. You are making a presentation on the topic of presenting to adults. You open with this small-group activity: "Compare presenting to adults and teaching students. Name what is similar. What is different? What conclusions do you draw regarding your work in this area?" You can also ask groups to list what they know, think they know, and want to know, about the topic.

Explore and Discover. You invite trios to observe a skillfully performed Cognitive Coaching[SM] transaction. At its conclusion you ask them to analyze the coach's use of language, interview the person being coached for his or her response to the coach's questions, and interview the coach to learn what principles and data were guiding the coach's decisions. As another example, you might elicit a partner's hypothesis about a topic and then read a document, seeking validation or reversals.

Organize and Integrate. You have small groups make graphic organizers that display the relationships of the concepts that have been learned. You might also ask the group to develop performance criteria at the expert, developing, and novice levels of a task, then present and self-assess performance.

The best design for learning can be further enhanced by attention to the physical environment. This is the next topic.

REMEMBER

1. Four questions drive design thinking: What do I want participants to learn? How will I know they are learning it? What strategies will I use? What can I learn by designing and delivering the content?

2. Adults have much information, but it is not organized in alphabetical order. Bring information to working memory by beginning topics with activating and engaging activities.

3. Activation alone produces little conceptual change. Have participants talk about what they know.

4. In the second stage of learning, exploring and discovering, content is provided in a variety of ways and processed by comparing, analyzing, inferring, and using other cognitive processes to tentatively consider new ways of understanding.

5. In the third phase of the model, organizing and integrating, learners process the data in a variety of ways to make it their own.

Prepare the Room

There is only one antidote to failure, and that is preparation.

I remember when a late flight forced an unscheduled overnight stay in a connecting city. My luggage caught up with me the next morning as I arrived in the city in which I was to present. The session was scheduled to start at 9:00 A.M., and I arrived at 8:55 A.M. after a frantic taxi drive from the airport. My first hour lacked artistry, and it wasn't until after the first break that I could catch my psychological breath and function with ease.

This all-too-real experience reinforced my awareness that attention to details before the opening adds elegance and focus to a presentation. For the presenter, getting there on time means getting there before time. Certain "before-the-opening" details, when unattended, allow problems to emerge. Because presenting is such a complex mental activity, speakers need to place 100% of their mental resources on what's most important—the audience's interaction with the content. The handling of minor decisions ("Where did I put the overhead pens?") draws important energies away from this task.

Prespeech jitters are amazingly common. While sitting on the dais, I have seen the hand wringing, trembling notes, and perspiration of well-known speakers. Experienced speakers anticipate this anxiety and increase their resourcefulness and effectiveness by settling certain presentation logistics before they begin.

They typically come early to do this. It's not unusual to see the most skilled speakers arrive a full hour before the presentation in order to attend to (a) the comfort and perspective of audience members, (b) the ambiance and utility of the presentation environment, and (c) the presenter's work space (Figure 2-2).

Figure 2-2. Before the Presentation

Arrive Early to Check
☑ Four audience species: habits and marking
☑ Nested levels of learning
☑ Efficacy as a road to learning, transfer, and application

Here are some before-the-opening tips I have learned from my own work and from other experienced presenters. These will help to ensure an environment geared for learning.

Comfort and Perspective

Walk the perimeter of the room to get a sense of its size and how much you will need to project. In your tour of the room examine the sight lines to flip charts and screens from various seats. Sit. Imagine a head in front of you. Note how much of the projection screen or easel can be seen over that head. (Usually this is only the top two-thirds of the screen.) Put masking tape on the side of the overhead projector and/or easel to indicate visibility zones. Check seating arrangements; crowded conditions contribute to comfort and attention problems.

Make a final check on refreshment arrangements. In the morning, fresh-brewed caffeinated and decaffeinated coffee, fruit juice, hot water, tea, and hot chocolate are sound basics. When snacks are included, participants seem to increasingly desire fruit in addition to or instead of pastries. Provide cold drinks in the afternoon. If the agency is on a no-frills budget, encourage participants to organize for their needs.

Establish a registration area with handouts, sign-in sheets (if required), and a person to welcome participants and answer questions. Provide preprinted name tags, or have a model name tag and instruct participants to complete theirs with felt-tip pens so that first names can be read 12 feet away. You'll want to be able to call them by name without squinting.

Plan to complete all preparations 30 minutes before your opening so that you can relax and personally greet participants; take this opportunity to learn about their interests, concerns, and experiences; and let them know something about you.

Mood

Provide music to set a welcoming tone and invite relaxation. Music affects the emotions, brain waves, and the in-the-moment learning capacity. Friend and colleague Michael Dolcemascolo (2004), assistant director at Onodaga-Cortland-Madison Board of Cooperative Educational Services in Syracuse, advises us to think of music as a movie director might. Directors choose music to set the mood for a scene. What moods might you want for different parts of a presentation? A simple rule is to play easy listening in the morning, something a little louder and more active as the day goes on, and music to move by in the afternoon (see chapter 5 for specific suggestions).

Technical Arrangements

Use props to create visual focus and make an aesthetically pleasant stage environment. A drama teacher in St. Louis once taught me about this "warming the stage" approach. The presenter's props are platforms, easels, screens, stools, and chairs. Arrange these to define (put boundaries on) the presentation area. Use colorful graphics that welcome people, name the session, and display a public agenda (see chapter 5 for more ideas).

Decide what your position should be in the room to give the majority of the audience the best visual access to you at the opening. Plan to be there and stand still (so they can take stock of you) for the first few minutes. If you have a platform, by all means use it for your opening.

Test the overhead projector. The two most common problems are poor focus and burnt-out bulbs. Be sure you have a spare bulb.

Check for ambient lighting when using an overhead. Close the drapes, turn off banks of lights, or reposition the screen, if necessary, to cut glare. Write notes to yourself on the cardboard overhead frames.

Check other audiovisual equipment, like an LCD (Liquid Crystal Display) on which you might present your PowerPoint slides. Beware the PowerPoint traps revealed in chapter 5.

Check the sound systems. A bad sound system can ruin your presentation. Check it early and get technical help before the group arrives.

If your face is going to be projected on large screens in an auditorium while you speak, prepare the room by preparing your face beforehand. Because any nervousness or uncertainty you feel will be projected on the big screen, you must overprepare. If you're introducing someone, you should be there long enough to get past your nervousness. Do some breathing exercises. Rename your nervousness as anticipation. It's natural. Overmemorize your introduction. Then, when you're at the podium, look into the bright lights behind the camera where the audience is and smile. Raise your eyebrows. Those big screens magnify all tense expressions, note reading, and loss of presence with the audience.

Room Arrangements

Decide what seating arrangement best fits the room and your learning objectives (Figure 2-3). A sample detailed room arrangement appears in Appendix D. The arrangements are described below.

Theater Style

If your presentation will primarily be a lecture and your group size is more than 50, consider using theater style, because this provides the greatest number of seats in the smallest space. The lack of tables makes audience member interaction difficult, however.

Chevron

Consider the Chevron style for groups of 30 to 50 when you want to promote presenter-audience dialogue but limit full-group discussion. This adds the advantage of tables but loses floor space. Hotels and conference facilities often set up a variation of this called *classroom style*, in which the tables are not angled but squarely face the podium, like desks in a formal classroom. I usually prefer chevron or the next arrangement, herringbone, over the classroom style; both are less formal and give participants greater visual access to other members of the group. However, they may take up more space than classroom style.

Herringbone

Herringbone is my favorite arrangement for most workshops. If your group size ranges from 30 to 150, use this alternative, which offers the advantages of classroom style to larger groups. In this arrangement, tables are angled so that participants seated on both sides have either their right or left shoulders pointing toward the speaker. This allows for lecture-style learning and easy access to small-group discussions with people at the same table or different tables. See Appendix D for an illustration.

Figure 2-3. Room Arrangements

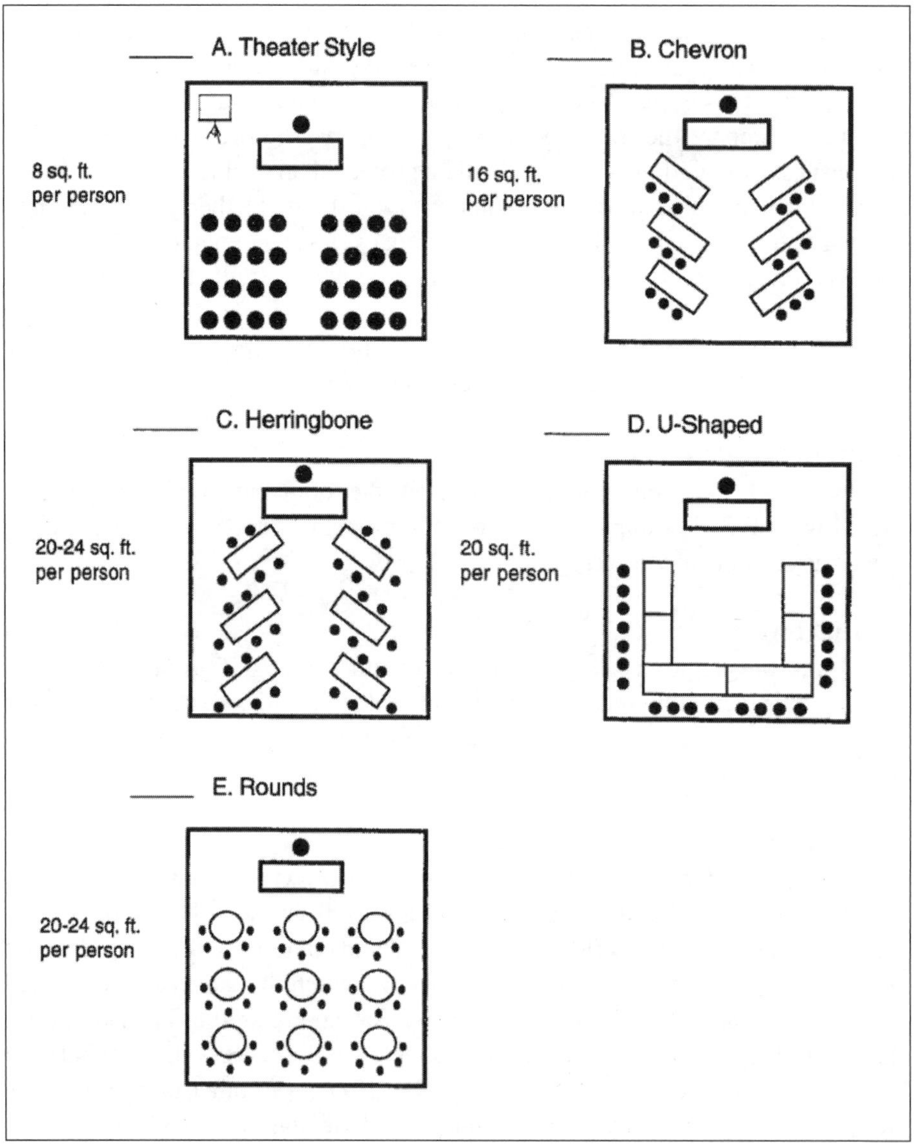

U-Shaped

To signal role equity and shared authority, use U-shaped seating for groups of 15 to 25. Here each participant can see all others, and this promotes interactions among members. The presentation focus is the open end of the U. Use semicircled chairs or tables for a variation of this design for smaller groups (up to 16).

Rounds

Use rounds if your audience ranges in size from 30 to 150 and you want participants to be actively engaged in learning activities a good deal of the time. From this arrangement, stable learning teams can be developed over full-day or multiday designs, yet enough flexibility exists to periodically assign participants across table groups for special activities. Seating participants in rounds facilitates group work and uses about 20 to 24 square feet per person. Both herringbone and rounds are supposed to take an equal amount of space. In my experience, however, the rounds arrangement will typically seat slightly fewer persons in the room, regardless of the shape of the room.

The Presenter's Workspace

This final domain is largely about routinizing a number of logistical considerations, so that during the presentation your precious and limited mental space can be reserved for monitoring the audience's interaction with the content.

Make final notes to yourself on your private agenda. Mark times in the margin to help you monitor and make adjustments as you present (Figure 2-4).

Figure 2-4. Presenter's Personal Agenda

Place one-inch strips of masking tape along the side of the flip chart for quick paper hanging during the session. Having tape strips handy allows you to maintain presentation momentum. Consider using two flip charts to allow for more visual memory. Tape pennies on the bottom of an 8½ x 11 inch blank page, which you can place under a transparency to control what you reveal. The pennies weight the paper so it will not fall off the overhead when you move it under the transparency.

Designate a space for pens, spare tape, blank overheads, and other necessary items. Always return items to that spot. This is particularly important if you are presenting with a partner.

A brief word on flip charts. There are some absolutely terrible ones on the market. What you want are firm, sturdy charts that hold a paper size of 27 x 34 inches. Chartpak™ makes a good easel, model no. E60, which adds the attribute of easy portability.

Use only water-based felt-tip pens. They do not bleed through chart paper or make permanent marks on clothing, walls, or yourself. Use bright colors. Charters™ pens are the best, in my opinion. They feature tips that hold up well over use and have a full range of bright colors: red, green, brown, blue, black, yellow, orange, and purple. They can be ordered from Grove Consultants International, at www.grove.com. The first six colors I consider basics. Orange doesn't show well. Purple is fine for those who like it; I just don't. Yellow is useful for highlighting. Adequate chart pens can also be found at Staples, Office Max, or other office supply stores. Sanford Flip Chart Markers™ or Sanford Mr. Sketch Water Color Markers™ are good buys. For creating graphics, see chapter 6.

For overhead projector presentations, arrange two sets of transparencies. In one stack, place transparencies in the sequence in which you will use them. Arrange them in a binder, housed in transparent sheet protectors that can be placed directly on the overhead. This system allows for organization by category and easy reference to related transparencies that you may use on an occasional basis. Spread the second supplementary set out on a table to allow you to respond to the unique needs of the audience. Keep your visuals bold, colorful, and simple. For PowerPoint users, print a copy of your slides—six or nine to a page, so you can look ahead while presenting, or use the three-to-a-page format with space for notes in the right-hand column.

If your session is going to be audiotaped, do a dry run to practice describing each visual that you use so the listening audience can derive maximum meaning.

Declutter the entire presentation workspace environment. Remove briefcases, extra handouts, and everything you do not need to present your material. This eliminates visual distraction for the audience and mental distraction for you.

Finally, place your private agenda at your fingertips so that you can unobtrusively refer to it at any time to stay on course. For presentations that accompany or are preceded by a written report, see Appendix E for guidelines.

The audience will expect to be with you, each other, and the topic. All of these preparatory tasks make these expectations more attainable. Of course, it helps if your plane (and you) arrive on time. If you are late, a simple comment acknowledging the difficulty for the group will do. Don't "overapologize." You won't be forgiven.

Next we will discuss some ways to resolve a major tension in selecting content—which content is most important.

REMEMBER

1. Attention to details before the opening adds elegance and focus to a presentation.
2. Arrive early to attend to the comfort and perspective of audience members. Be available 30 minutes before your opening to relax and interact with participants.
3. Check sight lines, double-check refreshments, provide music (see hapter 5 for tips on music).
4. Use props to create visual focus and an effective stage environment.
5. Check your audiovisual equipment several times. Nothing will break your stride like malfunctioning equipment.
6. Arrange seating to meet your design and purposes.
7. Organize and routinize your workspace so your mental space can be free to interact with the audience.

Decide What Content Is Most Important

The dilemma of too much content and too little time has several solutions.

Notes from a Safari Journal

In the crater, there is a moment-to-moment existence for resident animals and their human observers. Before 9:00 A.M. today two hyenas, rolling unconcernedly in the grass, caught the attention of a wildebeest scout. The herd became alert, and young and old ran for a safer part of the valley floor. Valley, I say, because the Ngorongoro Crater is like no other. It is 10 miles across, of rivers, lakes, and grassy plains with elephants, giraffes, rhinos, hippos, gazelles, lions, and probably hundreds of birds: flamingos, eagles, marabou storks, ostriches, ibises, kori bustards, and others. Film is expendable here; experiences are not.

The content of a presentation might be likened to a landscape. Many points of interest exist. Flowing rivers of energy carry a learner from one vantage point to the next. Some points of interest are worth close examination, others just a glance. What guides the selection of what is most important?

A continuing tension for presenters is what content to include in a presentation. Presenters often have far more to say than time allows. How do we decide what is essential to present and what is just nice? In this section I will address this question by examining seven purposes of content in a presentation.

Content means all the information provided by the presenter about the topic. Content, in the context of this section, does not include the processes that presenters provide to aid participants in learning the content. (The next section of this chapter will discuss the dilemma of selecting the proper ratio of content and process.)

Content serves at least seven purposes in a presentation (Figure 2-5). There may even be an eighth. Perhaps you will identify it before the end of this section.

Seven Purposes of Content
Inform

Content provides knowledge, opinions, research, and issues that are useful to participants. This frequently takes the lion's share of presentation time. (After actually watching lions eat, I can now appreciate the source of this expression.) This seems appropriate, especially in conference settings where people are hungry for information that they can take home to apply in their own situations. This purpose is congruent with the popular mindset that knowledge is something invented by others and given to us. Participants do indeed profit from listening to a knowledgeable presenter who distills information and experiences. Content presented to inform can be a valuable catalyst for learning. Content to inform is closely related to two other purposes: the communication of values and the provision of theory.

Figure 2-5. Seven Purposes of Content

1.   Inform

2.   Communicate values

3.   Provide theory

4.   Establish credibility

5.   Prime the learning "pump"

6.   Focus attention

7.   Set a course for action

Communicate Values

When values are clear, decisions are easy. One of the most potent forces for change is the conscious application of personal and organizational values. Too frequently a person's espoused values and acted-upon values are not the same. In a study of kindergarten teachers, for example, many teachers reported that each day they violated child growth and development principles in order to meet the requirements of the state curriculum guides. Content that is presented to illuminate values directs the participants' attention to the underlying principles of the work. (So does content presented to provide theory.) When the values you communicate are not yours, yet it is your job to deliver this content, maintain your integrity and fulfill your responsibility by presenting the information coming from a source other than you (see chapter 4 on nonverbal ways to do this).

Provide Theory

One could say that this chapter is about principles or theoretical knowledge. Knowledge of theory can help one to understand how something works, why it works the way it does, its relationship to other events and dynamics, and its contributions to the topic being presented. Knowing theory helps participants to make decisions—for example, when to use a strategy, when not to use it, and possible alternative approaches when a specific strategy is not appropriate. Theory then becomes a foundation for developing practices that utilize, in unique form, core principles. The theoretical information presented in this chapter is intended to influence presenters' decisions about what content to include in a presentation plan and what to eliminate during the presentation, if there is more content than time.

Establish Credibility

Speaker credibility and audience confidence in the sources of the material are important because without these, audiences may be polite but not receptive. Speaker credibility can usually be established with just a few comments: "Like me, how many of you find . . ." or "Every week when I work with students like yours . . ." or "Last week a group of teachers told me . . . ."

A workshop participant told me recently that she found me credible precisely because I did not introduce myself with an exhaustive review of titles, publications, and experience; instead I spoke with confidence and moved directly to the heart of the topic. Speaker credibility can be established at the opening of a session by succinctly citing relevant figures or other data. Speaker credibility can also be established at the opening of a session by referring to experiences you have in common with the group.

Sometimes you don't have experiences in common with the group. Never having been a policeman, I am feeling challenged about my upcoming work with police officers. "Have you worked with cops?" my contact person for the work asked. I said no, but I was in a lot of trouble as a juvenile. "That helps," he said. A safer strategy is to make reference to others who share experiences with this group. "Last week, teachers told me . . .", or "The literature on teaching for meaning is pretty clear."

Skillful speakers establish source credibility by referencing studies, commissions, or authors in relation to major themes in the presentation.

Prime the Learning "Pump"

Sometimes I tell participants a story about being on a zip line. I detail the experience of being terrified, looking down from the mountaintop to the valley below. I describe gripping the handles on the pulley mechanism that rides the cable over my head, perspiring, afraid that my hands will slip, causing me to fall, and how, at the moment I step from the platform and begin the descent, I pass from terror into ecstasy. Such a story primes the emotional "pump" for a group about to engage in a learning exercise involving some risk. That is, it encourages participants to locate within themselves the emotional resources that are necessary to risk and to learn. Similarly, cognitive pump priming helps participants to bring information from long-term storage into working memory. Presenters may do this, for example, by reminding participants of the attributes of a well-performed skill just before they engage in a practice session.

Focus Attention

Attention focusing is another good reason to invest workshop time on content because it helps participants to produce maximum learning from the skills-building processes that follow. To teach meeting facilitation, for example, I will demonstrate facilitation strategies before group members practice them. During the demonstration some participants are instructed to pay attention to what I say, others to notice the facilitation techniques being used, and still others to observe nonverbal communication. This is an effective process when teaching demonstration lessons to students. Focus detailed attention on important dimensions in a demonstration to stimulate high-quality practice and learning.

Set a Course For Action

Speakers may foreshadow two types of action for audiences. In one case, presenters prepare participants to practice and refine skills or to apply what has been learned. The second type of action is a call to communicate, influence others, vote, or engage in some other political activity. In each case, this is a valuable use of presentation time, for influencing what participants do after the presentation is usually the ultimate aim of the session.

Get participants started on a small step. The first step eases the others. A decision to act, followed by a modest start, done now, encourages action later. Have them create a "to do" list, write individual goals on 3 x 5 inch cards, or schedule appointments with another group member.

It may be a good strategy to deliver this type of content before nearing the end of a presentation. A time crunch usually becomes apparent near the end of a session, and a presenter may rush through the final content without communicating the full importance of an action plan. In addition, if people have to leave early, they will miss the action message.

Skillful presenters include four elements in a call to action. They provide a *rationale*, elaborating on why the action is important to the learner or the organization. They offer specific ideas, or *structures*, for how to proceed. They set *expectations* for frequency and timing. (For example, "Please complete two coaching cycles before returning here at the end of the month.") Finally, they *fore-shadow resistances*, procrastination, and awkwardness that learners might experience, and contextualize these as part of the normal learning process, something to be experienced with foreknowledge and perseverance. We will discuss follow-up at the end of this chapter.

An Eighth Purpose?

Is there an eighth purpose for content? I think so. Content can also entertain, relax, and increase audience receptivity to the other seven purposes in the presentation. Laughter is a particularly valuable resource toward these ends. It affects many positive physiological functions, including causing "a drop in the pulse rate, the secretion of endorphins, and increased oxygen in the blood. It has been found to liberate creativity and provoke such higher-level thinking skills as anticipation, finding novel relationships, and visual imagery" (Costa, 1991a). John Dyer is a very funny, peaceful, and knowledgeable man. He is my mentor for laughter. In chapter 3 I discuss what I have learned from John. When the audience is laughing, they won't leave the presentation before you do.

The Content Versus Time Dilemma

I have 2 hours of content and 45 minutes of time. What do I leave out? Four questions guide experienced presenters in resolving this persistent design dilemma. First, they remind themselves of the overall goal of the presentation, often stated in terms of what knowledge, skills, attitudes, or action is envisioned for participants. Second, they ask themselves what relevance this goal has to the longer-term goals that are related to the dispositions, capacities, or ideals described in chapter 1. Third, they examine the intended contribution of each content segment in relation to the seven purposes described above. Fourth, they ask themselves how essential each piece of content is to achieving the immediate and long-term outcomes for this session.

REMEMBER

1. Decide what is essential to present and what is just nice.
2. Content serves seven purposes: to inform, communicate values, provide theory, establish credibility, prime emotional pump for learning, focus attention, and set a course of action.
3. Provide four elements in a call to action: rationale, structures, expectations, and foreshadowing resistance.
4. Presenters pose four questions to themselves: What is the overall goal of the presentation? What relevance does this goal have to longer-term goals? What contribution does each content chunk make to the purposes of content? How essential is each piece of content to achieving immediate and long-term goals?

However, another consistent design tension exists. Once you have selected the content to fit the time of your presentation, how much time should you allow for *processing* the content? This is our next topic.

Tame the Content-Process Teeter-Totter

You can avoid some of my worst mistakes.

Several years ago I delivered the worst presentation I had ever done before or have ever done since. Not only did the audience know it was bad, but I knew it was bad, yet I couldn't stop myself from the behaviors that were creating agony for all of us. Such is the power of the untamed content-process teeter-totter. I persisted because of good intentions, overzealousness, and the misguided notion that delivering content is the sole purpose of presentations. I had been scheduled for a 3-hour Friday night presentation and a full day on Saturday. The topic was "Meeting Facilitation." A heavy rainstorm delayed my flight arrival time, so I missed the Friday evening session entirely. I resolved to "make up" the content that participants had lost by collapsing the $1\frac{1}{2}$- day presentation into Saturday. The distressed faces of those trapped participants are still burned into my memory, making the experience so painful that I learned an irreversible lesson about the content-process teeter-totter: My content is not as important as the audience's interaction with the content!

Presenters at the Bureau of Educational Research will often say, "We have enough time, we are right on schedule," rather than tell the audience they are slashing content. This keeps the group resourceful instead of worrying about what they might be missing.

Michael Doyle and David Strauss (1993) use the metaphor of gum chewing to describe the dilemma that meeting facilitators face with content and process. The issue for presenters is similar. Consider "gum" to be the content you bring to your audience. Consider "chewing" to be the interactive process you provide to assist participants in receiving, processing, and applying the content. How much gum and how much chewing you provide becomes a dominant question in presentation design.

What I learned on that painful rainy day is that the content I bring to a presentation has little or no value unless audience members chew it in some form. This simple realization has removed the burden of feeling that I must always follow my plan, report all my research, or use all my notes.

How does one know the appropriate ratio of content and process to provide? Decisions about this are made at two stages of the presentation. First, in the design stage, the types of presentation goals are determined, and decisions are made about the size of the conceptual units to present. Second, during the actual presentation, judgments are made about the degrees of learning accomplishment, unanticipated needs of the learners, rapport, and participant resourcefulness. These "show time" perceptions often override the decisions that were made during the planning stage.

Although content-process ratios can't be described in percentages, a logical progression of increased processing time exists as one's goals move from the acquisition of knowledge to the development of attitudes, skills, and commitment to apply what has been learned. To illustrate: In a World War II experiment that was considered a breakthrough in the social sciences, social psychologist Kurt Lewin tried to get Iowa housewives to purchase the less popular but highly nutritious cuts of meat, such as liver, heart, kidney, and sweetbreads. Lectures were given to three groups about the desirability of buying the organ meats; no group discussion was provided. Three other groups received the same information and, in addition, were given an opportunity to discuss the data among themselves. In follow-ups, it was discovered that the lecture plus discussion method was 10 times as effective at changing behavior. The first groups achieved a 3% behavior change; the second, 32% (Eitington, 1984). Figure 2-6 illustrates this theoretical need for a progression from less to more processing time depending on the type of goal, and it suggests intervals for processing activities. Please keep in mind that these are generalizations only, and that many good reasons can exist for deviating from these patterns.

The purposes and types of processes will vary also according to the presenter's goal. To develop awareness and knowledge, presentations are often information intensive. Listeners must be given opportunities to mentally organize the data, check their understanding, and compare the data to personal experiences. Without this, highly dense information presentations will put participants in the position of sustained passive listening, but not learning, because the learner's manipulation of information is essential to creating personal relevance and retention.

For attitude outcomes, the primary purpose of processing may be to help participants make meaning of an experience. Figure 2-6 shows processing occurring before content delivery to illustrate just one of many designs that will stimulate attitude change. In this design an experience (a process) is followed by an analysis (more process) of the experience. In another design, David Johnson and Roger Johnson (1994) describe an instructional procedure called "structured academic controversies." In this five-step process, pairs of learners (a) develop a position and decide how to present it to others, (b) present their position, then listen to and take notes of a presentation of the opposing position, (c) meet with the opposing pairs to discuss the two positions, criticize ideas (not people), and assess the degree of evidence and logic supporting each position, (d) reverse positions with the opposing pairs and present each others' views, and (e) drop all advocacy and work with the opposing pairs to present the best evidence and reasoning from both sides. The Johnsons report that these procedures produce high achievement, retention, transfer of learning to new situations, and generalization of principles. Marzano (2003) reports research finding that having students express and defend opposing positions is highly effective in correcting misconceptions about a topic.

Figure 2-6. Content-Process Ratios and Timing

TYPES OF PRESENTATION GOALS	CONTENT ------ PROCESS XXXX
Awareness	--------X-----------X----------X---------X-----
Knowledge Acquisition	--------X-----------X----------X---------X-----
Skills Acquisition	-----------XXXX-----XXXX-----XXXX----------
Attitude Development	XXXXXXXXXXXXXX------------------------------
Application	-----------X------------X-------------XXXXXXX

A colleague and I once used a variation on this theme with several school site councils in a workshop on "Living Effectively with Conflict." (I like that title better than "managing" conflict because it presumes that conflict is a natural consequence of living and that the human animal, like the wildlife in the Serengeti, can learn to work with it.) We introduced the topic in a 20-minute period of total silence in which each member (a) privately brainstormed his or her own assumptions about conflict, (b) selected the one assumption that had the greatest influence in affecting choices in his or her work setting, (c) wrote that one assumption on a sentence strip and—still silently—posted it on an easel, and (d) silently read the sentence strips as they were posted and recorded his or her intellectual and emotional reactions to other group members' posted assumptions in a journal. We then offered tips on safe ways of dialoguing about these assumptions. Before we offered any content of our own on this topic, most of the deep learning had already been done.

An important design decision that presenters make is how to organize concepts and information into presentation units. Because the limit of working memory is about seven items of information, in highly technical presentations no more than five important facts should be presented before participants have a chance to process the data. For less fact-intensive content, processing time might be planned to occur at regular 15- to 20-minute intervals.

When deciding about content-process ratios during the presentation itself, presenters need to be able to make decisions on their feet, even when they countermand the decisions made in the planning stage. I was recently reminded of this as I began the afternoon of a full-day session. The public agenda said "Coaching Competencies." Because the agenda was so artfully vague, I could eliminate portions of my planned (but not communicated) content without the participants feeling that they were missing out on anything. This allowed me time to address their need to interact and relate the content to their own experiences. In this case more process time than I had planned was crucial for participants to be able to accept a new perspective. My broadly painted public agenda and my reading of participants allowed me to drop content, meet the unanticipated needs of the group, and not repeat my earlier painful experience.

There are many other on-their-feet decision opportunities that presenters encounter. One of these is the after-lunch sleepiness syndrome. I explore in this chapter 3. In-the-moment choices to remove content is also facilitated by having the content organized in presentation "containers." Knowing a few ways of organizing content, which is what I mean by containers, can save planning time.

REMEMBER

1. Consider gum to be the content and chewing to be the processing people require for learning.
2. Provide adequate time to chew the gum you bring.
3. Your content is not as important as having the group process the content.
4. Information-intensive presentations can be effective as long as a great deal of processing occurs.
5. Processing requirements increase as the presentation goals move from knowledge to skills to attitudes.
6. Listeners must be given opportunities to mentally organize the data, check their understandings, and compare the data to personal experiences.
7. For attitude outcomes, the primary purpose of processing may be to help participants make meaning of an experience.
8. Presenters must be able to make decisions on their feet to modify the content-process ratio even when this overrides their design.

Use Organizers to Save Preparation Time

Relieve preparation stress and intensify learning.

In the next few paragraphs, some terms will appear in italics in parentheses. These are example of containers, or ways of organizing content. You will be able to easily refer back to these later.

(*Anecdote*) A few years before my wanderings in equatorial Africa, I took an assignment much farther north. It was a long weekend and a delightfully sunny one for Denmark for that time of year. Because of this, people had left Copenhagen for the countryside, and my wife and I were unprepared for the convoys of holidayers trying to ride the ferry from Odense back to Copenhagen on a Sunday afternoon. A friendly Dane in a Saab ahead of us explained what was happening and advised us that we would have about a 3-hour wait before we would be able to board. This being the case, I turned to the notes in my briefcase and, with Sue's help, began to plan the 2-hour presentation that I had been asked to make to members of the World Health Organization (WHO) the next day.

(*Problem*) Earlier, I might have agonized about the structure of that presentation for more time than it took to deliver it. This is often a problem for presenters, because they want to get the best possible results from a presentation but have limited time in which to prepare. As I've learned from painful experience, devoting energy to struggling with structure is not the best use of planning time.

(*Importance*) Deciding more important issues, like presentation goals, content, and delivery, is a better investment of time because these get to the heart of the learning experience—its essence and achievement, not the mechanics of organizing it.

(*Credibility*) Bruce Wellman and I wrote a book on presentations for the Association for Supervision and Curriculum Development (ASCD) (Garmston & Wellman, 1992) and in the process discovered the notion of organizers—formal structures, frameworks, "baskets," or "containers" into which the presenter can "drop" his or her content. Since describing some containers in the first edition of this book, I have found more, which appear here.

(*Solution*) Use presentation organizers to save planning time.

(*Subpoints*) To use them a presenter must know three things:
- Type of presentation goal and available time
- Information about the audience
- A variety of presentation organizers, from which the presenter can pick the best fit for the first 3 considerations

Type of Goal and Allocated Time

We speak to inform, to request action, to motivate, to entertain, and to instruct. Or, as Nick Morgan suggested at the beginning of this chapter, we should consider all of these as persuasion presentation, because this thinking focuses attention on the audience. To help you think about the organizers, try relating them to the scenarios described in Table 2-1.

In each case, materials, time constraints, and the presenter's goal—what he or she wants participants to do as a result of the presentation—interact to affect the type of presentation container that will be most useful. My purpose in Denmark was to motivate and instruct, and I guess, also to persuade.

Table 2-1. Which Container Might You Use?

Scenario 1:	A 15-minute presentation to a parents club to request volunteers for a project. You have printed materials.
Scenario 2:	A 40-minute keynote to a large group in an auditorium setting. You have no printed materials.
Scenario 3:	A 90-minute follow-up session in which teachers are bringing student work to share. You have rubrics.
Scenario 4:	A 30-minute board report requesting project approval for an innovative program serving handicapped students. You have printed materials.
Scenario 5:	A 10-minute presentation to an administrative team, requesting its participation in a moderately high-risk leadership professional development project. You have no printed materials.

Information About the Audience

Two types of audience information are useful in selecting containers. First, what is generally known about the audience? Is it a decision-making group, and if so, what formats are typically presented to it? How will furniture be arranged, and what limitations might that create? What are the norms for this group for interaction in presentations? Some high school faculties, for example, sometimes expect more lecture and less processing time than elementary school groups.

The second type of information concerns the immediate emotional environment. Is this a mandatory meeting? Is there anything in the recent history of this group that might affect its receptivity to you, the topic, or any presentation made to them at this time? For example, I was once asked to speak to a group that had recently received a memo explaining that in this first year of a new employee performance review system, far too many "excellents" were awarded. The situation was to be corrected next year by increased training of supervisors. Can you imagine this group's state of mind regarding any presentation, particularly a mandatory one (which this one was)? I also once used a puppet with a high school audience to develop a concept. Never again! They thought I was talking down to them.

What did I know about the group I was to work with in Denmark? It was an ad hoc group of WHO professionals. They would attend the session voluntarily out of a desire to increase the effectiveness of presentations they made; they each spoke several languages; they gave presentations in formal and informal settings, to large and small groups, to government officials, and to professionals and citizens interested in the field of health.

Presentation Containers

In this section I present eight time-tested containers, four more than in the first edition. Research shows that listeners remember better and remember more if they know the organization of the talk. The best presenters, then, are not only deliberate in choosing the organizing features of their presentation but also make these boldly obvious to the audience. Containers may sometimes be the entire organization for a presentation. (For example, the first three containers described below can be used for an extemporaneous speech.) At other times a presentation may employ several containers within the context of a formal opening, body, and closing.

Time Sequence

In the time sequence, you explain something in the exact order in which it occurred or happens in real time. For example: "First we discovered that students had rote knowledge of math and limited problem-solving capacities. Next we explored alternative approaches to our curriculum, and finally, we decided to incorporate manipulative materials into our math program. Let me describe our central findings at each of these stages."

Question-Answer

The question-answer container is built from answers to one or more key questions. To create this structure, first identify all major questions you think need to be answered, then add any extra questions your audience will likely want answered. Consolidate both lists of questions into one unified sequence (which becomes your question-answer framework). For example:

Opening.   "Today, we'll answer three basic questions:

First, how did the project begin? Second, how has it evolved? And third, how is it unique?"

Body.   "Let's start with how the project began."

"Now, let's see how it has evolved."

"Finally, how is it unique?"

Closing.   "So, in summary, we have answered three basic questions."

Three Ideas

The three-ideas container is used to focus listeners on important concepts or issues related to a topic. You might use this as an advanced organizer from which you could provide extensive elaboration or to highlight areas a group should consider in reaching a decision.

Opening.   "There are three components of self-directed learning: (a) self-managing—to set goals, success indicators, and timelines for one-self, (b) self-monitoring—to pay attention to where you are in your planned action and how you are doing in relationship to your success criteria, and (c) self-modification—the in-the-moment and post-event changes you make based on information from the first two stages."

Body. "Let's start by defining what we mean by self-managing, and its relationship to self-directed learning."

Closing. "So today we have identified three components of self-directed learning."

These first three containers can also serve as lightning-quick organizers for impromptu speeches. When the board president asks for your input on a topic, between the time of her question and you positioning yourself in a speaking posture, you can have arranged in your head a simple, logical set of mental notes from which to speak.

Startling Statement, Reasons, and Solutions

The fourth container opens by boldly stating a problem in a manner designed to achieve arousal, a psychological state of intense alertness and focus. This results in listeners' undivided attention. The speaker then follows with possible causes and a call to consider certain solution approaches. For example:

Startling statement. "After several years of steady gains, progress was stalled this year. The high school results are especially discouraging. Just 35% of 10th graders scored at the proficient level or above in English Language Arts, and a mere 6% of sophomores who took the algebra exam showed mastery of its standards."

Reasons. "An independent review of the exit exam found that students had not yet benefited from extensive educational reforms initiated by the state. Many of our teachers are working harder, but not differently, than before. Furthermore, most of our high schools are still using 50-minute instructional periods, inadequate for many forms of constructivist learning, and exhausting teachers and students as they move from subject to subject and room to room day in, day out, throughout the year."

Solution. "We must support teacher development and work to develop cultures of professional communities in schools. We can start now in two areas: (a) provide professional development on the rationale, forms, skills, and structures of professional communities; and (b) develop capacities for collaborative problem solving to develop standards and accountability for student success. Here are some practical ways we can pursue this."

Compare-Contrast

When you're presenting a choice between two or more alternatives (people, programs, equipment), an excellent organizer is the compare-contrast container.

This approach gives your audience a detailed, side-by-side comparison of each alternative. To compare teacher evaluation with supervision, for example, you would list the key attributes: who sets the observation and conference focus, who makes judgments about what is good or bad, and what is done with the data. Then you would speak about each attribute and how it is treated in the two systems.

Topical Grouping

If your topic is large and no other container seems exactly right, you might try a topical grouping. Design this by dividing the topic into several smaller subtopics, each of which is discussed in turn. For example, you might organize the topic "Facilitating the Learning Organization" in terms of three main sub-units: skills, structures, and leadership functions. You might discuss "The Human Body" by looking at each of its major subsystems: skeletal, circulatory, digestive, and so forth.

Topical grouping is a very common pattern and is usually easy to create (all you do is subdivide the whole into smaller parts), but it's also less original and less compelling than other options. Given the choice, you might consider another container first.

Cause and Effect

Cause and effect describes how one action leads to another. For example, when teachers extend wait time, the length and quality of student answers increase dramatically.

Problem-Solution

Problem-solution is one of the most exciting containers for me because of its versatility and logical appeal. Developed by Communication Associates, it is a nine-step organizer delivered in this sequence. It can also be used to organize writing.

I've used this container to organize this chapter. The problem is "best use of preparation time," and the solution is "containers." (If you like, return to the italicized words at the opening of this section that reveal five of the steps of this container.)

1. *Anecdote.* Tell a brief story in which a problem is illustrated that relates to your topic.
2. *Problem.* State the problem that the anecdote illustrates.
3. *Importance.* Tell why this is an important issue.
4. *Credibility.* Here you establish your own expertise. What gives you the authority to speak on this topic? Perhaps it is reading you have been doing, personal experiences, or people you have consulted.
5. *Solution.* Name or state the solution.
6. *Subpoints.* List about three supporting ideas for the solution. (In this chapter they are (a) type of goal and allocated time, (b) information about

the audience, and (c) information about containers.) Completing these first six steps provides the frame for the body of the presentation, which you will make in the next step.

7. *Essential details*. Now elaborate on each of the subpoints. This becomes the body of the presentation.

8. *Future*. Provide examples of how the solution will benefit the audience. (For example, in this chapter I stress that one of the major benefits of containers, as long as you have routinized a few, is that they save preparation time, freeing you from planning to focus on other important issues related to the presentation.)

9. *Action*. This is the close of your presentation. Now you ask for approval— a vote, a signature, an allocation of funds, or a commitment to try the ideas you have presented.

(Action) To save time in the preparation of your next presentation, I invite you to inventory the presentation containers you currently use and determine which of these might augment your repertoire (see Table 2-1). When you do that, I think you'll find that the time you've saved and the increased confidence you feel make it well worth the effort.

In the next section, I present a ninth container that I have recently learned.

REMEMBER

- Using organizers saves planning time.
- A presenter must know the presentation goal and available time; information about the audience; and an array of organizers from which to pick.
- If this is a decision-making group, learn what typical furniture arrangements are used and what limitations that might place on your design and outcomes.
- If this is a mandatory meeting, is there anything in the group's recent history that might interfere with their receptiveness?
- Research shows that listeners remember better if they know the organization of the talk.
- Inventory your repertoire of presentation containers and add two or three from which to choose.

Give a 2-Minute Speech

Be quick, be elegant, be persuasive.

The setting was Budapest. I was there with the Step-by-Step Program, an effort to democratize former communist schools and bring constructivist learning principles to teachers and students. This was sponsored by the Soros Foundation and was beginning its work at the preschool level and working up the grades.

I was to work with representatives of 27 countries, almost all of them former Soviet bloc nations located in Eastern Europe or the portion of Asia close to Mongolia. We worked at the Art'hotel Budapest in a room too small for even 20 participants. (Because public gatherings were illegal under communist rule, adequate meeting rooms did not exist.) Project staff joined us for the 2-day seminar on presentation skills, and there were 35 to 38 persons in the room. The staff sat in a row at the back wall because there was not enough table space. Five rounds, with six to eight chairs each, filled the space so tightly that to do a walkabout exercise on the second day I first had to remove some chairs. The cramped quarters did not produce crazy energy, however, as it usually does with American audiences. I suspect that this is because many of these people are used to too little space, families of five or more living in two-bedroom apartments. A book that captures the living conditions for many in this group is *How We Survived Communism and Even Laughed* (Drakulic, 1993).

Among the things I learned on this trip is that many of these people have limited time in their crowded agendas to influence or persuade. Almost everything is stacked against them. They are usually not members of the groups to which they present, the groups are policy bodies with limited time, and they have even less attention to give to dozens of reports and supplications they hear at each meeting. While we were together, drawing on other resources, including some notes from my father and other documents of uncertain origin, we developed and practiced the following presentation container.

I call this the "Get to the Point" container. It is useful for brief, even 2-minute, presentations or speeches. In this format the first sentence of your speech should break through any audience apathy or uninterest that may exist.

Next, build a bridge to the listener's interests. Remember the hierarchy of needs developed by psychologist Abraham Maslow. At the bottom of the pyramid were physiological needs, followed by safety, then social needs like love and belonging, ego needs like self-esteem, and finally self-actualization. Decide at what level on the pyramid you are going to focus your presentation. The lower the level, the more it will connect with the group if it is real. Political speechwriter Nick Morgan notes that in the 1992 presidential election in the United States, Bill Clinton spent time "feeling our pain." It wasn't until his message became "It's the economy, stupid" that he caught the electorate's attention. In a parent meeting in the Bronx recently, we said to parents, "Although the test is important, there is much more at stake. You want your children to be safe and able to make good judgments even when you are not there."

Give examples. Resist the urge to say more about your primary assertion. Finally, close by telling the audience what you want them to do about the information you have provided.

Table 2-2 summarizes the container.

Table 2-2. The "Get to the Point" Container

1. Ho Hum!
   - The first sentence of your speech must crash through your audience's apathy.
   - Kindle a quick flame of spontaneous interest.
   - Smokers do not like matches that fail to light with the first scratch.
   - Listeners do not like speeches that do not light with the first sentence.

2. Why Bring That Up?
   - Build a bridge to the listener's interests.
   - I bring up this subject because what happens to young children seems remote, but in reality it affects your future.
   - Until this bridge is built you are not ready to begin the body of your speech.

3. For Instance!
   - Resist the urge to say more about your primary assertion.
   - Plunge immediately into examples.

4. So What?
   - What do you want the audience to do about all this?
   - Ask your audience for some specific action which is within their power to give.
   - Join, contribute, convince, visit, vote, write, e-mail, buy, or investigate.

Here is an example of the container in action:

About 60% of all beginning teachers leave the profession within the first 3 years.

This is costing the state millions of dollars in lost tax dollars for teacher preparation and in poor achievement for students.

For example, in school district X in southern California, there was an 80% loss in 3 years. The least prepared teachers are teaching the children in this city. In some of the rural areas the dropout rate is as high as 70% (Harvey Hunt, personal communication, 2004).

We must find ways to retain our teachers in the profession. I advocate a system of one-to-one support for beginning teachers and am asking for funding for a teacher mentor program at a ratio of one mentor for every three new teachers. To start, I am asking you to authorize a university and school district task force to explore ways this can be accomplished.

Now you have a ninth container (organizer) for your content. Next we will consider issues related to follow-up.

REMEMBER

1. The 2-minute speech can be used when you have limited time on crowded agendas. It is good for policy groups.
2. This is a speech of persuasion.
3. Build a bridge to the listener's interests at lower levels on Maslow's hierarchy of needs.
4. Resist the urge to say more about your primary assertion. Move directly to examples.
5. The container can be summed up as follows:
   • Ho hum!
   • Why bring that up?
   • For instance!
   • So what?
6. Be brief, be sincere, be seated (Winston Churchill).

Design Effective Follow-Up

Leave them learning.

Recently I was invited to Laos to deliver a 2-day training, then help plan follow-through. On concluding the training, I met with the Professional Development Committee of the Vientiane International School. Four teachers serve on the committee (which is 25% of the faculty). The headmaster, myself, and two spouses (also teachers) brought the meeting size to eight.

Persistence is the key to the mastery of skills taught in professional development sessions, but how do we achieve it? This was an informal Friday evening after-dinner gathering. Our purpose was to begin the design for follow-up. Knowledge of implementation outcomes and principles were musts.

Implementation Outcomes

Two generic outcomes are appropriate to programs that develop skills: unconscious competence and the integration of new skills into work habits. A third outcome, reculturing, is necessary when the skills being learned relate to developing work cultures of collaboration.

The first outcome, unconscious competence, was especially challenging. This had been a 14-hour seminar in what normally would have taken 24 hours over several months. I am finding that in geographically isolated settings, such as rural areas in North America and in many international schools, professional development activities are often condensed into tighter than desirable time frames.

Unconscious competence (I know it so well my performance seems effortless) is an ultimate goal. As described earlier, it follows unconscious incompetence (I don't know that I don't know), conscious incompetence (I know that I don't know), and conscious competence (I know that I know). Aikido Master George Leonard (1991) regards the third stage, conscious competence, as where the deepest learning occurs. Here neurological and psychological adjustments are made. Old patterns of responding are unlearned. Persistence during the mechanical state of conscious competence is required to achieve this.

During training, foreshadow unconscious competence as a goal. Explain that only 20% of learning will occur inside the room and that 80% comes from practice outside the seminar setting. Provide between-session assignments and record-keeping devices for continuing practice.

The second outcome, integration of new skills into work habits, requires teaching for transfer, as transfer does not happen automatically. In transfer, knowledge and skills associated with one context are extended for application in another. Transfer is enhanced when a presenter persistently mediates the processes of abstraction and connection making to new contexts. In the Laos training, for example, participants were asked to explore how a teacher planning conversation protocol could be used in a parent conference. Help participants build the metacognitive skills to guide new systems of behavior. When, in what ways, and to what ends do I use my new skills?

Reculturing is our third goal. In the case of the Vientiane School, we were working on 2 of 11 factors found by Marzano (2003) to affect student achievement. One factor is collegiality and professionalism; the second is the instructional decisions made by individual teachers. Our vehicle was Cognitive Coaching[SM], which means that the habits and skills of mediating thinking and collegiality would become values, skills, and norms permeating classrooms, staff meetings, parent conferences, and lunchroom talk.

Designing Follow-Up

Table 2-3 summarizes seven questions that drive well-formed implementation design. The answers to each are dependent on principles of learning and the skills being taught.

Quantity

How many repetitions does it take to learn a skill? This answer varies according to what is being learned and, indeed, what standards you set for mastery. Studies in Cognitive Coaching[SM] suggest that six to eight coaching cycles may mark a threshold in which the person being coached has internalized the coaching voice. This is less practice than is required for applying moderately complex teaching strategies. Why? For each lesson taught, there are seven mental engagements, which, in a sense, are really additional practices: (a) develop a plan, (b) have a coaching conversation about my plan, (c) continue to reflect before teaching, (d) access components of the plan (goals, success indicators, approaches) while teaching by working memory with a special clarity because of the planning processes, (e) reflect after the lesson, (f) have a reflecting conversation with a coach after the lesson, and (g) probably continue to reflect after the conversation. Furthermore, because of the nature of reflecting conversations, the teacher moves beyond episodic learning, composing generalizations and commitments to action that extend beyond the nature of the particular lesson.

Table 2-3. Implementation Design Questions

1. Quantity

   How many practices are there?

2. Frequency

   How close together should they be done?

3. Relevance

   How relevant is the new practice?

4. Integrity

   How true is the practice to the original model?

5. Intensity

   Are more skills or training needed?

6. Transfer

   How will the transfer of skills be taught?

7. Ownership

   How will program implementation be managed?

Normally these seven questions are addressed in the initial stages of planning a training program. In Laos, they became the questions around which the professional development committee would design the follow-up work.

Frequency

Is there an ideal frequency of practice in the beginning of implementing to support the development of new habits? Two middle school English teachers and I kept journals during a semester in which we engaged in Cognitive Coaching[SM]. One finding was that for about 2 weeks after a coaching session, the coach's voice was still in the teachers' heads. However, early in the project, teachers reported that beyond 2 weeks, old mental habits took over, and the daily demands of teaching crowded out self-coaching thought. Set expectations and provide time for frequent practice.

Relevancy

Can I use it tomorrow? Help teachers see the relevance of what they are learning. When new behaviors are considered to be of limited benefit, it is natural to avoid practice. Withdrawing from practice creates a landslide in which quantity of practice, frequency, relevance, and integrity (the next question) are affected. Combined, these affect the teacher's perception of learning, which is itself a motivator.

Integrity

Will the practice of skills learned in seminars be true to the initial instruction? Implementation mutations are natural. Some are benign, some are useful and should be shared with others, and some are destructive. Gather, analyze, and apply data to determine if the intervention is being implemented widely and properly; if not, devise corrective steps. In Cognitive Coaching[SM], for example, losing intellectual rigor will reduce value. Reduced value affects relevance, which tempers satisfaction and ultimately affects quantity and frequency.

Intensity

Is the initial training enough? Are additional skills required? For the Vientiane School, because the training was an abbreviated version of a full program, certain concepts and skills were not developed during the initial training. More training was needed, so they made arrangements for follow up training.

Transfer

How will you support teachers in transferring coaching skills into other venues—students, parents, full groups? Some transfer may occur naturally because of an overlap in surface similarities. A planning conversation with a teacher is similar in many aspects to a parent-teacher conference. However, most transfer requires a deliberate, studied application of a skill from one context to another. Until concepts and skills are transferred into the broader fabric of school life, neither integration nor reculturing can be done.

Ownership

Finally, establish governance structures that provide for teacher involvement in decisions. Every new program needs a watcher. Someone must tend, take the pulse, watch for mutations, encourage, assess, and solve implementation problems. It became clear to the Professional Development Committee that follow-up required more persistence and greater resources than did the training itself.

As the evening ended, we said our goodbyes and the teachers rode off in old Volkswagen Bugs or astride motorcycles, ponchos and helmets gleaming in the light Laotian rain.

REMEMBER

1. Persistence is the key to mastery.
2. Two generic outcomes are developing unconscious competence and integration of new skills into work habits.
3. Unconscious competence follows conscious competence, in which people can perform a skill, but at a mechanical level.

---

cont.

4. Integration into work habits requires deliberate teaching for transfer.
5. Reculturing is often the most important and most difficult goal.
6. During the planning stage, consider seven questions for sound implementation design.
7. A workshop is the least of the work; maintaining the learning is at the heart of effective professional development.

Summary

Fundamental to presentation design are four questions: What do I want participants to learn? How will I know they are learning it? What strategies or approaches will I use? What can I learn by designing and delivering the content and how can that inform refinements?

Also fundamental to good design is knowledge of how meaning is constructed by learners. We examined the three-phase teaching-learning model developed by Lipton and Wellman (2003), which represents a synthesis of current research in learning theory.

Several issues related to design were developed: what to do before the opening, how to arrange the room for participants, use of music to enhance learning, and paying attention to what is often overlooked—the presenter's own workspace.

Several continuing tensions for presenters as they design are deciding what content to include in a presentation, managing the content-time dilemma, and determining content time versus process time. Finally, this chapter presented nine presentation organizers, the awareness of which saves much valuable planning time.

CHAPTER 3

How To Deliver Effective Presentations

Have more influence with less effort.

Plan before you act. Chapters 1 and 2 explored issues related to planning and laid the foundation for effective design. In schools, teacher planning has significant impact on student learning. Planning produces the greatest effects when it is based on deep knowledge of subject matter, information about students and how they learn, and age- and content-appropriate teaching strategies. With the exception of subject matter, chapter 1 addressed these elements for adult learners and provided a vision for transformational learning. Chapter 2 added details to the work of design.

This chapter begins to explore the intricacies of delivery. There are many platform skills that can turn an ordinary presentation into an unusually effective one. In the next chapter, Kendall Zoller will add further depth in a discussion of the unusual impact that nonverbal communication has on learning.

This chapter is contained within bookends, so to speak, appropriate to the topic of presenting: ways of opening and closing a speech, presentation, or workshop. Within these "bookends" are thoughts on audience rapport, uses of and tips on humor, and considerations for speaking with parents and other audiences. Next are strategies for maintaining momentum through predictable and unusual slowdowns (like after lunch). Responding to questions can be tricky and is often where presenters lose credibility. I've included some research on this topic and tips from accomplished presenters. Finally, before the section on closing, there are ways to give value-added presentations through providing "triple track" agendas.

How to Open

*Get the group on your side of the room
in the first 3 minutes.*

The connection with Juma was immediately good. From the moment he met us at the Kilimanjaro airport, we felt comfortable and in good hands. I have come to believe that this sense is essential for a successful opening.

> *Notes From a Safari Journal*
>
>   *I'm very pleased that Juma is our*
>   *guide. Sue is, too. We both like him and*
> *can't imagine what it would be like to be in such*
> *close quarters for so long with a guide with whom*
> *we felt tense.*

I've searched for years for the perfect opening, but there isn't one. All depends on the group, the setting, and what is real for me in the moment. This shouldn't take a rocket scientist to figure out, but sometimes I am slower than I would like to be.

I have, however discovered a practical template for openings and clear purposes for its use. My personal notes now generically contain the list shown in Table 3-1. These are five opening organizers within which I work to energize, intrigue, focus, and develop a rapport with the audience. They are applicable—as a model to be used flexibly—in a third-grade classroom, a high school history unit, a university class, a speech, or a workshop.

Table 3-1. Presenter's Notes

- Welcome
- Connections with the Audience
- Purposes
- Agenda
- Activator

The Magical Word *Begin*

Insert "to begin," at any point in your opening comments. The subliminal message is that you have begun, no matter what you are doing. For those anxious to get on with the content, this is satisfying.

A Theory of Openings

The first 3 to 5 minutes are critical in developing expectations, receptivity, and relationship with a group. Consider an opening from the audience's point of view. They want to know who you are, what the topic is, and what's in it for them. Tell them that within the first few minutes. Now consider an opening from the presenter's point of view as an opportunity to send the following five important signals:

- I know who you are.
- I will not waste your time.
- I know my subject.
- I am well organized.
- I am approachable.

Openings create conditions for receptiveness. Table 3-2 shows goals and important ideas to communicate within the first few minutes.

Table 3-2. Conditions for Receptiveness

Goals	Communicate
• rapport, focus, energy • presenter credibility • participant benefits	• presuppose learner sufficiency, efficacy, and nobility of intentions • concern for creature comforts • a cognitively safe enviornoment

Nick Morgan (2003), editor of the *Harvard Management Communication Letter* and founder of Public Words, a communications coaching company, recommends making an "elevator speech" as part of your opening. This is what you would say on the top floor of an elevator to a person who is deciding whether to attend your seminar. The elevator is going down. You don't have much time. Make it one sentence, Morgan proposes, in which three elements are present: the benefits to the listener, the word *you*, and an emotion, because emotion is ultimately what motivates us and guides our decisions. Thus, a sample "elevator speech" would be "In today's session you will learn to overcome apprehension about public speaking and move audiences to take action."

The audience wants to perceive you as credible. Help them out by standing still during the first moments of introduction so they can "take your measure." Let them know you are paying attention to them. If you say hello, wait for a response. If you don't get one, elicit a response. There are many ways of stating your credentials indirectly without bragging. If your resume has been read to the group, decrease the psychological distance that might have been created with the group by making a personal comment ("What I didn't hear in that resume was my interest in backpacking," or "Hmm, it didn't mention my grandchildren. Any other grandparents here?"). Credentialing can be accomplished by referring to your time with a similar group ("Last month I was working with mentor teachers in X and learned that Y"). You can also refer to your own experience if it is appropriate to your topic ("My 15 years as a history teacher have taught me . . ."). Another credentialing move is to state your association with known experts in the field ("When Sigmund Freud and I were working together . . ."). Oops, I didn't want to reveal my age!

Address creature comforts early—but, as a rule, not before statements of welcome, connections and purposes (unless someone is introducing you—then let him or her do it). Creature comforts, at the minimum, include bathroom locations, coffee, and breaks.

In our discussion of transformational presentations in chapter 1, we noted that the work of transformation starts even before the opening. Have your demeanor and comments reflect your suppositions about the audience: They are sufficient (not deficient and you are here to "fix" them), they have noble intentions, and they have efficacy and can take care of themselves, their comfort, and their learning. Communicate your respect for individuals, for the group, and for the knowledge, skills, attitudes, and experiences that learners bring to the educational setting. Use names and thank people for comments or questions.

To learn, one must feel safe to take risks, to be a "public learner"—that is, to reveal one's own lack of knowledge in front of others. You can create a learning environment of safety by scaffolding tasks for success, by humor, by exchanging learning partners for paired or small-group activities, and by revealing your own learning and mistakes. It is good to keep in mind that safety is different from comfort. Discomfort is often the avenue to learning, yet we must feel safe enough to take that risk.

Energy is also required for learning—the energy that is beyond fatigue, the energy to care, and the energy to want to learn, to be able to concentrate, and to believe one is capable. One-minute stretch breaks and a variety of other movement options contribute to keeping the physical sources of energy in place. Structuring learning tasks for maximum safety (pairs are always safer than larger subgroups) also keeps energy available for learning.

Although these conditions can be evoked in the opening, it is important to maintain them across the entire learning experience.

Table 3-3 shows sample expressions for the welcome, connection, and purposes portions of an opening. In what ways might some of these elicit energy, focus or relationship? In which comments are references to presenter credibility and respect for the audience? With which of these might you be most comfortable? (Having written this last question, I am reminded that the most important issue is never what are you comfortable with; it is rather, what is most effective.)

Recognizing Conditions for Learning

How will you know if the opening comments you select are getting the results you want? What might you pay attention to to determine if the environment is learning-ripe? Look for full attention on you as presenter and the participants' responsiveness to directions. Also, seek indicators that the collection of individuals is becoming a group: movements in unison (like laughter or opening books on command); heads and shoulders leaning into the group during small-group activities; and participant voice qualities that are conversationally normal for the culture. Other cues include facial animation, erect body postures, and heads up rather than down. You can also watch for an absence of cliques, isolates, or other disaggregations in grouping.

Table 3-3. Sample Opening Comments

WELCOME STATEMENT	ALTERNATIVE STATEMENTS
Good morning! I'm Bob Garmston and I'm delighted to be here.	• Good morning! Say hello to the real experts in the room, the people sitting before, behind, and on either side of you. • Good morning! I've spent this last year interviewing teachers who do the type of work you do. I am even more proud of our profession than I was before. I hope to share some of my excitement and what I have learned with you today. • Good morning! I'm Bob Garmston. My job is to talk and your job is to listen. If you get through before I do, please let me know. • Good morning! I am glad to be here for three reasons: (1) I am an avid _____'s [the local sports team] fan, (2) the topic is critical for you, and (3) I work only with bright audiences.
CONNECTION STATEMENT	ALTERNATIVE STATEMENTS
You know teaching is the most cognitively complex of the professions—more complex than law, architecture, or medicine. Imagine, a surgeon works on only one person at a time, and that person is usually anaesthetized. [*pause*] Maybe some days, that's not a bad idea.	• You have one of the toughest jobs in education today because _____ . • I imagine that some of you might be thinking, "I could be making this presentation." You are right, and I feel both honored and humbled to be addressing this topic, given all the expertise in this room. • I've promised [a member of the group] not to share pictures of my grandchildren on the screen today [*pause*] unless someone requests it. • Of all the roles I've played in education, _____ is closet to my heart because _____ . • I talked with quite a few [the role in this room] before coming here and learned that _____ . • Thank you for the glowing introduction. What I would like to add is that I also have four preschool grandchildren, each of whom is cute and bright.

cont.

PURPOSE STATEMENT	ALTERNATIVE STATEMENTS
My purpose is to support you in the work you are doing refining mathematics skills for students. To that end I will be sharing some research about students' mental processes, some practical strategies for you to consider, and some time-saving tips.	• Today's purpose is to extend the capacities of teams to work effectively together so you can be more comfortable and effective in truly meeting student needs. • Our purpose is to support you in your challenging roles as teacher leaders. To that end we will explore practical tools and strategies, what teachers want from you, and some tips on trust. • My intention today is to support the collective deepening of knowledge about _____ . • Our goals today are in two parts: for you, tools to increase your leadership comfort and confidence; for those you work with, a sense of direction and greater effectiveness in their work. *Notice that none of these statements is detailed. Later is the time to present specific learning outcomes. At this point your purpose is let the group know what this is about and align them with the broad purposes.*

Consider these as signals that the group has energy for learning, feels comfortable and respected, is present, and is open to ideas, information, and experiences.

Too Much Energy

How might you know that you don't have a learning environment? Here is one example and an in-the-moment response. It was the first day of the work year for 30 administrators. Jeff Peltier—at that time the professional developer for the North Thurston School District in nearby Lacey, Washington—and I opened a 2-day session on supervising teachers. We had planned an opening that concluded with a small-group discussion of what was pleasing them and troubling them about supervising teachers. As Jeff and I listened to people and observed the pre-opening energy in the room, we were clear that our planned opening had a good chance of failing. We had energy in the room. That was good, but it was ricocheting off the walls and the people in ways that defied our attempts to focus the group.

We anticipated that a lack of energy would not be a problem with this group. In fact, there was abundant energy, but none of it was headed in the direction we wanted. Prior to our opening, the group was animated and so engaged in informal discussions of personal topics that Jeff and I actually felt excluded from the conversations of participants. Our challenge was to ride the high energy in the room and redirect it to our topic. Without this, we would have a congenial carnival climate, but not a learning climate.

We rode the energy by inserting an activity for trios after saying hello. An administrator is like what kind of exotic food, we asked. Suddenly, the camaraderie and liveliness was focused on the task. The reporting out, and laughter, helped the group to begin to function as one group with a common purpose. In this case we entered at the group's level of energy, which gave us permission to move from there to a common focus.

One mistake I am finally beginning to overcome is rushing to content too soon with faculties back together for the first time after a summer break. They need a great deal of reconnection time.

Tools for Openings

The group is always the group's group, says Michael Grinder. Tacitly, the group gives you permission to present. You've achieved permission when you have focus, energy, rapport—and breathing.

Focus

Normally, focus can be achieved through a variety of rather straightforward strategies. Describing the goals and agenda, eliciting participant concerns about the topic, delivering a startling statement or statistic related to the topic, or posing a problem question is an effective way to get started.

These examples are in addition to paralanguage moves that we will explore in chapter 4. Both are important. In fact, without sufficient attention to nonverbal aspects of communication, the words are often ineffective.

Below are some elaborations on the generic elements of openings and additional moves that will focus a group.

State the purpose. Brief, clear statements let participants know why they are there and how the topic relates to them. Notice that the comments in Table 3-3 are statements of sufficiency that presume that knowledge and resources already exist on the topic. Notice, too, that each is artfully vague. Such statements are best made within the first minute or two of your comments. Later, if appropriate, specific learning goals for the session can be identified.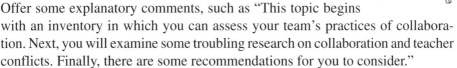

Preview the agenda. Use a posted public agenda, preferably on chart paper so that it can be used throughout the presentation to mark where you are. Even if you are using PowerPoint and the agenda is on one of the slides, you should still have it posted. It serves as an organizing system for the rest of the presentation. Offer some explanatory comments, such as "This topic begins with an inventory in which you can assess your team's practices of collaboration. Next, you will examine some troubling research on collaboration and teacher conflicts. Finally, there are some recommendations for you to consider."

Your comments help group members to make sense of the visual agenda, serve as an advanced organizer for their learning, foreshadow key points you wish to make, and underscore the relative importance of sections ("You may find this section of the presentation the most important for you to take home and use immediately").

The posted public agenda for this session might look like the following with some appropriate chart art (see chapter 6):

- Welcome and overview
- Inventory
- Research
- Recommendations

The agenda uses artfully vague language so you can adjust the emphasis as you learn more about the audience's interests. Items should also be stated without reference to times, except for the opening, ending, and lunch times. This gives you maximum flexibility in making decisions on your feet, without a group member at any time feeling "behind" because you aren't on topic X at exactly 10:00 A.M.

Make a provocative statement. Bypass the conventional pleasantries and go for shock value. Attention and focus is immediate. Following are some examples:

> Good morning. As you remember your last walk by the primary grades, you may recall the location of the kindergarten classes. Can you see some of these kids in your mind's eye? [*Long pause*] Ten of them will not make it through your school system. Which ones? What can you do about it today?

> You can close your eyes because I don't have any transparencies. But I hope you will keep your ears open because I have something worth hearing.

> I do not have much time with you today. In fact, I only have time enough to annoy you, and I plan to do this, much like a grain of sand annoys an oyster.

> The Sprinthalls [Sprinthall & Thies-Sprinthall, 1983] report disturbing findings about adult development. On tests of cognitive development, ego development, and moral reasoning, adults in fields of work other than teaching demonstrated continuing growth over the course of their careers. Teachers, measured on the same instruments, did not. Why? What organizational culture factors might contribute to this? What might be the implications for professional development?

I have used the latter opening several times in sessions about teacher cognition. Attention and curiosity are immediate. Be sure to have data to support such assertions. It gets attention, so be prepared to elaborate later about the research. Educators get hooked, and rightfully so.

Cite searing statistics. Appropriately related statistics and facts can also grab an audience's attention. Consider the following:

> Context: Imagine the 3 billion years of human existence as one cosmic super-month. Each second represents 2 years of time. [*pause*] Until 2 hours ago we were locked in the age of hunting and gathering. [*pause*] Lasers, satellites, com-

puters, biotechnology, satellites, cyberspace, and color televisions have appeared in only the last 20 seconds.

Complexity: Tiny events cause major disturbances. A change of one half-degree Fahrenheit on the surface of the ocean can change a tropical storm into a hurricane.

Priorities: In 2002, Americans spent more money on fast food than on higher education (Schlosser, 2002).

Pose a problem. Another move that can rivet a group's mental energy is to describe a perplexing and persistent problem and then add that the purpose of today's work will be to address that issue. Here is an example of a problem:

A problem: In examining student mathematics scores, a faculty predicted that basic math skills would be weakest. The faculty articulated these predictions and described the assumptions that led them to that conclusion. However, the actual scores revealed basic facts to be comparatively high, but number concepts were low. Yet in designing solution procedures, the faculty concentrated on improving basic skills. Why?

Energize

Why are some groups "energyless"? Participants report a range of reasons for opening "blues" and nonparticipation. These include not wanting to be there, social discomfort from not knowing other participants, and feeling low in the role hierarchy represented. Participants sometimes report low energy related to a limited understanding of the topic's relevance, not knowing why they are there, anxiety about "performing" well in the workshop, organizational stress, or just plain fatigue. Since mental and emotional energy can be directed either internally (my thoughts, feelings, concerns, sensations, and attitudes) or externally (the environment, the topic, other participants), and a presentation requires commonly focused internal and external energy, the presenter's job is to get the energy flowing in roughly the same direction.

Because physiological changes ensure changes in energy and emotional state, one road to energizing is to get people moving. Have participants sit with someone they don't know, do a birthday lineup, stand up and interview several other participants, or rearrange the furniture. Another approach is to direct their collective attention to some topic-related activity. In pairs, have them list and share personal goals for the workshop, or have them list what they know, want to know, or think they know about the topic. In small groups, have them list their concerns or develop causal theories for a current situation (e.g., many of our most intellectually capable teachers are leaving the profession) and give possible solutions.

I've found that such opening idea-generating exercises with pairs, trios, or quartets not only energize, they also illuminate the purpose for being there and help me establish rapport with the group. In addition, they are sound instructional practices because they support learners in activating their prior knowledge, their thinking about their knowledge, and their engagement with other learners.

Establish Rapport

During the first few minutes of a presentation, most audience members are hard at work making judgments about the presenter's credibility, the topic's relevance to their interests, and the personal benefit-loss ratio of attending the session. As described earlier, it's useful for the presenter to stand still at the opening to aid participants in making judgments—but not for too long. Many presenters make it a rule to engage the audience within the first 5 minutes in the types of idea-generating, small-group discussions mentioned above. This shifts attention from the speaker and redirects it where it most properly belongs, to the relationship with the audience and the collective expertise in the group.

Because rapport is the product of credibility, respect, and perceived personal concern and similarities, a range of beginning activities can hasten this connection between the presenter and the participants: pre-opening one-to-one conversations (I care about and am interested in you); presentation of an agenda (I'm organized, know where I'm going, and respect your time); invitations to proactively attend to comfort and learning needs (I know you're adults with unique styles and interests, and I respect that); use of names and eye contact (this is a personal communication between us); humor (let's not take this or me too seriously, we have permission to have fun); and clear and visible motives (I am personal with you when I share, without pretense, my intentions in this relationship, and you don't have to worry about hidden agendas).

Focus, Energy, and Rapport

Is one of these three significantly more important than the others in a presentation opening? Yes and no. No, because all three are inextricably intertwined in their support of quickly producing an optimum learning environment for adults. For example, when Jeff and I were able to focus the administrator group described earlier, we also drew ourselves into their inner circle of energy, and we developed focus and rapport. Yes, because relationship is the ultimate context and foundation for learning. In fact, rapport most often generates responsiveness, as it did with our administrator group.

Focus, energy, and rapport are all enhanced by humor. Humor also assists learning, as we shall see in the next section.

REMEMBER

1. The first 3–5 minutes of a presentation set tone, expectations, and relationship with a group.
2. A generic template for openings includes a welcome, connections with the group, purposes stated with artful vagueness, an activating exercise, specific goals, and the agenda.

cont.

3. Practice developing an "elevator speech" to use in your opening.
4. People want to know who you are, what the topic is, and what relevance the topic has to them.
5. Credential yourself briefly, without bragging.
6. Create a safe learning environment by scaffolding learning tasks for success.
7. Your first goals are focus, energy, and rapport.

Do's and Don'ts of Humor

You can get them laughing without being funny.

Caution! Potential risk ahead! The anecdote below is neither a suggestion nor a standard for podium humor.

About the time this book went to press, John Dyer, independent consultant and associate of the Center for Cognitive Coaching, presented in Singapore. He was to make a keynote speech on "The Power of Laughter in Learning" to 1,000 people, following a serious message from the welcoming principal, a sober presentation by the minister of education, and an opening address (read: boring) by a professor from England. I offer this anecdote not as an exemplar of what you might do, but as an example at the extreme end of the comic scale, which only a very gifted and loose individual like John would even think of performing.

When John (who is Canadian) began, the audience never knew what hit them. He wrote to me as follows:

> Some advance preparation was obviously required, as I had to review my material and eliminate any references to North American culture with which they would not be familiar. I also had to delete anything that was linguistically based. As it turned out, the choices I made were effective. During the break after the presentation I felt something like an aging rock star.
>
> I got a lot of attention and multiple compliments on the keynote. I definitely got off on the right foot by getting on the stage and taking a picture of the audience as the first thing I did. I got them to stand and wave and say, "Hi, Canada!" Their reaction was hilarious. Due to my own nervousness and oversight, for the first couple of pictures the flash on the camera didn't go off. I looked at the camera and said, "This camera must have been made in Japan." It turned out to be a good use of local humor.

John is my humor guru, but his form of humor is unique and doesn't fit well on me. Many accomplished performers would be mortified to think of using any form of physical humor, yet they engage audiences in laughing together. So as you read on, trust and be true to your own style.

John is funny because he looks for humor in his environment. He describes it as a state of mind or a way of interacting with the world. At both the conscious and subconscious levels he searches for the humor that surrounds us. Like any skilled artist, he practices. One of my favorite stories is of John alone in his car at a traffic light on his way to work, practicing some new lines, slapping the dashboard and laughing uproariously as drivers in nearby cars looked nervously in his direction.

John's greatest gift to me, and one I hope I can adequately pass on to you, is that the best presentation humor comes not from the presenter but from the audience. Perhaps it would be slightly more correct to say that it comes from interactions within an environment that the presenter sculpts and then steps inside of to watch, participate in, and enjoy. Once, when I was presenting in Jerusalem to a group with the Branco Weiss Institute for Thinking, I found myself trying to explain the term *strange attracters*. A woman from the back of the crowded room stood up and said that she had a science background and would be happy to clarify. I watched the group nod and make other signs of attentiveness and understanding as she spoke for about 4 minutes in Hebrew. The group thanked her, turned to me, and I commented, "Now what she said was . . ." The group and I laughed until tears were in our eyes. What made that funny, in part, was that it was humor directed at me, as the one with limited language skills.

One of the benefits of laughter is a momentary increase in pulse and blood pressure, which then drop to levels lower than before, reaching an ideal learning state. Laughter also causes the secretion of certain positive endorphins that are critical elements of the human immune system. Laugh and stay healthy.

Humor clears the mind and opens the brain to higher levels of thinking. It reduces stress and anxiety. A learning environment that supports fun is motivating for the participants. Information connected to an entertaining event is more readily committed to long-term memory. Humor refocuses individuals whose attention has drifted away from the topic of the presentation. Because humor results from lateral thinking rather than linear thinking, the intentional inclusion of it encourages divergent thinking, imaginative problem solving, and creativity. Humor helps to build relationships within the group. It contributes to the establishment and maintenance of the learning community.

Getting Laughs

One of my most serious dilemmas regarding humor is that the more I read about it, the more depressed I become about my own comedic abilities. I've come to the conclusion that to get any better at all, I have to stop reading. In fact, a major motivation for writing this chapter was the selfless belief that in passing on to you some of what I've learned, I might also ease my depression. The late comedian Steve Allen (Allen & Wolliman, 1987) said that not everyone is funny, but everyone has a sense of humor. We may not become professional comedians, but we can increase our humor quotient. What follows are ideas that I'm learning about presentation humor, some of which I've read and much of which John has taught me.

John says that the real goal is to create an environment for humor. Most of us are not stand-up comics, but we can become environmental architects for humor. We can intentionally craft the conditions in which humor can flourish and give permission to the participants to enjoy their learning. We can let them know that it is okay to have fun here and acknowledge the importance of releasing the child within. We can allow the participants to contribute to the humor rather than trying to be the sole source of it ourselves. There are three stages for these special design considerations: before the opening, during the opening, and throughout the body of the presentation.

Before the Opening

John advises that we set expectations for humor through our first contact with participants. We signal a lighthearted tone to the participants when the written announcements of the presentation or the signs on the workshop door contain clever graphics, cartoon characters, or cute text. This indicates to the participants that they can anticipate a comical touch in the session. Unexpected interactions before the session can also serve this function. Sometimes I will whisper to a small group of early arrivers, "There's a rumor going around that this is the smart table." This usually evokes laughter and some funny comments from the participants. I was joking like that once with a group in Georgia, and a woman asked me in an exaggeratedly drawn-out voice, "Tell me, is that a genuwine California accent?" Everybody within earshot cracked up laughing. When someone extends a handshake and says to John, "Hi, I'm glad to meet you," he may laugh and respond with "You don't know that yet." (Without a playful smile and a twinkle in your eye, this one might backfire.) Because rapport is never made with a group but only with individuals, personal contact and light bantering before a presentation can give permission for that tone to carry over into the work period.

During the Opening

As I mentioned earlier, the first few minutes of a presentation are important and set norms for the rest of the session. Four ways to stimulate opening humor are autobiographical comments, cartoons, synectic exercises, and fast-break statements. Kendall Zoller sometimes opens with "Thank you for being here [*pause*] as if you had a choice." Art Costa and I are co-founders of the Institute for Intelligent Behavior. That name occasionally evokes a giggle, so I sometimes build on that reaction by adding that my job is to make others feel intelligent and well dressed by my mere presence. Or sometimes I reveal that I'm an "empty nester" and then define that as a parent who has grownup children who have left home (and returned), left home (and returned), and so on. Many people relate to that and the group usually laughs. Another autobiographical line is to say, "I'm glad to be here. Actually, at my age, I'm glad to be anywhere." That used to get good laughs for George Burns, and, increasingly, I'm discouraged to note, it does for me.

Self-deprecating humor is the safest. (I really like self-deprecating humor, but I am not very good at it.) By taking ourselves lightly, we can more readily communicate with others.

As noted earlier, not everyone is funny. For the comically impaired, like me, there are a number of strategies that I use to include humor without having to be the source of the humor. Cartoon transparencies are good at getting laughs. (Always get permission to use published work from newspapers or other sources.) I've found it best to cover the caption until people have absorbed the picture. The laughter increases when we display and read the caption aloud. If the cartoon consists of a series of frames, cover all of the frames at the beginning, then display them one at a time, saving the disclosure of the punchline to the very end. Self-stick notes do this well.

Most people recognize if they are a good joke teller or not. If you are not a good joke teller (e.g., you don't remember them, you forget punchlines, or you aren't confident about how timing and intonation are part of the delivery), then I recommend that you don't use them. Jokes can be an entertaining part of a presentation but there are some conditions for success: (a) The presenter has to deliver the joke well; (b) the joke has to be congruent with the presenter's character—the presenter has to be comfortable and relaxed with the humor that he or she is using; (c) the joke has to have a direct relevance to the content; and (d) the presenter can't pretend to have made up the joke if he or she got it from somewhere else. Personalizing a joke is usually good. Pretense, however, reduces one's credibility. This can happen when you tell a joke as if it happened to you, and members of the audience have already heard someone else tell the story.

John confesses that one of the ways in which he has developed a joke repertoire is by noting what spontaneously created laughter in a presentation. Sometimes it was something he said, and at other times it was something a participant said in response to the presentation material. John records the comment so that the next time he presents the material, he can intentionally use that humor with the same material. He might, in fact, even pretend that he just made it up and imply that it was an impromptu remark. It's sleazy, he admits, but it works. I will sometimes ask, "Remember Jonas Salk, the man who invented polio?" and wait to be corrected.

Synectic exercises that evoke metaphorical thinking can tap creativity and tickle the funny bone. The presenter asks pairs or trios to answer the question "What game are you playing in this organization?" The answers can get an audience roaring. "We're playing badminton in a hurricane," or "Parcheesi™, because the name sounds really interesting, even though we don't really know how to play it," or "Hide-and-seek, because no one ever knows what the goals are; they keep changing so frequently!"

Finally, fast-break statements that employ both incongruity and syntactic structure—"We promise to adjourn promptly at the scheduled time of 4:30" (the real ending time is 3:00)—surprise people with the unexpected final thought and alert people that you are encouraging a playful atmosphere.

Throughout the "Bawdy" of the Presentation
Participants value energizers, particularly in long sessions. Bruce Wellman, my Vermont-based partner in the Adaptive Schools work, and I will frequently

engage a group in singing "My Bonnie Lies Over the Ocean," during which participants shift between standing or sitting whenever the B sound is sung. Silly instructions lighten moods. Sometimes we will designate as the reporter in small-group activities the person who is wearing the most elaborate shoes. We work to sprinkle funny lines into our most serious content.

Co-presenting offers an additional vehicle for humor. After some antic of mine, Suzanne Bailey used to look at audiences, point to me, and say, "I dress him up and can't do a thing with him." See chapter 5 for more on using a partner to keep an audience engaged.

For longer workshops, when John Dyer wishes to help people loosen up, he might get them on their feet to do something silly. "Humorobics" is one form that this can take. John explains that humorobics are uncomplicated laughing activities. He will model and invite people to (a) yawn and get ugly; (b) put both feet flat on the floor, shake the right hand and say EEEEEEEEE, shake the left arm and say AAHHHHHHH, shake the left leg and say BL-BL-BL-BL (i.e., blow through the lips), shake the right leg and say BLAAGGHHH, and lift both feet off the floor and say OUCHHHH; or (c) force laughter in unison, HA, HA, HA, HA, HA, HA, and continue until everyone is laughing naturally. Another exercise John does is to have a "laugh-off." People force themselves to laugh wholeheartedly and listen to everyone else's laugh as they do so. This frequently becomes uncontrollable.

You yourself must be comfortable leading any physical exercise. If you are not, don't do it. The group will sense your discomfort and will not fully participate. Also, explain why you are offering an activity. Link the rationale to the benefit you wish the group to receive.

I used the title of this section intentionally. *Bawdy* as a play on the spelling of the *body* of a speech is all right, but bawdy in tone is not. Occasionally a double entendre might emerge spontaneously from either you or the audience, and everyone will have a hearty laugh. However, my experience is that deliberate comedy based on sexual innuendo is not okay. Slapstick humor may also have limited appeal. I have met very few—if any—women who enjoy a Three Stooges routine. Many people (both women and men) do not like jokes that involve aggression, sexuality, or gender or ethnic stereotypes—they find them offensive. Even though I know individuals for whom this is not true, this is a sound guideline when working with groups. The line between "good taste" and "distaste" is in many shades of gray, depending on the character and perception of the listener. Be cautious not to offend. You cannot fail with good, clean, wholesome humor that everyone in the room can enjoy.

Why People Laugh

> The funniest animal is a duck.
>
> —Tad Friend

We don't know why people laugh, but this doesn't stop us from making theories about it. The source for the quote above is Dr. Richard Wiseman, professor of psychology at the University of Hertfordshire in England. He has been conducting a global humor study in which people rate other people's jokes on a 1 to 5 scale. Comparing scores for the same joke with names of different animals inserted in it, he found that the funniest animal is a duck.

Again we don't know why, but here is a possibility. One set of researchers has concluded that the left hemisphere of the brain is an efficient but narrowly programmed computer, whereas the right hemisphere would make a good audience for a humorous silent film (imagine a waddling duck). Perhaps the left side of the brain follows the story line about the duck and the right side of the brain sees the duck. Only the two hemispheres working together can fully appreciate a funny moment.

What we do know is this: When we laugh, the coordinated action of 15 facial muscles begins. What follows are spasmodic skeletal muscle contractions, a quickened heartbeat, and rapid breathing. The diaphragm contracts in clonic movements and then diminishes. Kendall Zoller elaborates on the brain's need for oxygen in chapter 4 and describes how oxygen allows access to the neocortex. Laughter refreshes the oxygen supply to the brain.

What is laughter really about? Evolutionary biologists are considering that laughter may occur in response to a perception of threat that shifts to a perception of safety. The cortex signals something alarming, and then the anterior cingulated gyrus, which detects incongruities, responds, "Don't worry, no threat." The laughter may alert others in the social group that the disturbance is trivial.

How to Increase Your Humor Quotient

Presenters get better at facilitating laughter in three ways: developing knowledge about and a repertoire of humor, practicing, and developing a humorous state of mind. For those who have a comic gift and want to expand it, some theories about what constitutes humor may be useful. For others, this may not be of interest and you may wish to move on to the section of humor resources.

Superiority Theory

Plato and Aristotle initiated what is called "superiority theory." The story provokes a "sudden glory" attending a perception of some deformed aspect of another or of our own powers. Here is an example:

> Some people my age are being diagnosed with AAADD: Age Activated Attention Deficit Disorder. The other day, I decided to wash my car. I started toward the garage, and spotted the mail on the hall table. I should go through the mail before I wash the car.

> I lay the car keys on the table, put the junk mail in the trashcan under the table, and notice that the trashcan is full. So, I put the bills back on the table and take out the trash first.

Since I'm going to be near the mailbox when I take out the trash anyway, I might as well pay the bills first. I see my checkbook on the table, but there is only one check left. My extra checks are in my desk in the study, so I go to my desk, where I find the bottle of juice that I had been drinking . . . and so on.

Below are some additional theories about humor.

Incongruity Theory

Incongruity is a disproportion between one's expectations and what one hears. The listener experiences surprise, then coherence—thus the laugh. Ken Zoller's "Thank you for coming—as if you had a choice" is an example. I once heard Garrison Keilor, comedic writer and radio host of National Public Radio's *A Prairie Home Companion*, respond to a question about what was his favorite book as a child. When his grandfather died, he gave him a book, and he treasured that book, carried it with him, read it and reread it frequently. He then explained that his grandfather had 14 grandchildren, and each one got one book from the grandfather's set of encyclopedias. Garrison got the M, and to this day he could tell you all about Mississippi, Mojave (the desert), Moibus strips, Macedonia, molecules, mummies, and other interesting facts about words that started with M. We were laughing so hard we had tears in our eyes before he was done.

Social Identity Theory

In social identity theory, a person esteems one's own group and disparages alien groups. These are generally no-no's for educators. There may be some exceptions, like the following story of a phone conversation with a tech support person:

Tech Support: "I need you to right-click on the Open Desktop."

Customer: "Ok."

Tech Support: "Did you get a pop-up menu?"

Customer: "No."

Tech Support: "Ok. Right-click again. Do you see a pop-up menu?"

Customer: "No."

Tech Support: "Ok, sir. Can you tell me what you have done up until this point?"

Customer: "Sure, you told me to write 'click' and I wrote 'click.'"

(*At this point the tech support person put the caller on hold to tell the rest of the tech support staff what had happened. She couldn't, however, stop from giggling when she got back to the call.*)

Tech Support: "Ok, did you type 'click' with the keyboard?"

Customer: "I have done something dumb, right?"

Theory of Three

Leo MacCarey, who directed early Laurel and Hardy films, says it is an unwritten rule that we laugh when there are two straightforward examples to establish a pattern and then a third, to shatter it. For example: "My favorite books are *Moby Dick*, *Great Expectations*, and *Rock-Hard Abs in Thirty Days*."

Fast Break or Syntactic Theory

In fast break, or syntactic, theory, the punch word comes at the very end of the sentence. Example: "A bicycle can't stand alone because it is two tired."

Humor Resources

For increasing comic knowledge and repertoire, read books about humor. Amazon.com has many listings with intriguing titles like *365 Instructions for Hysterical Living*, or *Unusually Stupid Americans: A Compendium of American Stupidity*. Read comedy books or the joke sections in *Reader's Digest*, scan newspapers and magazines looking for cartoons that are relevant to your presentation topics, remember accidentally funny lines that emerge in your presentations, and watch comedians on TV. Try a Google search for "humor." At my last check I found sources like Joke Data Base, the Comedy Board, and Unprinted News—a collection of news, and bizarre stories from around the world.

One of my favorite comics is Steven Wright, whose humor is dry, unexpected, and zany. One bit I've borrowed from him is to walk across the stage, stop suddenly, take off my glasses, and stare at them and say, "What do you know—my prescription just ran out!"

As in any skill development, knowledge is not enough. Practice teaches timing and refinements and ultimately contributes to unconscious competence in the use of humor. You develop the capacity to deliver a funny line or gesture without conscious thought. Off-stage is as good a place as any (and safer) to experiment with comedy.

Finally, acquiring a playful state of mind is the most powerful self-development strategy. You probably have experienced times in which humor came naturally. It's likely that you just saw the comedy in the events around you and took things less seriously. We can all enter this pleasant state of lightness, either by willing it to be so or asking ourselves the question, "If there were something funny about this, what might it be?" Entering this state gets easier with practice. By setting one's ego aside and not worrying about looking foolish or failing to get a laugh, we make the journey smoother. Jim Huge, a Colorado-based consultant and master of presentation humor, taught me to say, "That's humor!" after saying anything that fails to get a laugh. Bruce Wellman will often add a stage whisper to me, "Bob, if they don't laugh, it's not humor." We get laughs at two places. As professional comics know, that sort of poking fun at one's own failed attempts does produce laughter. Probably the core and real gift of John Dyer's humor is that he never tells a joke at someone else's expense, and he reveals himself through his humor to be a genuinely caring and gentle man.

Humor forms a bridge for you when you are talking to parents or other special groups. It is also a good bridge between yourself and any audience unlike you.

REMEMBER

1. In most cases, the best presentation humor comes from the audience, not the presenter. Create an environment for humor.
2. Humor clears the mind, reduces stress, and opens the brain to higher forms of learning.
3. Set expectations for humor before the session starts in informal interactions with participants.
4. If you are not a good joke teller, don't tell jokes.
5. One source of humor is something said by accident in an earlier presentation that got a laugh. Use it again as if it were new.
6. Bawdy humor is not OK and will be offensive to someone in the audience.
7. When we laugh, 15 facial muscles interact, skeletal muscles contract, and heartbeat and breathing increase. This pumps the brain with oxygen, an essential fuel for learning.
8. Having a playful state of mind is the most potent self-development strategy for humor.

Speaking to Parents and Other Audiences

Remember your humanness and forget your role.

At the end of a presentation a woman said, "Thank you for speaking in a language I could understand. I'm a community representative on my school district's strategic planning commission, and often I go home after a meeting wondering just what it was the educators were talking about." Her comment caused me to reflect on the changing nature of schoolwork and a rich learning experience that I had had with parent members of school advisory committees the week before. Both perspectives reminded me that educational jargon belongs in the faculty room and not in public meetings.

North American schools are being tossed on many waves in the name of "reform." Three currents influence communication with school communities. One current is the emerging reality that parents are partners (not clients!) in the school enterprise. Parent participation in school site committees has increased, and community members at large are taking greater part in public meetings, councils, and task forces. The second current is about changing demographics, spurred by an unprecedented immigration wave from all over the world. Public school classrooms—particularly in the Canadian provinces of British Columbia and

Ontario and in states such as California, Florida, Texas, and New York—are filled with a rainbow of races and hundreds of different ethnic, cultural, and national groups. The sounds of nearly 100 different languages can be heard in many schools. Into this milieu steps the educator, presenting to increasingly mixed adult audiences. The third current affecting schools and community communications is the emphasis on accountability measures, high-stakes testing, and public access to records of school performance.

Below are several ideas for clear speaking on complex topics.

Slow Down

Recently I conducted a 2-day seminar for school advisory groups in which half of the audience was parents, some spoke no English, and many were from low-income homes. Because in any group one feels resourceful only to the degree that one is familiar with the topic, it is important to judiciously pace the flow of ideas on complex topics. I realized that in this setting of parents and educators, my typical speaking pace needed to be altered. Presenters have many ways they can slow the flow and make the content more user-friendly. These include speaking more slowly than usual at the beginning of a session so that participants can get used to your speech patterns and style, pausing more frequently and for longer periods, consciously using nonverbal skills to illustrate concepts, paraphrasing oneself, and repeating key ideas.

Enunciate

Unfamiliarity with the sounds and patterns of a speaker's language can contribute to miscommunication. If many audience members speak English as a second language, learn to enunciate clearly the sounds that are unusual in languages other than English. Stephanie Nickerson (1995) notes that people whose native languages lack sounds such as the *th* in *then* and the *th* in *thin* typically substitute a *z* or *d* sound for the *th* in *then* and an *s* or a *t* for the *th* in *thin*. She writes that her French-Swiss grandmother used to say "zeeze leetle seengz zat confuse me" ("these little things that confuse me"). Such substitutions can make communication difficult.

Teach Vocabulary

Presenters can teach vocabulary that has special meaning and is central to a session by alerting the audience that they will be talking about a word, using the word, defining it, giving an example, and perhaps eliciting a choral repeat of the word if it is unusual enough. Once, at the International School in Aleppo, Syria, I asked the group for the Arabic word representing the concept I was portraying. I used the Arabic term repeatedly, to the audience's delight and comprehension.

Request Translators

Arrange for language translators in advance. In addition, ask for a show of hands to see who else is multilingual and can assist with translations and clarifications during a presentation. Even better, create subgroups across roles and language groups for any group activities. Mary Bailey, a principal in the Fresno Unified School District, used to conduct some of her parent meetings in Spanish and provide an English translator so that all could appreciate the energies that go toward participating in a meeting conducted in another language.

Resist the Tendency to Consider Differences Inferior

Anthropologist Edward Hall notes that Americans have a tendency to consider differences inferior. Studies also reveal that many Americans have a tendency to unconsciously judge people who speak nonstandard English as less trustworthy and less intelligent. Nothing could be further from the truth than this assumption of limitation. I will always remember a graduate student in one of my university classes who opened his strongly accented presentation to classmates with this statement: "Please because I do not speak good English, do not consider me not smart. Remember that I am speaking to you in my second language, and I speak two others as well."

Beware the Hidden Cultural Chasms

Cultural differences aren't just about geography, relative wealth, skin color, or national origin. Culture has to do with how one thinks about life and work. Forms of reasoning are culturally influenced. For example, people in Asia do not share the Aristotelian mode of reasoning prevalent in the West. Workers in an engineering firm are likely to approach problem solving differently than many teachers do. A superintendent whose total work history had been in private industry told me that 6 months after being hired to lead a school district, he came to appreciate the differences between education and the private sector. "We do the same work," he said, "but we live in different worlds." He explained that the social, political, and financial fabrics of the two worlds were as different as night and day, and that this led to work domains driven by different assumptions and peopled by different human resources. So when I speak to parents, the public, or a gathering of public service representatives, I must remember to forget my culture and remember my humanness.

A few years ago I was working with teachers in Singapore schools and was forewarned that the group tended not to be very interactive in learning. Because of this, and because I was teaching instructional skills related to thinking, I developed a rich rationale for why student learning is enhanced by verbalization with other students. For participants to experientially understand the value, I suggested it would be important for them to engage in some interactive strategies I had designed.

I found the predications were accurate. Reticence to speak, answer questions, or comment on observations was common. Special strategies were required to get verbalization within the full group. One technique was to designate a "special person" within a group to respond, such as the person who had risen the earliest that morning or who was wearing the most jewelry. Now, with access to groundbreaking international research in cultural psychology, I'm wondering if I was assisting or complicating learning. See comparing Eastern and Western ways of thought (Nisbett, 2003).

Culture also has to do with terms of respect. I was told of a high school in an African-American community in which classified personnel wore name badges displaying their first names only. The morale was low among the instructional aides, clerks, safety monitors, custodians, and others. Then someone noticed that students were calling these adults by their first names, which did not feel at all respectful. The badges were changed to titles and surnames—Mr. X and Ms. Y. Students responded and morale improved.

Recently I was in a parent meeting with 1 father and 16 mothers. My colleague, an African-American woman, told me, "In our community, the polite form of address to women is Ms., a form of address that does not specify their marital status." She explained that, partly in response to the uncertainty of knowing if there was a father in the household, *Ms.* became a generically respectful term for a woman. I've learned to address parents in these settings as Mr. or Ms. until given permission to be more familiar.

Remember That Parents Are Partners

I believe that the metaphor of parents as clients is harmful. Thomas Sergiovanni (1992), professor of education and administration at Trinity University in San Antonio, reminds us that schools are not businesses, armies, or fast-food chains. Schools are closer to families (i.e., functional ones) or communities than they are to these formal organizations. Educators need their own metaphors of leadership and must stop borrowing from the private sector those that are inappropriate for schools.

Consider the parent-as-client metaphor. How does one work with a client? One has a service or a product to sell. One seeks to satisfy needs and interests, conducts polls and information surveys, and reveals some (but not all) information about the operation. One assumes a position of superiority regarding knowledge, expertise, and intention.

Relationships with partners are different. We jointly define intentions, set goals, discuss problems, search for resources, and own the challenges and the successes. Educators don't know more than parents; we know different things. Remembering this can help us to speak beyond "educanese" when we present.

The next section explores an issue common to working with any group: how to maintain momentum even through interruptions and unanticipated events.

REMEMBER

1. Regard parents as partners. We speak to partners differently than we do to clients.
2. With partners we jointly set goals, discuss problems, search for solutions, and own the challenges and successes.
3. Eliminate educanese—speak plainly.
4. Know when to slow down, enunciate carefully, and explain vocabulary.
5. Be alert for hidden cultural chasms.

How to Maintain Momentum Even in Slowdowns

Keep the group focused through unexpected delays and frustrating interruptions.

Notes From a Safari Journal

We started at the break of dawn and went nonstop till mid-afternoon. At one point I realized I was nodding off. How was that possible? The Land Rover bounces, lurches, and jostles its way across the plains; my right hand grips a handle high over the door in the back seat. I struggle to stay alert, yet my eyes close involuntarily and I drift toward sleep. A hard bounce. My eyes open. I glance toward Sue. She, too, is nodding off. Somehow, Juma has kept us on the run all day, every moment an adventure, until at last we are exhausted.

Final attention to detail can make the difference between a premier presentation and a second-rate one. Experienced presenters, like skilled train engineers, keep passengers steadily moving toward a final destination. Because it takes less energy to keep a train rolling than to start it again, certain preparation strategies and en route procedures are important to a good trip and a smooth ride. Presenters use certain procedures to maintain this comfortable momentum for individual "passengers" and the group.

To maintain a learning momentum for an audience, three questions must be addressed: (a) At what points can I anticipate that the "train" might slow down? (b) How do I know when it is slowing down? (c) What can I do to either prevent loss of speed or provide sudden acceleration?

Several hills, tunnels, or turns exist that can predictably slow the "train" without proper preparation. Transitions, unclear directions, elicitations, and break-time returns are some of these. You can develop preventive routines to deal with these potentially momentum-breaking situations.

Transitions

Link the past with the present, the present with the future, and all three with why the audience is there in the first place. Transitioning from one topic or activity to the next may lose participants' focused attention when they struggle to make connections from what happened to what is about to occur. Jon Saphier (Saphier & Gower, 1987), of Research for Better Teaching, masterfully prevents this by frequently providing "train schedules" in his presentations. For instance, he might say the following:

> We've just examined things teachers do to check whether students are with them or confused. Next, we are going to watch a videotape to see which of these things are going on. Then, this afternoon, we will look at the broader picture—what teachers do to keep students with them. From all of this, you will become a better observer and commenter on these aspects of instructional management.

In this example, Jon links past, present, and future, then links all three with why the audience is there in the first place. The "passengers" need not worry about which "stop" they are at and which "station" is coming next.

What, Why, How

Laura Lipton and Bruce Wellman (2003) describe a pattern for effective transitions in which momentum is maintained. Tell groups what topic is being introduced, why it is beneficial to them, and how the group will work. You can vary the order in which you address these. Here is an example:

> *What (is the topic)*: Our next topic is group development. Effective groups manage two areas: (a) their interaction with their external environments, like school boards, state or provincial departments of education, or parents, and (b) their internal dynamics for effective task accomplishment. To do this, groups need skills in six domains. (*Display them*)
>
> *Why (this activity)*: The purpose of this next activity is to overview these domains so you can learn where your group is hot and where it is not.
>
> *How (you will work—or pay attention to make the best learning for you)*: You will use a strategy called "say something." The purpose of this strategy is to support you in making connections with the content, both from your own perspective and the perspective of a colleague.
>
> Choose a partner and read silently to a designated stopping point. When each partner is ready, stop and "say something." The something might be a question,

summary, key point, or personal connection. Continue the process until you have completed the section.

Unclear Directions

People often feel stupid when given confusing directions. Once direction perplexity occurs with a group, it takes an enormous amount of energy to get the "train" chugging confidently down the "track" again. Any preparation time to make directions clear, explicit, and elegant (minimum words, maximum understanding) pays handsomely. Graphics help. Congruent paralanguage is essential. Here is a way to use your nonverbal knowledge effectively.

Present visual directions. Carefully describe these directions in a credible voice (see chapter 4). Stop; breathe; step to a new location. In an approachable voice, check for understanding: "OK, what's the first thing you will do? What should you be focusing on during the activity?" In this routine you are giving the message from one location with a credible voice. Then, with a pause and a movement to a new location, and in a new voice, which signals that this is a different communication, you check the group's understanding of the directions. You are going slow in direction comprehension so that the group can go fast with the activity without interruption or confusion.

Eliciting Audience Responses

Recording audience responses can occasionally cause deadening time lags. Ask yourself, "Do I have a purpose in recording this?" If the answer is yes, recruit one, two, or more recorders from the audience to chart audience comments while you stay engaged with the group and keep the "train" rolling.

Break-Time Returns

Another unscheduled delay can occur after a break or a lunch period. You can prepare audiences before the break for what is to follow and privately rehearse the opening statement during the break so that minimum strokes and maximum movement can be maintained. Sometimes I gather the on-timers around me after lunch and weave topic-related yarns as "icing" for them. This also serves as a reminder to latecomers that these sessions start exactly when announced.

Madeline Hunter was an influential American educator who developed a model for teaching and learning that was widely adopted by schools during the last quarter of the 20th century. She popularized a tactic she called *sponges*. Providing an activity at the beginning that will "soak up time" has value to those present but will not put latecomers at a disadvantage. Structure the activity so that latecomers can be folded into it whenever they arrive. One example is to have trios review yesterday's material. Provide a structure, such as 3-2-1: Each person writes three ideas from yesterday, two insights, and one question. Then they share and compare.

Another example is four-box synectics. On an overhead screen are four items. Groups are asked to pick one and describe several ways the item is like or unlike today's topic. Members coming in late are easily folded into the groups. The activity spurs metaphorical thinking, reveals participant knowledge and attitude on the topic, and generates laughter and energy.

A third strategy is to display a brief series of contextually appropriate cartoons immediately after a break. The bursts of laughter will draw people from the hallway into the room like a friendly magnet.

Sensing the Slowdown

Many presenters miss the subtle and sometimes not-so-subtle cues that the audience has already left or is leaving. In fact, this is a key survival tool for beginning teachers—to detect student mood shifts (from attending to interested and from understanding to confused, frustrated, despairing, angry, or resistant).

Presenters who sense the "train" slowing down do so in a variety of ways. A physical reaction is often my first alert. Something just feels wrong! When this occurs, I search for visual cues to confirm or explain the feeling. Blank faces, side conversations, doodling, purse packing and paper stacking are some of these. Other presenters rely on auditory cues to monitor purposeful activity in a group. They listen for the natural rhythm in a pattern of surges and rests that occur when people are working in buzz groups. Whenever the pattern is interrupted, a rest comes inappropriately in the rhythm, or the volume gets unpredictably high or low, it may signal that momentum has been lost. At that point, presenters gather visual information about what is wrong and how they might intervene. Those with keen auditory acuity learn from experience that certain activities have distinctive sound patterns. In brainstorming, for example, volume dips as people reach the stage at which the group experiences a natural slowing of ideas. A fresh line of thinking, more ideas, and a rise in the noise level usually follows this.

Some presenters sense momentum shifts more readily than others. This probably has to do with how much they allow themselves to check in and out from an egocentric state of speaking (How do I look?) to an allocentric (other-centered) perspective of seeing, hearing, and feeling the presentation from the audience's perspective. The ability to be sensitive to momentum shifts may also be related to a presenter's ability to keep foremost in his or her mind the goals and plan of the presentation.

Taking Action

As suggested in addressing rapport, if what you are doing is not working, do anything different. This simple adage eloquently applies to jump-starting the "train" back into motion. Do something differently, even if what you are currently doing "always" holds audience interest and attention. Pick up the pace, call for buzz groups, tell a story, take a break, or restate the purpose of the current topic or activity. Here is an example of how far you might go in changing what is not working. One Thursday morning late in the school year I found myself presenting to a group of administrators who looked and acted like zombies. I adopted a rag-doll, head-sagging stance and said to them, "This is what you look like. What's going on?" They informed me that yesterday they had passed out reduction-in-force notices to their teachers and that this was the fourth morning this week that they had been in meetings away from their buildings. "What should our agenda be this morning, then?" I asked. They told me, and we changed topics. The group energetically engaged on an issue that had meaning for them.

Signaling Your Most Important Points

A well-known educational consultant used to give audiences "research" findings that claimed that at any time during a presentation, 15% of the audience was gone, thinking erotic thoughts. "That," he would say, "is one of the reasons I like to speak. I enjoy watching people have a good time!" Although I can't locate the research base this consultant used in his assertion about audience attentiveness, there is much evidence to support his general thesis: A certain percentage of the time, a certain percentage of the audience will be following its own thoughts and not attending to the speaker's message. The problem that speakers have is knowing how to break through these reveries to get the major points heard by everyone. An important fact to understand about attention is that very little is under voluntary control. People in an audience cannot make themselves listen. Attention is automatically switched off by repetitive stimuli. For example, if you are in a room with a clock that is ticking quietly, you will soon habituate to the sound, so that after a while you no longer seem to hear it. Nevertheless, the sound is still being heard by the brain, and if the clock were to suddenly change volume, stop, or speed up, it would be noticed. Good presenters know this and vary their speed, volume, rate of ideas, and other factors to help keep people alert.

Many ways exist to keep a group focused. In the next section we address eight useful strategies.

REMEMBER

1. It takes less energy to keep a group moving than to restart it.
2. Anticipate and recognize slowdowns—take action.
3. Invest time in clear directions and checks for understanding.
4. When whatever you are doing is not working, do something different.
5. People cannot make themselves listen.

Eight Strategies to Keep Your Audience Tuned In
Because humans are not in control of their listening,
sometimes you need to tune them in

Table 3-4 lists eight specific strategies that invite attention. They are all based on two notions. First, the speaker has a few key points that are essential to be heard. If those points are missed, people may feel shortchanged. That is because they would be shortchanged if they left without knowledge of some critical assumptions, steps in a process, cautions, statements of purpose, or other points essential to getting value from the presentation. Second, audience members may need, and even appreciate, some sort of signaling system that tells them when to tune out their inner thoughts and tune in to the speaker.

Table 3-4. Eight Moves to Keep Audiences Tuned In

1. Here is my most important point
2. Pauses
3. Visual paragraph
4. Megaphone
5. Echo
6. Numbers
7. Physical signals
8. Choral repeats

Here Is My Most Important Point

Ed Wohlmuth (1983) has written a short, readable, and timeless book on presenting, *The Overnight Guide to Public Speaking*. He identifies six signals that audiences want to hear. "Here is my most important point" is one of these. Wohlmuth suggests sending this message in two parts because it takes a moment for people to leave their inner thoughts and rejoin the speaker. An example: "If you don't take anything else away from my talk today, I hope you'll remember this one point [*signal*]. It is, in fact, the key thought [*reinforcing signal*] that I came here to deliver."

Pauses

Employ an extended period of silence before making a point. This returns people from personal trances and focuses their curiosity on what is about to be said. Speakers who do not pause enough (or long enough) may sound subordinate, says Iain Ewing (1994). He reports on a study that analyzed the speech patterns of prominent French politicians, such as President Francois Mitterand.

The findings indicate that the more prominent the speaker, the more slowly he or she speaks, and with more and longer pauses. Table 3-5 displays some interesting data that seem to support this point. I don't know of similar studies with English speakers, but my memory of speeches by very powerful persons—Maya Angelou, Winston Churchill, Ronald Reagan, Martin Luther King, Jr., and John F. Kennedy, for example—all reinforce this concept.

Table 3-5. Power Pausing

Person and context of speech	Percentage of pause time in speech	Average length of pause
1974, Mitterand as opposition politician running for president	30%	0.8 seconds
1984, Mitterand at the peak of his power as a popular president of France	45%	2.1 seconds

Visual Paragraph

In chapter 4 the use of space as a presentation tool will be explored. Here is a simple example. To execute a visual paragraph you make a statement, pause, break eye contact, step to another part of the room, and make the next statement. Visual paragraphs help participants to tune in. This is television jargon for moving with deliberate silence to some new spot on the platform. This alerts an audience that something different is going to be said. Take advantage of the many natural transitions in your presentation by signaling these changes with your position in the room:

- After your introduction and as you start the body of your speech
- As you move from your first main point to your second
- As you pause to listen to a question, then move to answer it
- As you move from the body of your work into your conclusion

Megaphone

Speaking through a megaphone is also effective at getting the audience to tune in. Since I don't own one, I sometimes cup my hands on either side of my mouth to speak. Like a human megaphone, I lower my voice and boom out a statement. Because this signaling procedure lacks the two parts that Wohlmuth describes as necessary for audience members, I often combine this with the next strategy. Nothing is perfect, though. A participant in Buffalo told me that the megaphone covered my mouth enough to garble my words. She didn't like it.

Echo

To echo, I will simply say the sentence again, with the same phrasing and the same intonation. I've found the echo to be an effective strategy, with or without the megaphone.

Numbers

Numbers also capture people's attention. Occasionally I use them to create advance organizers and focus attention. "There are three important things to keep in mind during implementation. Number one [*said with inflectional stress*] is . . ." I'm always amazed at how many people will reach for a pencil when I start this pattern.

Physical Signals

Numbers can be combined with visual paragraphing: "Number one [*the speaker makes a point and then moves to a new location*]. Number two [*the speaker makes the next point*]," and so on. Numbers can also be combined with physical signals such as raised fingers. In fact, as suggested earlier, the more the presenter speaks simultaneously to the right and left sides of the brain, the more potently and clearly the signals are received. A variation of this is "Show, don't say." The presenter says you will have a certain number of minutes for an activity. Instead of just saying the minutes, hold up the corresponding number of fingers. Since the brain is attracted to novelty, this simple strategy can tune folks in when you are giving directions.

Choral Repeats

Playfully engaging the audience in choral repeats will also bring focused attention to key points. In a choral repeat, the speaker says a phrase and asks the audience to serve as a chorus, repeating the line in unison.

Soundbytes

There are, of course, other strategies, but I think that you will discover, whatever the strategy, that the most effectively delivered important points are sent as "soundbytes." These are pithy information capsules that can be received, recorded, and repeated by persons reared in the television era. Some examples: "Adults do not learn from experience, they learn from processing experience." "Any group too busy to reflect is too busy to improve." "Paraphrasing is not a language skill, it is a listening skill." Analysts say that speaking in soundbytes became a potently effective communication strategy in the 1988 presidential election (Noonan, 1990). In 1970 the average soundbyte length for candidates on network evening news was 42.3 seconds. In 1988 it was 9.8 seconds. By 1999 it was 7.3 seconds, about 20–25 words. (See Table 3-6.) If your sentence is so long that you have to take a breath, it may be too long for your audience to understand easily. Keep it short.

Of course, all the strategies for keeping groups tuned in require that participants be awake. Sometimes this is difficult for audience members no matter how brilliant your presentation. Read ahead for some ideas on keeping them awake at times when people are most likely to feel drowsy.

Table 3-6. The Shrinking Soundbyte

Year	Average Length of Candidate's Statement Broadcast on Evening Network News
1970	42.3 seconds
1988	9.8 seconds
1999	7.3 seconds

REMEMBER

1. Ask yourself at what points you might anticipate slowdowns, how you will know things are slowing down, and what you might do to either present a loss of momentum or provide sudden acceleration.
2. What, Why, How. Introduce topics or activities by telling the group what the topic is about, why it is important to them, and how they will work or best pay attention.
3. Confusing directions make people feel stupid.
4. Ask yourself if you have a purpose in recording comments from the group. If there is none, don't.
5. Attention is automatically switched off by repetitive stimuli.
6. Signal your most important points.

How to Keep Them Awake and Learning After Lunch

*Overcome the vexations of
stragglers and mealtime blahs.*

Even a 10-minute talk includes at least 1,000 words. When those 1,000 words are directed at audience members right after lunch, the combination of full stomachs, midday fatigue, and lunch-topic diversions can potentially convert the sound of the speaker's voice to something akin to the drone of lazy afternoon flies and sleepy lullabies. As far as I was concerned when I stepped out of the safari vehicle, all resident hippos were asleep. It turned out not to be the case. I would rather have dealt with that problem than the one I encountered.

Notes From a Safari Journal

Not all learning is pleasant. It is late morning. I've been drinking coffee. I step cautiously from the safari vehicle to adjust the balance between my fluid intake and outgo. Suddenly from behind me appears a hippopotamus, the animal responsible for more human deaths than any other on the African continent. He, she, or it is enormous (we decide it's a she), with canines up to 18 inches long. The guidebook says that this one weighs somewhere between 4,000 and 7,000 pounds. Grunting and snorting, glistening and terrifying, she comes charging directly at me from the waterhole from which she emerged. Sue and Juma are yelling for me to get back in the vehicle. The hippo is oblivious to us, our noise, and our fear. I get in. We grab cameras and click, click, click; our shutters record her as she slips into the muddy water to our side.

Presenters may encounter a concern for drowsy participants (people, not hippos) in three types of after-lunch presentations: the banquet speech, the workshop that begins at 1:00 P.M., and the presentation that is a continuation of a session that began in the morning. This chapter focuses on the third type, but several of these ideas are applicable to the first two as well.

There are at least three issues that presenters encounter in getting a workshop restarted after lunch: (a) stragglers, (b) post-lunch blahs, and (c) contextualizing.

Stragglers

Bruce Wellman and I anguished over the straggler problem in a 10-day training program that was scheduled over 18 months with bright, competent, overworked, and busy professional developers in a major U.S. city. There were two approaches we could use: be flexible and cope with the situation, or help the group change its norms. Ultimately we did both.

We hit upon the idea of offering a special (but unessential to skills development) learning "dessert" for persons who returned on time after lunch. We developed several criteria for these "desserts." First, they were yummy, with the capacity to captivate, focus, and physically bring the audience together. Second, they were related to the topic of study. Third, they added new depth, nuances, special perspectives, or understanding to the topic. Finally, the knowledge was not essential for the entire group to be able to complete the balance of the afternoon's learning tasks. I've referred to these earlier as activities (sponges) that soak up time that otherwise might be lost.

Stories nicely meet these four criteria. Lunchtime frequently found Bruce and I taking inventory of our repertoire of stories to find an appropriate one for the post-lunch session. Now I plan these in advance.

Physically arranging the seating for story time adds to the focusing effect of the story and provides a sense of intimacy and specialness for the group. I often invite the on-timers to bring their chairs forward to create an informal storytelling circle. Latecomers are drawn to the hushed atmosphere of the group and seat themselves on the periphery, sometimes encouraged by an inviting wave of my hand. When most of the participants are present, I can segue into the afternoon's agenda.

The simple act of starting on time regardless of how many people are in the room helps to develop on-time starts as expected behavior. Nevertheless, group norms run deep, and sometimes more direct approaches are necessary. Whatever topic Bruce and I are presenting, we routinely hold a simple "pluses and wishes" evaluation session with participants at the end of the day. With the 10-day train-ing group, many comments showed up in the "wishes" section on the third day indicating that they desired more modeling and skills practice. Bruce and I used this information to engage the group in problem solving. Without any judgment or blame, we described the start-time behavior pattern of the group, which was creating less total time together for learning. The next morning (for morning starting times were also a problem), the entire group was there on time. One person even confided, "You know, this is the first time I've ever been on time for anything in my life!" From that moment on, the norm for the group became punctuality, despite their continuing heavy and unpredictable demands from out-side.

Post-Lunch Blahs

Frank Koontz, a leading provider of professional development and training resources for the Bureau of Education and Research, tells me that the first period after lunch is the most difficult for participants and presenters. He advises that the afternoon break be scheduled no later than 1 hour into the session. Because pulse rates slow significantly after about 12 minutes of sitting, any physical ac-tivities that can be appropriately included in the afternoon presentation make good sense. I use a number of interactive patterns that get people talking and/or moving. Some of these are: (a) partners take inventory and compare notes; (b) partners take turns summarizing; (c) participants get up, select a new partner, and begin a new activity together; and (d) individuals move to different corners of the room to express an opinion and, once there, tell a neighbor their rationale for making that choice.

As one speaker puts it, if adults sit too long they will "smush" (sit on) their intelligence. To prevent this from happening, much movement is encouraged. The walk-around survey is an excellent device for stimulating brain cells and learning. In this strategy, participants interview at least six other persons in the room, collecting three recalls and three insights from the day's work to date.

This takes about 5 minutes and is gratefully received by participants at starting time or 30 minutes or so into the afternoon session.

Contextualizing

It's 1:00 P.M. People attending the workshop have enjoyed lunch and are now settling into their seats for the afternoon session. What is most prominent in their minds is the lunchtime conversations, not the teaching points that seemed so engaging that morning. The presenter's task is to overcome inertia, refocus the group, and make connections among what occurred in the morning, the point of reentry, and the participants' own interests and goals.

One device for this is the cliffhanger. Just like the old Saturday afternoon movie serial that ended with the hero in some precarious position (Is there anyone out there as old as I am who still remembers those?), the presenter closes the morning session with a verbal tease for the afternoon. "What single, simple strategy can teachers use to get a 300% to 700% improvement in student performance? That's the question we'll address immediately after lunch."

After lunch, the presenter says the following:

> As you will recall, this morning we explored ways to increase student participation in class. We identified three and suggested that there was one more that has been shown to produce as much as a 300% to 700% performance improvement in complexity of thinking. (See Rowe, 1986.) Please turn to your neighbor, recall this morning's three strategies, and share what you think the next might be.

This activity bridges participants' morning learning with the afternoon's focus and can also help with the straggler issue if people are not too late getting back.

Another strategy that accomplishes this goal is paired verbal fluency. In this approach, people are paired off; A speaks to B for 1 minute, telling B everything he or she remembers from the morning. B then speaks to A for 1 minute. This pattern repeats for two or three cycles, each time getting just a bit shorter. I will usually position myself at the rear of the room during this activity so I can catch latecomers as they enter and direct them immediately into the activity.

Other Ideas

Many of these strategies for dealing with stragglers, after-lunch blahs, and contextualizing are also useful at the beginning of the morning and/or at midmorning or afternoon breaks. So is humor. Songs or camp games can produce this. As described in the section on humor earlier in this chapter, singing "My Bonnie Lies Over the Ocean" and shuttling between seated and standing positions at every B sound in the song evokes laughter, adrenaline, and energy to carry people into the next learning task.

You have kept them awake, kept them tuned in to important points, and provided valuable learning experiences. Participants are attentive and learning. Your credibility is high. Then you are asked questions. The next topic deals with some common errors in responding to questions and ways to respond that extend participant learning and maintain your credibility.

REMEMBER

1. Even a 10-minute talk includes at least 1,000 words.
2. To start sessions on time, start them on time.
3. When there are stragglers, offer special content, valuably related to the topic but not essential to inform further learning. This is a learning bonus for the on-timers.
4. Because pulse rates slow after about 12 minutes of sitting, use a variety of physical activities to keep bodies and brains in motion.
5. To change energy at any time, get people to move, talk, or reflect.

Respond to Questions and Maintain Your Credibility

Some simple ideas allow you to
respond with ease and spontaneity

Don't you think that if we implement this program, it's just going to cause teachers a lot more work, with no benefits for students?

—Angry Workshop Participant

The workshop is 30 minutes old. The participant who is speaking seems tense. His face is strained, his voice is loud. Other participants focus intently on him. They are very interested in the presenter's response. The presenter, seemingly at ease, draws from a practiced repertoire and responds elegantly. The questioner is satisfied. The workshop moves on.

How does a presenter know how to respond to the various questions and comments by participants? I have come to some tentative conclusions as a result of reflecting on my own continuing efforts in this area, watching master presenters with different styles, and examining the literature on response strategies and decision-making processes.

Use Personal Pause Time

The more aware presenters are of their thinking processes, the more focused and effective they can be at reaching outcomes. I've recently given myself permission to pause before responding. I consciously ask myself three questions, not necessarily in the following order: (a) What are the possible ways I could answer this? (b) What's my desired state for participants? (in the moment and for an ongoing ecological learning environment), and (c) What is the source of the participant's question?

I also consider, on an intuitive level, all that I know about the group, this particular participant, and the setting in which the group is working. This helps me to understand the reason for the individual's question and tailor a response that answers the thinking behind it. My three questions, posed consciously, create a simplified map for me of a complex dynamic situation. This frees me to work straightforwardly, in an uncomplicated manner, trusting my intuition and experience to guide me in the nuances of my response.

Author Michael Grinder taught me that I have permission to think in front of an audience and that a few nonverbal tools help. Be still and allow your gaze to fix on some distant point. For most of us, this is a thinking posture that is recognized and respected by others. Freezing a gesture, stretching out one's hand, or putting a hand on one's cheek all communicate to people that you need time for your own processing. Michael's advice to presenters is "Choose a gesture that makes you look intelligent, then freeze it while you think." I will sometimes just say to a group, "Let me think about that." I am still searching for a gesture that makes me look intelligent.

Be Strategic

With the third question I ask myself, what is the source of the participant's question, I get intrigued with the possible reasons. Sometimes the question is straightforward. "Are there credits for this course?" At other times it may be useful to ask yourself why this question, from this person, at this time? I am not exactly aware of how I consider this in selecting an outcome and a response. My hunch is that although I always intuitively think about it, I only consciously put energy here when strong emotional signals accompany the question. In these cases, I strive to tune my acuity to the speaker so finely that I can make adjustments in the second half of my sentence based on the nonverbal feedback I receive from the first half of my sentence.

Choose Your Outcomes

What outcome do you want to produce? You might want to satisfy a participant's curiosity, set a mood of inquiry, or evoke laughter. These outcomes may be intended for the individual participant, a subgroup, or the entire audience. This may be the most important stage of presenter thought, for without clear intentions, responses are likely to produce random and sometimes undesirable results. In my work, I am conscious of at least five classes of response outcomes: (a) validating data, (b) building a knowledge base, (c) shifting perspectives, (d) understanding participant thinking, and (e) extending thinking.

To validate data, for example, presenters give direct answers to questions like "Could you give me an example?" or "What is the research?" or "Who were the authors?"

To build the group's knowledge base, a presenter might give data, provide references, tell an anecdote, give an example, or affirm or correct the participant's contribution. Presenters also build knowledge by eliciting audience responses through questions like "How do other people handle that?" or "Turn to your neighbor and list four additional strategies."

To shift perspectives, an anecdote or a metaphor might be appropriate. Other techniques can also be used: humor, presenting data from another person's perspective (such as a child's or a parent's), or responding at a logical level that is different from the one at which the question was asked. For example, to the question "Why doesn't the district provide more mathematics manipulatives?", a response might begin with the paraphrase "You want students to have the benefit of concrete experiences with number concepts." Turning to the rest of the group, the presenter asks, "For how many of you is this an issue?" If several hands are raised the presenter might ask, "What do you think you might do to make this need known?" If no one else is concerned, you might suggest that the person explore this with others at his or her school.

To understand participant thinking, the presenter paraphrases, asks for examples, or probes for relevance, intentionality, values, metacognition, or application.

Finally, to extend thinking, presenters may use wait time, give content-neutral acknowledgments (such as *uh huh, yes, ok,* or *thanks*), paraphrase, or ask for clarification, elaboration, evidence, and information about thinking processes.

Criteria for Responses

In selecting a response, consider the effect it will have on the learning environment. If the response will (a) maintain the momentum toward meeting the workshop goals in a timely manner, (b) keep the presenter's credibility intact, (c) encourage continued responsiveness from the group, and (d) contribute to feelings of individual and group efficacy, the response is truly elegant.

Expand Your Repertoire

Be on the lookout for ways to increase your response repertoire. Here are a few ideas. When conducting a question-and-answer period after a presentation, tell the audience that there will be a period (e.g., 10 minutes) for questions and answers. Recruit a timekeeper to help you stick to this time allotment. This puts the idea of brevity into the audience's mind before anyone rises to ask a question, and it decreases the chances of rambling questions.

Identify the next three people you plan to recognize. This helps people to relax to participate in the conversation and also sends a signal for brevity—theirs and yours.

Use the Research on Presenter Responses

Listen for the syntax of a question to determine whether it is true-false ("Should we announce this to all seniors?"), multiple choice ("Should we buy the equipment now or later?"), short answer ("How many?" "How much?" "When?" "Who?"), or essay ("Why have we changed the policy?"). Answer the question, initially, in the syntax matching the way the question was asked (Table 3-7). Then explain your rationale. ("Should we change the schedule?" "Yes! Here are three reasons.") Short answers, according to research conducted by Communication Development Associates, are more credible than long ones. CDA advises answering the question in summary form first and then elaborating.

Table 3-7. Answering Questions

Type	Syntax	Response
True-False	Should we change the policy?	Yes. For these reasons (list and elaborate).
Multiple Choice	Should we modify the policy now or wait?	We should change now. For these reasons (list and elaborate).
Short Answer	How much? How many? When? Who?	$1,000 30 Monday Sue
Essay	Why should we change the schedule?	It's an issue of efficiency. Elaborate. It's a question of . . . It's a matter of . . . The central issue is . . . Simply . . .

Another strategy is to summarize the question first. Your summary does not have to be a full repetition of the question, but it should clarify what was asked. There are three powerful reasons for making a simple summary of a question before answering it: (a) the questioner is assured that the speaker understands the question, (b) the rest of the group can hear the question, and (c) it focuses the presenter's attention to the exact question. If there are several questions wrapped into one, enumerate them as you respond.

I started this section with an example of a tough question. "Feel, felt, found" is a strategy the speaker in this example might have used. The participant asked, "Don't you think that if we implement this program, it's just going to cause teachers a lot more work, with no benefits for students?" The presenter might have replied, "I know just how you *feel*, because when I was first exposed to this program, I *felt* the same way. All I could see was the bookkeeping. It looked as if I had to spend time learning new systems and it was going to increase my preparation time. What I've *found*, however, as I began to work with it, is that while there was some initial upfront work, my load is actually easier now, and student work has improved tremendously."

Speakers must be very careful with the first step of this response. If you don't really know how the person feels (and it's likely that you don't, unless you have directly experienced it), you can't say, "I know how you feel." What is possible to say, however, is, "I know that many teachers feel that way when they first come into contact with the program." Another caution with this response is to keep in mind that your intent is not to persuade this person about the value of the program. Your job is to give information, to support participants in having access to the internal resources needed for learning—energy, interest, and emotions—and to offer them choices.

You are now providing great value to participants and maintaining your own resourcefulness and credibility as you respond to questions. Next we will discuss how to add extra value, particularly for your concrete sequential learners.

REMEMBER

1. Give yourself permission to think before responding. (See chapter 4 for nonverbal help.)
2. Be curious about the source of the question.
3. What outcomes do you want to produce with your response? (Validate data, add to knowledge base, shift perspectives, understand participant thinking, or extend thinking.)
4. Consider the effect your response will have on the rest of the group.
5. Listen to the syntax of the question and answer that first.
6. Use "feel, felt, found" to overcome objections.
7. Your intention should never be to persuade—just inform. When you find yourself trying to sell an idea, you are retreating from your effectiveness.

How to Teach Triple Tracks

To keep yourself out of trouble, satisfy a range of learning styles
and add value for everyone with this simple strategy.

Like the experience with the hippo in Ngorongoro Crater, some experiences in a seminar room can be painful but can also be a source of learning. It was immediately following a presentation at a national conference that Bruce Wellman and I first realized the extraordinary usefulness of teaching on triple tracks. While scanning the post-session participant evaluations, we were stung by one in particular. According to this person's experience, we had been abstract, vague, and theoretical, and our work had lacked utility because of the absence of concrete examples. We were stunned by the anger in the participant's language. He had given us his valuable time and was going away empty-handed. We were also puzzled because we thought we had designed the presentation with specificity, examples, and applications in mind.

Our reflection led us to two hypotheses: (a) the writer was a concrete sequential processor in the extreme, and (b) something had happened in our opening that interacted with his perceptions in such a way that he missed the concrete portions of the presentation and focused only on what was conceptual. With this in mind, Bruce and I began deliberately tuning and refining a process that he and Laura Lipton had intuitively begun to use when they presented together.

We call this approach triple-track presenting (Figure 3-1). Its benefits include satisfying a range of learning styles, transferring learning to a range of applications, assisting memory, and making a public record of the interactive strategies used in a presentation. If you'd like to test this approach in your own presentations, here are some ideas to get you started.

Figure 3-1. Triple Track

First Track	• Use a learning activity to support group learning.
	• Post the name of the activity on butcher paper on the wall.
	• Describe the learning theory being employed.
	• Describe conditions under which it would and would not be appropriate.
Second Track	• Give examples of how the same activity can be used in classrooms to support student learning.
Third Track	• Give examples of how the same activity can be modified to support groups in faculty meetings, curriculum committee work, site-based decision-making groups, etc.

Set the Stage

During your opening invite the audience to attend to certain experiences at three levels.

First, advise them that you will use interactive learning strategies that are designed to support their learning throughout this seminar. You will comment on the rationale and the intended contribution of each of these strategies to their learning.

Post a chart labeled "Strategies and Moves." Hang it high on a wall so that it maintains visual prominence throughout the presentation. Each time you engage the audience in an interactive learning process, name the process, write it on the strategy chart, give origins and a pedagogical rationale for the strategy, and describe specific ways to apply the strategy. Have participants keep a record of strategies as they are used.

Strategies are planned, multistep processes that engage people in acts of learning, A strategy also has structure and sequence. For example, in an "AB teach strategy," participants pair off, then A teaches B and B teaches A. *Moves*, on the other hand, are quick, discrete remarks or behaviors that take only a moment to perform. Instead of being planned, they are often spontaneous. Presenters use them to intervene, amplify, or direct. A frozen gesture is a move; switching to a credible voice is a move.

Second, explain how each strategy might be adapted for classroom work with students.

Third, describe how the same processes can be used to support other adults with whom these participants might work.

Model the Process

Use the following process in the beginning of a presentation:

In just a moment you will engage in an inclusion activity. On page XX of your handout you'll find a section to record ideas. You may wish to take some notes there regarding the purposes of inclusion activities and some specific inclusion strategies you can use in meetings, seminars, or with students.

Give a rationale for the strategy:

Inclusion strategies typically serve four purposes. They help people know who they are in relation to the entire group, they focus the group's mental energy inside the room, they establish a norm of participation, and they begin the journey from "me-ness" to "we-ness"—the progression toward interdependence.

The inclusion strategy we will use to help you get a sense of who is here today is called "like me." In a moment, I will make some statements. For each statement that is like you, stand, look around, and see who else fits that particular category.

Some generically useful categories for the "like me" strategy are roles, time in a district, the state one was born in, up before 6:00 A.M., experience with the topic, and a passion for chocolate. Be sure to include "other" as a role category. Persons left out at this stage will often feel unacknowledged for some time into the seminar.

Now give specific examples of how the "like me" strategy can be used in other settings. Tell how it can be modified for parent meetings, at beginning-of-the-year faculty assemblies, in other seminars, or with students. As much as I would like the transfer of ideas to be automatic without my giving specific examples, for most people it seems not to occur.

The transfer of learning is facilitated when presenters provide proximal or distal bridging (Perkins & Salomon, 1991).

Proximal bridging involves giving examples in which the new situation so closely approximates the situation in which the learning occurred that the application is fairly obvious. In this case, we've used the "like me" strategy in a seminar, then described how it might be used by these participants as they conduct their own seminars with other groups. *Distal bridging* refers to more distant, remote, or obscure applications in which the elements are greatly dissimilar to those in which the skill or concept has been learned. With the "like me" strategy, this might include descriptions of applications at a parents' back-to-school night or examples of changing the text of the "like me" statements to fit a special circumstance. For example, in a community forum gathered for problem-solving purposes, statements such as "I have more than three solution suggestions," "I have an idea from which I will not budge," "I know someone in another school who has a successful resolution," or "I'm willing to explore options but I don't think some of my neighbors are" might be used in place of the more generic inclusion statements. To provide proximal or distal bridging examples adds another level of detail to your preparation work. It also multiplies the usefulness of your work threefold.

For each strategy used, you can choose to add to the group's repertoire other strategies that would accomplish similar aims. For example, you might describe other inclusion activities and record their names on the public strategy list. In "Peter Paul," two people interview each other, then they introduce their partner to the group. "Cash flow" is another inclusion activity and mixer in which everyone gets money (Monopoly play money) at the door. The task is to look for people with whom all the money adds up to a predetermined amount, and form a group with them. However, because transfer is generally enhanced when learning has been constructed out of personal experience, these described strategies may not transfer as well as the experienced ones.

There is one unexpected benefit of triple-track presenting for the presenter: It requires us to be more articulate about why we are choosing particular learning strategies. You might want to take an inventory of the processes you use to support adult learning. Reflect on why they are used, what is known about the principles of learning that support their use, and what other strategies might be used or invented that could produce similar learning benefits.

Participant Responses to Triple-Track Learning

Here are some responses I've learned to expect when using the triple-track pattern. First, in the post-session evaluations, many people comment on how appreciative they are of getting many concrete strategies. Partner huddling during the session is frequent, with one partner explaining a strategy to the other if the person has forgotten any details related to the strategy or has come in late and missed the experience and explanation altogether. Often participants will approach me at break time, notes in hand, asking an application question about a particular strategy. I also observe many participants visually scanning the strategy charts during reflective periods. Both Bruce and I get requests for permission to take the charts and post them in staff rooms as reminders of strategies.

I have returned to settings in which I have used triple-track learning and have been astounded at how often the moves and strategies modeled in an early presentation have been adopted and applied by workshop participants. Conceptually, I know this will be enhanced by the degree of modeling I provide, the opportunities in the seminar for mediated reflection on the strategies we've used, and the degree to which the organizational environment signals compatible values and provides opportunities for practice, experimentation, and application of concepts.

Finally, as this chapter nears the end, I offer some ideas for closing a seminar.

REMEMBER

1. Satisfy a number of learning styles; add to the teaching, presentation, and facilitation repertoire; and support the transfer of learning with this approach.
2. Post a chart labeled "Strategies and Moves."
3. Record teaching strategies you use on the chart and provide a recording page for participants.
4. Explain the use of each strategy at three levels—why it is being used now for this group, how it might be used in the classroom, and how it might be modified for use with other adult groups. Do this after using the strategy.
5. Periodically give the group time to review the strategy chart and ask application questions.
6. You will discover that participant satisfaction with your sessions increases.

When and How to Close

Close the way you want people to remember
you . . . and the message.

Don't summarize. So advocates Nick Morgan (2003), who believes that the adage "Tell them what you are going to tell them, tell them, then tell them what you told them" is outmoded in the 21st century. It's sure to put people to sleep at the end of your presentation.

Instead, when concluding a speech, give a call to action, inspire, or stir community. When conducting a workshop or a seminar, help participants to organize and synthesize their own learning and/or foreshadow their journey toward application.

Some people believe that the ending is nearly as important as the rest of a speech. Put yourself in the audience's perspective. From that vantage point you want clarity, you want to feel good (or aroused for action), and you want it to end.

Close Early

Speeches and seminars typically close at the end. However, for workshops in which groups are learning skills, concepts, or new knowledge, processes before the close are needed. Suzanne Bailey calls these "early closes." They help participants to organize and integrate what they have learned.

One form of "early close" is called "sort and store." This happens an hour or so before the end—or even midway through a workshop, perhaps as a transition step between two topics. "Sort and store" is simple and takes little time. In one version participants are encouraged to write a word or phrase that is important for them to remember on each of three imaginary balloons. They then share these with another participant and explain their choices. Other "sort and store" examples include asking participants to outline a personal action plan, list key points they plan to tell someone, or write a brief narrative summarizing concepts important for them to remember.

Laura Lipton and Bruce Wellman (2003) describe organizing and integrating activities in their presentation of a teaching-learning cycle in which the last of three phases supports learners in making the new learnings theirs. "Activities during this phase include summarizing, categorizing, mapping or graphic outlining, confirming or revising hypotheses and predictions, and generating examples and non-examples to test out new theories" (p. 13).

To Conclude

"To conclude" says that you are about to end. Resist the temptation to add another thought or two after saying that. You will have lost three-quarters of the group, anyway, and they will not hear your final bursts of brilliance. Be sure that logistics are dealt with before your conclusion so that you don't experience the awkwardness of making an emotional close only to have to follow it with mundane items, such as requesting that a certain form be turned in. If logistical announcements must be made after your close, have someone else make them. In the next chapter, Kendall Zoller will explain why they must also be made from a different place in the room.

Because a group can especially recall what occurs at the end of a session, the closing deserves your best craftsmanship. Here are some general tips:

1. Save time for your closing.
2. Plan your closing in detail.
3. Appeal to emotions—pride, love, hope. Political speeches sometimes appeal to fear or to noble intentions—determination, a better world, all students succeeding, a pioneer spirit.
4. Keep it brief.
5. Then be silent.

Call to Action

What do you want people to do? Do you want them to tell others, turn out for a bond election, restructure homework activities for their children, or practice a skill a day? Perhaps your call to action is less specific and more artfully vague—love one another, keep the faith, stay the journey. Rhetorical calls can move people to action. President Kennedy, near the end of his inaugural address, said, "And so, my fellow Americans, ask not what your country can do for you, ask what you can do for your country." Later he said, "My fellow citizens of the world, ask not what America will do for you, but what together we can do for the freedom of man." This call was answered with thousands of young Americans serving in the Peace Corps all over the world (Morgan, 2003).

Bruce Wellman and I sometimes use a metaphoric call to action to close an adaptive school seminar in which we've focused on developing collaborative work cultures. We recount the possible origins of collaborative community in Africa in which the drum plays such an important function. The drummer, we say, calls people to the dance by naming their ancestors. Bring all of who you are to the center and dance. The villagers do, but in a polyrhythmic fashion, dancing off the beat, adding their own signature rhythm. To heighten the effect, softly in the background, we play West African drum music.

We close with this:

> You don't have to dance on the beat to be part of the village, but you are expected to hear the beat and blend your movement with the movements of others. In fact, to dance with disregard to the beat is considered to be mentally disturbed, because this represents a breakdown of communication, awareness, and community.

Actually, our final words as we say them are more like poetry than prose (Garmston & Wellman, 1999):

> The goal is to find the beat,
>
> honor the beat,
>
> add your voice,
>
> and dance.
>
> Welcome to the dance. (pp. 273–274)

A call to action can also be literal and specific: " I ask you to do three things upon leaving here: Locate another person in this group to talk to; tell them what, for you, was the most important idea; and tell them what you intend to do about it."

Inspire

Poetry inspires. An appropriate poem can make a good closing. You can design your memorable closing with a technique developed by Winston Churchill. The acronym is CREAM, which stands for contrast, rhyme, echo, alliteration and metaphor. "Just as cream rises to the top in a bottle of unhomogenized milk, the lines created with these five elements will stay uppermost in a listener's mind" (Humes, 2002, p. 127). In *Speak Like Churchill, Stand Like Lincoln*, author James Humes offers examples. I have added others.

Contrast

To use contrast, pick your concept and work with a thesaurus to find the right antonym.

There is only one answer to *defeat* and that is *victory*. (Churchill)

As I would not be a *slave*, I would not be a *master*. (Lincoln)

We realize that no one sex can govern alone. I can conceive of nothing worse than a *man-governed* world except a *woman-governed* world. (Lady Astor, first female member of the British Parliament)

Finally, here is a quote from Martin Luther, the German founder of Protestantism. Speaking in his defense before Emperor Charles V, he said that he would not recant anything he had said, for it cannot be right for a Christian to speak against his conscience. "Here I stand; I cannot do otherwise."

Rhyme

Lord Byron, before he came of age, exhibited political and cultural defiance. "I'll publish right or wrong: Fools are my theme, let satire be my song."

"There is no hope for those who use dope" (Rev. Jesse Jackson, civil rights activist).

"There is no dream without reach, when we work as a team" (a Bristol-Meyers executive).

Echo

In the following examples, a significant word is repeated.

"Any group that is too busy to reflect upon its work is too busy to improve" (Garmston and Wellman).

"The only thing we have to fear is fear itself" (Franklin Roosevelt, in his first inaugural address).

Then there is Lincoln's famous line "that government by the people, of the people, and for the people shall not perish from the earth."

Alliteration

"Judge not, that ye not be judged." Jesus of Nazareth, in an English translation of the Sermon on the Mount.)

"You, like peak performers everywhere, live at the edge of your competence. Living there, you fail frequently, and when you do you fail, you fail forward" (Garmston).

President Kennedy: "We shall pay any price, bear any burden."

Metaphor

"I learned that . . . the politician who persistently lifts his wet finger to test the political polls before he acts usually leaves office with a wet finger." (Jack Valenti, presidential aide to Lyndon Johnson).

"Teachers are overworked and underpaid. How true. What energy it takes to turn a torrent of energy into a rivulet" (George Leonard in Ecstasy in Education).

Stir Community

> Let every female heart become united.
>
> —Social reformer Maria Stewart, advocating education for Black women in 1832

When your goals include collegiality and teamwork, it might be appropriate for the closing moments to extend a pathway into those feelings and behaviors. In one form of this closing, the presenter invites open-ended comments about "this experience or anyone in the room." The presenter employs extended wait time and a simple nod or "thank you" to acknowledge contributions.

Acknowledging audience members is another way to recognize community. I once heard Carl Glickman, an educational author and researcher, say the following in closing:

> I appreciate your acknowledgement of me. But you must know that if there are any heroes or heroines in education, it is the people in this room. I come to speak and am gone. But you are here; in good weather and bad, under stressful times and peaceful ones, whether you are well or feeling poorly, you are staying the course for students.

Foreshadow the Journey

All journeys begin with desire. Any goal, and the steps leading to it, is first represented in one's mind. These representations, which are often unconscious patterns of pictures, feelings, sounds, smells, or tastes, can be coaxed to consciousness and shaped to not only foreshadow growth but to support attainment. The presenter stimulates and accelerates growth toward personally defined workshop-related goals by inviting participants to envision themselves engaged in future activities in which they successfully employ the new skills they are refining. The following is an example:

> As you think about a presentation you will make in the near future, see yourself experimenting with a closing that you wish to use. You are with a particular group and you've selected a specific closing for the ending. Envision the room and see what you are wearing and how you appear to the group. Now hear the words you say, noticing your tone of voice and rhythms of speech. See the audience's reaction. Notice how you feel. Watch the group in your mind's eye and adjust your closing until you have it just right and are getting the desired response.

In this example of a mental rehearsal, the presenter literally engages participants' minds in producing the neurological responses necessary for successful task completion. Notice that the language is very broad and nonspecific, allowing the presenter, like a tailor, to provide the fabric and the listeners to construct from it their own garment. Notice, too, that most of the senses are used. The richer and more varied the internal representation (pictures, sounds, feelings, smells), the more complex the neurological activity and the more likely the actual attainment.

In another type of foreshadowing, alert people to the challenges they might face and some suggestions for overcoming them: "People at work like you just the way you are and may be uncomfortable with changes you wish to make. You might find it useful to say, 'I'm working on improving these skills. Will you support me?'"

To close skill-building workshops, it can be useful to remind a group that when applying new skills, we often get worse before we get better. Help them to normalize predictable discomforts or declines of confidence. The key to mastery is perseverance. Help participants to psychologically prepare for this journey.

Commitment

Finally, presenters can close in ways that extend and support participants' own commitment to action. Providing a structure and time in which to outline the next steps in a plan, formulate objectives, and identify potential barriers to overcome will move participants one step closer to action. Sometimes, in closing a Cognitive Coaching[SM] seminar, trainers have participants conduct a planning conference with each other regarding personal plans they have formulated. Talking out loud with a colleague who nonjudgmentally responds in ways that evoke greater clarity, detail, and imagination is an especially powerful aid to action.

REMEMBER

1. Your closing may be as important as your opening.
2. At the closing, an audience wants clarity, wants to feel good, and wants the presentation to end.
3. Save time for your closing, plan the closing in detail, appeal to emotions, and be brief.
4. Memorable closings are remembered.
5. Use literary devices (CREAM): contrast, rhyme, echo, alliteration, metaphor.
6. Use preclose activities that allow participants to organize and integrate what has been learned.
7. Close for action, commitment, inspiration, or foreshadowing.
8. The closing is your last, and should be your best, shot.

Finally, from Ken Blanchard, author of *The One-Minute Manager* and other popular leadership literature, I learned a closing that comes at the beginning of a session! Ken notes that the typical Likert scale evaluation form distributed at the end of a presentation is received too late for the presenter to alter his or her behavior. He distributes it first, and asks if anyone objects to the workshop quality being a straight 5 (the top of the scale). Hearing no objections, he encourages people to let him know "the moment he is drifting from a 5." In that way, he shares the responsibility for presentation success with the learners, an effective strategy for closing the psychological distance between presenter and participants and for increasing adult learning.

Summary

This chapter examines many of the major issues related to the delivery of instruction. Providing quality openings is the first. In the best ones the presenter has clear outcomes in mind: to focus, intrigue, energize, or build rapport. This is true for keynote addresses, workshops, university courses, or classroom lessons. Several strategies were presented related to these goals, and a practical generic template for openings was provided.

Humor clears the mind and opens the brain to higher levels of thinking. Because humor reduces stress and anxiety, it has an important place in presentations, yet not all presenters are funny. John Dyer revealed his secret to laughter in a workshop: Provide an environment in which it can emerge. We also explored why people laugh as well as some strategies to invite laughter.

Another challenge is presenting to parents. It is the same as, yet in some ways different from, presenting to educators. A critical idea to keep in mind is that parents are partners in the educational enterprise, not clients. As partners we relate to them and communicate to them more richly and equally than we do with clients. Ideas were presented for speaking to parents clearly on complex topics.

All presentations can suffer from unexpected challenges. One of these is lagging momentum. Presenters were encouraged to prethink about this issue with three questions: (a) At what points can I anticipate the "train" might slow down? (b) How do I know when it is slowing down? (c) What can I do to either prevent loss of speed or provide sudden acceleration? Another challenge is that most groups will periodically need some sort of signaling system that tells them when to tune out their inner thoughts and tune in to the speaker.

There are other challenges: the post-lunch blahs, on-your-feet responses to questions in a way that maintains your credibility, and how to have value added to any presentation by bringing attention to the learning strategies you employ. The chapter ended with an examination of concepts and tools for closing presentations.

In chapter 4, Kendall Zoller will build on this foundation by offering a number of nonverbal strategies that enhance memory, create psychological safety, focus groups, and direct energy.

CHAPTER 4

The New Science of Nonverbal Skills

Kendall Zoller*

---

*Increase your credibility and influence
with your body and voice.*

> After years of vain familiarity, some distant gesture or unconscious behavior,
> which we remember, speaks to us with more emphasis than the wisest or kind-
> est words.
>
> —Henry David Thoreau

Nonverbal communication in itself is not new. What is new is a body of knowledge and credible research that details the results of various nonverbal skills on
memory, energy, and learning environments. Like any intriguing natural phenomenon, such as the ripples produced by skipping rocks on the surface of water, or the
falling rain, what we see looks simple but what lies underneath is rich with complexity and nuance. This is true, too, about nonverbal communication.

This chapter is organized into five sections: (a) an introduction to the science of nonverbal signals, (b) the influence of nonverbal communication on the
flow of information in a seminar or classroom, (c) the use of nonverbal signals to
increase or deflect energy, (d) the effects of nonverbal skills on memory, and (e)
conditions for creating psychological safety, which is necessary for learning of a
demanding nature.

A caution to the reader may be in order about this chapter. The skills we will
explore can be understood at several levels of complexity. For some, the information will be simple and direct. On a first read these skills may seem simple,
like a good habit you already do. In fact, one of the values of this chapter is to
bring to consciousness patterns you are already good at but are perhaps unaware
of. Other skills are situated within deep levels of communication complexity. To
understand these and be able to perform them may require a return visit and/or
conversations with another with whom you are exploring and testing these skills.

---

*With the exception of the introductory section and the summary, Kendall Zoller is the author of
this chapter.

Marzano, Pickering, and Pollack (2001) show that an individual teacher can have powerful effects on his or her students even if the school doesn't. The teacher's use of *instructional strategies* is the determining factor. Later, Marzano (2003) examined classroom management. This chapter addresses both building on instructional ideas in chapter 3, and introducing potent ways to manage seminar and workshop dynamics.

Kendall Zoller, the author of the bulk of this chapter, and I each owe a lifelong debt of gratitude to Michael Grinder (2000) who has helped us to enhance our own effectiveness by teaching us about nonverbals. Kendall and I refer to gestures, voice qualities, breathing, eye contact, and other nonverbal skills as *paralanguage*. *Para* means alongside, in this case alongside the spoken word. (Think of *paramedic*, *paraprofessional*.) Technically, in educational research, paralanguage is narrowly defined to include the audible sounds, intonations, inflections, speed, and volume characteristics that accompany speech (McNeill, 1992). We will use the term in its more generalized meaning for simplicity in this text.

Why Blind Children Gesture

*You have the power to help groups feel safe as you direct energy
and information flow and learning—not so much by what you say,
but by your use of universal nonverbal communication.*

How deeply hardwired in the human brain is gesturing? Is gesturing so linked to the verbal component of communication that the two co-develop as we mature? Blind children gesture to sighted people. Blind children even gesture when speaking to other blind children! This section provides an entry point for bringing to our consciousness what we say beyond our words.

Whether you are a teacher, a leader or a presenter, you can quickly identify and evaluate the quality of a presentation. Your judgment is often unconsciously based on reactions to the choreography of nonverbal (paralanguage) features used by the presenter. Each of us is intuitively knowledgeable in this area. The purpose of this chapter is to bring your intuition to consciousness, to enable you to have more control and effectiveness.

Juma, Bob's guide in Africa, "consistently sees more than I do," Bob says, even though both of them are looking at the same things. Let us begin to see what we have always been looking at but not always seeing. I (Kendall) am reminded of my first session with my friend and mentor, Michael Grinder. It was 1997, on day 1 of a 5-day session on nonverbal classroom management. I was a captive audience member sent by my boss upon my appointment as the 7–12 science curriculum specialist for a large school district in California. I sat in the back, arms folded, with skepticism emanating from my face. My resistance was high; my tolerance threshold for poor content was low. I did not want to be there because I had better things to do. Besides, being a product of the late '60s and the 1970s, I already knew about body language.

Within 20 minutes of day 1, I was learning forward—intrigued, captivated, and engaged. As I was later to find out, my shift was generated by Michael's conscious and strategic nonverbal strategies. His deliberate intention was to try to shift my breathing and influence my thinking. This moment was my first step on a journey that has not slowed—a journey that, like Robert Frost's fork in the road, was the path least traveled and the one that has made all the difference. When we finally "hear" our first nonverbal conversation, no verbal message will ever sound the same. No meeting will ever be the same; no classroom will ever be the same. Like Juma, we will begin to consistently see what others just look at.

My curiosity has also been stirred by a phenomenon I hadn't noticed before. Why do blind children gesture when in conversation with another blind child? Might it suggest that gesture is part of speech, inseparable from the spoken word? Indeed, we find this to be true (Roth, 2001a). Later I will distinguish among several classes of gesturing that assist speech.

Think about a good presentation you attended recently in order to respond to the questions in Table 4-1. Most readers will not have many *conscious* answers to these questions; this is the author's intention. Each "learn how to" statement in the table serves as an organizer for the chapter. Next, a focus question narrows to the specific paralanguage moves associated with the learning. The focus questions allow us to explore the paralinguistic "dance" of the presenter. Read each focus question and think about your response. Then look at the "learn how to" statements of interest to you.

Table 4-1. Organizing Questions

Learn how to	Focus question
1. Influence the flow of information	Can you identify the voice pattern the speaker used, the varying volume or modulation?
2. Direct and redirect the flow of energy	What hand gestures were used and what effect did they have on you? on the group?
3. Affect individual and group memory	How does the presenter use location to enhance content? Was the use of space congruent with the content?
4. Develop group safety	When participants asked questions, what paralanguage skills did the speaker use as the answers were given?
5. Become aware of your influences	What were the influences of the paralanguage skills on you? The group? Your learning? Your level of engagement?

These questions are often not asked, yet the answers are critical to utilizing one of the five states of mind—craftsmanship (see Appendix A). Our drive to extend our knowledge of content and teaching strategies may have distracted us from learning about the paralanguage "dance" of the presenter or teacher. There is good reason to deepen content knowledge, for teacher knowledge of a discipline is highly related to student learning. However, as professional educators, we are also committed to the continual enhancement of our effectiveness, regardless of where a search for that might take us.

REMEMBER

1. We intuitively recognize quality presentations but may not be able to describe why.
2. Allow yourself to notice what you have not been noticing before.
3. One goal is to bring to consciousness patterns you are already good at but are perhaps unaware of.
4. Paralanguage includes the audible sounds, intonations, inflections, speed, and volume characteristics that accompany speech.
5. Gesturing is deeply hardwired in our brains.

Influencing Information Flow

Without relationship, there is a decreased flow of information. Without information, there is no learning. According to Wheatley (1992), leadership is always dependent on the context, but the context is established by the relationship we value. Our relationships influence the flow of information. With relationship, information flows. Without relationship, information is impeded. The paralanguage moves that enhance relationship and thus facilitate information flow are explored in this section.

Information flow can be enhanced through the conscious use of paralanguage. What you do with your voice, body, breathing, and gestures adds information to your verbal content (Kelly & Barr, 1999) and helps to develop your relationship with the audience. You can increase your influence through the conscious use of certain paralanguage moves. Planning paralanguage moves is as important as planning teaching strategies and content. Planning allows you to do proactive presenting. To be reactive restricts your options. If we can plan and anticipate, we have at our disposal our entire tool kit of paralanguage skills. Let's revisit the four audiences described in chapter 1 (see Figure 1-2) and offer specific suggestions for each.

- The *What* group (the "Professors," who want data) can be addressed using a flat voice (credible) with high eye contact.

- The *So What* group (the "Friends," who want to know how the learning relates to them) can be addressed most effectively using various locations in the room, adding bounce to your voice, and smiling.
- The *Why* group (the "Scientists," who are curious about reasons) can be served by using location and placing ideas in containers for easy access.
- The *What If* group (The "Inventors," who want to tinker with new learning) can be influenced using animated voice patterns and frozen hand gestures to create visual imagery.

Four specific moves from Grinder's work (2000) influence information flow: *choose voice, pause, ABOVE (pause) whisper,* and *freeze* body. Let's examine them one at a time and relate them to the work with the four audiences above. As you learn more about these moves, you will recognize that the above ideas are merely suggestions. Your focus can then be the following: What move will I use? When will I use it? How will I know if it is effective?

Choose Voice
Skill

Choose voice infers a conscious selection of voice modulation. The modulation continuum can be labeled "credible" at one end and "approachable" at the other. This continuum is chosen with intention by the speaker and evokes a perception from the group. Credible, in many cultures, is represented by a flat tone that drops at the end of a sentence. For example, think of the following pattern spoken by former news anchor, Tom Brokaw: "This is Tom Brokaw, and this is the news." A voice and chin drop at the end of the sentence signals to the group that information worth hearing is going to be conveyed.

On the other end of the continuum, the approachable voice sounds a bit—but not exactly—like asking a question. In fact, it is the voice you want to use when eliciting information—it sends the message that this is about interest, not interrogation. The approachable voice signals that the speaker is seeking information or being tentative in the delivery of the message.

The speaker's intention should be supported by the appropriate paralanguage pattern. If the intention is to send information, select the credible voice. If the intention is to seek input and ideas, then use the approachable pattern. Congruency of words and voice make a good oration. This is especially important in light of the work of Miller (1981), which reports that 82% of communication in the classroom is nonverbal, and of Goldin-Meadow, Kim, and Singer (1999), which reports that students who are taught by teachers who are incongruent in their verbal and nonverbal signals achieve at lower levels than students with teachers who are congruent in their verbal and nonverbal signals.

Practice

To become aware of your own personal range of voice pattern and to explore beyond that range, the following exercise can be useful. Using a credible voice, say aloud the phrases below, which might be used to open a meeting. Notice your voice and the emphasis on the last word of each line:

Welcome to the meeting

On the agenda

The new curriculum

Now repeat the same script using a very approachable voice with bounce and rhythm. Lift your chin at the end of each line to accentuate the voice modulation. Notice the effect on the message delivered. The credible voice sounds right; the approachable is not congruent with the message.

Reflection

• What do you notice about the intent of the message when using the credible voice and then the approachable voice?

Pause

Skill

A second skill, pausing, enhances message delivery and acceptance by allowing the speaker and the listeners to breathe while the message is delivered. Breathing is essential for supporting cognition, not to mention life in general. The importance of breathing can best be understood by recognizing that the human brain is approximately 3% of the body mass and can consume up to 37% of the oxygen. Breathing is controlled from the pons and medulla oblongata at the base of the brain (Campbell, Reece, & Lawrence, 1999). When we hold our breath, the carbon dioxide levels in the blood increase. The body reacts to the carbon dioxide increase in much the same way that it responds to threat—by releasing hormones that support the fight-or-flight response. In addition, the human brain is hardwired to detect threat, which results in a decrease in blood flow to the frontal lobes and an increase in flow to the brain stem. When we hold our breath or perceive a threat, thinking is negatively impacted (Garmston & Wellman, 1999). Action, not thought, becomes the priority. Pausing in appropriate places during the delivery of content supports group breathing and establishes a low-threat environment, thus allowing both presenter and audience to think more clearly and effectively.

To understand the difference between high (shallow) and low (deep) breathing, we must first recognize breathing on a conscious level. Try the following: Recall a situation that was difficult. Stay with it a moment and reexperience it. Notice that your breathing is probably high and shallow. Now, in contrast, recall a vacation that was pleasurable. Notice your breathing. It is probably deep and slow. Both presenter and audience members should stay as much as possible with the second type of breathing to maximize their mental functioning.

Pausing is particularly effective in four different contexts:

1. After you ask a question
2. Before a person responds
3. After a person responds
4. When a group pauses collectively to think

Whether you use pause as a presenter depends on your intention. Your intention might be to focus the group on a question, to build anticipation for what you are about to say, to provide think time, or to provide process time for integration and reflection. Individuals need time to process and construct their thinking, and the pause provides that time. Pausing promotes thinking. Not pausing can get in the way of learning and inhibit the flow of information. A colleague observed a leadership team of teachers, parents, and the principal from an elementary school in California as they developed their collaborative skills to support cross-grade teaming. During the meetings, whenever someone was about to finish what he or she was saying, the principal was already starting to inhale and would begin to speak before the previous speaker ended. There was no pausing, no thinking, no progress—the team was stuck in the sense that new ideas were not surfacing and conversations were not focused on students and student learning. The staff did talk, but not about the most important thing, improving student achievement, nor did it talk in the most effective ways. The principal's failure to pause inhibited the flow of information, because when she talked, others were silenced—their ideas, ways of thinking, and solutions were never put on the table for consideration and dialogue. Ask yourself if there is someone at your school or in your office who silences others by never pausing.

Practice

Using the same script as in the previous exercise, insert a pause at the end of the second line. Using a credible voice, say the first two lines, and at the end of the second line, on the word *agenda*, pause. To support the pause, internally count backward (3, 2, 1) before saying the last line.

> Welcome to the meeting
> On the agenda
> The new curriculum

Reflection

- What did you notice about the impact of the pause?
- How is the effect on the message different from not pausing?
- When have you made a conscious decision to pause? What was the influence on the group?

ABOVE (Pause) *Whisper*
Skill

The *ABOVE (pause) whisper* skill is also grounded in the work of Grinder (1993). It can be used with almost any size group. In Breckenridge, Colorado, the National Academy for Science and Mathematics Education Leadership was having its annual summer institute for more than 120 educators committed to professional development and leading change. The presenter modeled *ABOVE (pause) whisper* by dividing the room in half. Half the room was told to talk to each other. The presenter then turned to the other 60 participants and spoke to them about voice modulation and how we, as presenters, can influence the metabolism of a group and affect the flow of information when we teach. As the presenter talked to the one group, she increased her voice volume in steps with each statement, getting louder and louder, almost to the level of yelling. While this was going on, the other half of the room raised its collective volume to match her volume—unaware of the influence and the catalyst. When their collective volume decreased, the presenter said in a very loud voice (the "ABOVE" step), "The next—." Then came the pause, and, using a soft stage whisper, she continued, "The next step is to stop." The room of 120 fell silent. The surprise for the group with whom the presenter was speaking was how quickly the independent half of the group fell silent. Faces registered shock and surprise as they recognized the effectiveness of this skill on getting the attention of a group.

The speaker's "ABOVE" is slightly louder than the loudest noise in the room. Figure 4-1 illustrates how the collective voice volume of a group cycles from louder to softer every 8 to 10 seconds. To effectively use the "ABOVE," simply wait until the collective volume of the group begins to decrease before speaking. You need to deliver only a word or two in the "ABOVE" voice. Next comes the pause, the single most powerful nonverbal. It is a skill that allows the speaker to breathe and to more effectively observe the group. The pause also provides a break in the pattern. Because our brains are hardwired to detect changes in patterns, the pause influences the listeners, especially the kinesthetically oriented participants. Last is the whisper. Think of the soft stage whisper. The whisper offers another change in pattern and quiets the group. At this point, you can face the independent group and continue with a polite "thank you." An effectively delivered *ABOVE (pause) whisper* is a sophisticated management tool that can reap respectful results with adults.

Figure 4-1. ABOVE (Pause) Whisper

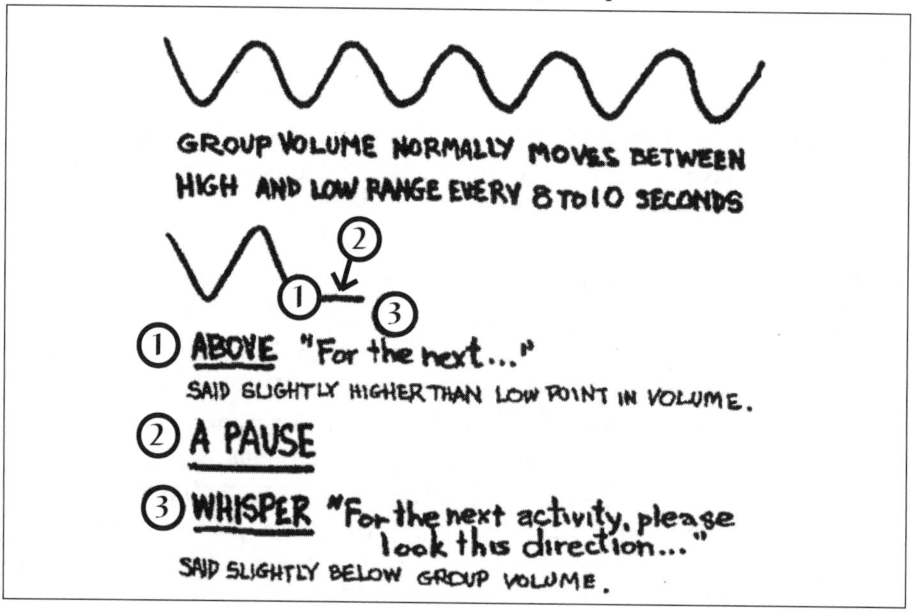

GROUP VOLUME NORMALLY MOVES BETWEEN HIGH AND LOW RANGE EVERY 8 TO 10 SECONDS

① ABOVE "For the next..."
SAID SLIGHTLY HIGHER THAN LOW POINT IN VOLUME.

② A PAUSE

③ WHISPER "For the next activity, please look this direction..."
SAID SLIGHTLY BELOW GROUP VOLUME.

Practice

This one is a bit tough to do alone; however, it is essential to practice the skill if your goal is to be smooth and artistic in your implementation.

The task is to first say, "As we stop" in a loud voice. Think about a presentation you have led when the volume of the room was high; and top that volume with this phrase. Next you pause and internally count backward (3, 2, 1). Then whisper, "As we stop [pause and count internally 3, 2,1] and shift to reflect on the topic."

Reflection

- What did you notice about yourself when you did this exercise?
- What part is difficult for you? If there is an awkward or difficult aspect, how might you get past the awkwardness?
- Think of your next presentation and plan when you will use this strategy. Are you willing to try this?

Freeze Body
Skill

A fourth skill for information flow is *freeze body*. This is designed to get the attention of the listener by visually representing "Listen to me." You can think of participants as having visual, auditory, and kinesthetic preferences in the way they process information. *Freeze body* draws the attention of the audience to the speaker and is particularly effective with kinesthetically oriented individuals. These are students in a classroom or participants at a seminar with whom the teacher has the hardest time gaining their attention. Since kinesthetically oriented learners often do not process the information they hear or see, the *freeze body* skill indicates to them, in a respectful manner, "Be quiet and pay attention!" We all know how quickly an adult group can shift and resist when they perceive overt management tricks. Our challenge is to learn how to manage the group in a nuanced manner that models respect and safety to support cognitive challenge. The successful implementation of *freeze body* is simply to freeze your body when you talk and during the subsequent pause. To write about standing still is bit ridiculous, so let's move to an exercise.

Practice

You can try this exercise two ways. First, practice the least recommended way to kinesthetically experience what it feels like when body movements are not frozen. This will be followed by the most recommended way.

In the least recommended way, walk across the room toward the front, where you will present, and say, "Thank you, and look this way please," as you walk.

For the most recommended way, stand still as you deliver the above line. And insert a pause after "thank you" and after "look."

Reflection

What did you notice about the differences between the most recommended and the least recommended ways you practiced?

Example

A good friend was presenting to a group of 65 staff developers from around the state. We all knew each other quite well; in fact, I had led several trainings for them on facilitation and presentation skills. On this particular day, my friend was going to practice *ABOVE (pause) whisper* while presenting. As the group was coming back from a break, my friend wanted to quicken the return time. He stood about 6 feet from the overhead projector and made little eye contact with the group. As the group volume started to drop, he said in a flat voice, different from anything in the room, and using a *freeze body* said, "half a minute." He listened to the group volume, and as it began to decrease even more, he moved toward the overhead. What happened next was the surprise. The group actually stopped talking before he got to the overhead and looked at him in silence. My friend froze midstep with a deer-in-the-headlights stare. Someone said, "Say something!" The whole group started laughing and applauding because they realized the *ABOVE (pause) whisper* worked in spite of the fact that they knew the skill, too. He made it to the overhead as the applause quieted and began a great session. In short, it worked! Nonverbals are what we react to first and pay attention to last.

REMEMBER

1. Information flow can be enhanced through the conscious use of paralanguage.
2. Have the words you are speaking match the message in your voice.
3. Use a credible voice for giving directions.
4. Pausing in appropriate places during the delivery of content supports group breathing and establishes a low-threat environment, thus allowing both presenter and audience to think more clearly and effectively.

Influencing Energy Transfer

The group's eyes will follow yours.
Where do you want them to look?

When we are presenting to a group, there is energy present in the room. Energy emanates from the presenter, the group, and from individuals within the setting. The direction of the energy, or focus, can be influenced through paralanguage moves. This section explores how paralanguage moves can influence this vital resource for learning.

I am tired this morning; the night was long with grading papers. I do not want to stand in front of a group of university faculty and do a presentation of my research in education and then be forced to defend it. —A university professor

You may not be a university professor, but I am sure there have been times when you were not looking forward to giving a presentation. When you find yourself in a situation in which you would like to redirect the energy, consider the following paralanguage technique.

Third Point

Get the group to look at a screen or easel. The key idea is to get them to look at something other than you, at a third point. (The first two points are yourself and the person or group to whom you are talking.) The listener's eyes follow the speaker's eyes, so as you turn to the screen, use a frozen hand gesture to direct the group to the screen and, most important, you look at the screen, too. Then walk away without making eye contact with the group. The group will continue to look at the screen. You can repeat this skill several times during a session, even if it is only a 30-minute presentation. In the case of the professor quoted above, she used a frozen hand gesture and the concept of a third point to influence the listeners to look at her work and not herself. In doing so, her comfort level was increased, and the conversation after the session was positive. Did the nonverbals made a difference? They certainly did from the perspective of the presenter; she was successfully able to redirect the energy from her to the screen. From the perspective of the group, they made a difference, too; the group was able to view her work at its own pace, and people's breathing was low and comfortable.

Bob watched an eighth-grade teacher in Kuala Lumpur greet his class the first day back from a weeklong field trip. The kids were extremely energized, and the instructional period had been shortened to 40 minutes. How could he focus them, he wondered, in these circumstances? As the students entered the room, he stood by the chalkboard and with a frozen gesture, pointed to a task the students were to start when they entered. The students quietly fell right to the task. This was the first time the teacher had used this skill, and he was amazed at its effectiveness.

An understanding of nonverbal choreography includes use of space. Table 4-2 lists verbal messages and identifies the nonverbal skills of directing and redirecting energy from one location to another. The verbal message is "As you look at the data, what patterns do you see?"

The key to redirecting the energy from "eyes on the speaker" to "eyes on the screen" is to stand to the side of the screen, so that you, the audience, and the screen form a triangle. This shifts group energy and guides attention (Grinder, 2000; Goldin-Meadow, 2002). For example, as shown in Figure 4-2, if you stand in front of the screen (between the group and the screen), as you turn to look at the screen the group has to look past you, but in a direct line. Then when you turn around, the group easily shifts back to looking at you, and you become the focus of energy. In this in-line position, there is no escaping the eyes of the audience. When the audience is looking at you.

Table 4-2. Choreographing An Opening

Verbal	Nonverbal
Thank you for coming this morning,	High eye contact with audience. A mix of credible and approachable voice with an open, palms-up gesture.
As if you had a choice!	Pause with the hands vertical. Wait for a laugh.
On our agenda are 4 topics.	Credible voice, look at agenda, pause after each topic. With the last topic stated, turn to the group, freeze body, and count internally, 3-2-1.
Before we get started,	Walk a few feet from the easel (presentation space). Pause.
Think how many of you would like to be prepping your classrooms today. There are a lot of things to do other than being here today.	Gesture outside, toward the classrooms. Pause periodically. Use credible voice, pause, and count 3-2-1. Then move halfway back to the easel.
There is good reason to want to be in the classroom. It is where our passion is. Our drive is to support students and the desire to provide the best science experiences for them.	Approachable voice. Palm-up gesturing to group. Inclusive language. (our)

Redirecting energy is very useful from a personal standpoint. Consider the times you had to present when you were tired, sick, or just having a bad day. This skill provides you with the opportunity to shift the energy to a location other than yourself, permitting your audience to look, think, pause, reflect, or process. By developing our skill at redirecting energy, we can establish and maintain positive rapport with the group, and rapport is essential to learning (Brekelmans, Wubbles, & Creton, 1990).

Let me add one caution: Adults have a low tolerance if they perceive they are being managed or manipulated. The onus is on presenters to have intentions that support the learner and to be skillful and genuine with their paralanguage.

Figure 4-2. Triangular Setup

REMEMBER

1. The listeners' eyes follow the presenter's eyes.
2. The key to redirecting the energy from "eyes on the speaker" to "eyes on the screen" is to stand to the side of the screen or easel and the audience so that you, the screen, and the audience form a triangle.
3. By refining your skill at redirecting energy you can establish and maintain positive rapport with the group. Rapport is essential to learning.

Affecting Memory

Save time and increase comprehension
with strategic use of space.

Recent research links paralanguage to improved memory. In this section we will examine a study that sought to find out if teacher gestures could increase student memory in a mathematics class. We will also explore how presenters can set specific locations from which to communicate types of content and how that enhances participant understanding and memory.

Locations evoke memory. We all hold special memories that resurface when we return to their origin: vacation, a favorite restaurant, Grandma's kitchen. Location is also tied to historical events. We all know where we were and what we were doing when we heard the news of the Challenger disaster or the day the Berlin Wall came down. In the classroom, locations are full of memories: the disruptive table, the teaching position, the spot where a student failed a test, and even where content was taught.

Grinder (1997) suggests that we use location in the room to separate management from teaching, as well as to teach different content. In professional development sessions, we can and should establish a content location, a management location, a process location, and an announcements location.

I watched Bob Garmston and Bruce Wellman in a weeklong Adaptive Schools seminar. They consciously and deliberately used location brilliantly to facilitate learning, group comfort, and announcements. The room was large, sufficient to seat 100 people at round tables. There were four doors, one at each corner, and a wide presentation space up front (Figure 4-3).

Figure 4-3. Four Locations

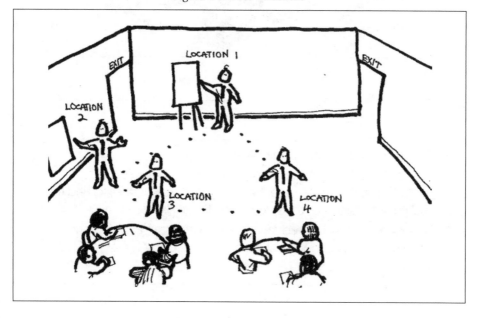

Location 1 was used for content and presenting chunks of information. Location 2 was used to go over day-to-day logistics such as lunch sign-ups and hotel procedures: announcements were made from here each morning. When the speakers wanted to break the chunks of content into smaller bits of information, they moved from location 1 across the presentation area to locations 3 and 4.

Once the content was delivered and as the participants asked questions, the presenters would either move to the location from which the content of the question was delivered or gesture to that location as they responded. This technique boosts memory. Locations 3 and 4 served as new containers to anchor additional content and enhance participant memory and thinking. (See organizers, chapter 3.)

Location is often established through gestures. Gestures alone also affect memory. Cross and Franz (2003) found that people remembered a majority of phrases spoken with relevant gestures. Recall dropped substantially for gesture-free phrases and was even worse for phrases accompanied by irrelevant gestures.

In an intriguing parallel, researchers (Goldin-Meadow, 2002; Goldin-Meadow, Wein, & Chang, 1992) wondered if student gestures informed teachers about what their students knew and understood. Their findings are powerful. They found that teachers impacted students whose gestures were incongruent with their verbal messages more than they did the students who either did not gesture or displayed gesture-verbal congruence. This suggests that gesture may provide a view into Lev Vygotsky's "teachable moment." In a mathematics study (Goldin-Meadow, et al., 1999), teachers taught a lesson twice—once without gestures and again to a new class of students using gestures. Students taught with gestures demonstrated a better memory of the content than those students taught by the same teacher without gestures.

Gestures can be categorized into two groups. In one group are the gestures used to represent concrete things, like a book, a car, or paper. The other category consists of gestures that represent images or abstractions. An example of this is using the hand to represent a person running over a hill. Gestures are believed to emanate from our visual cortex in the brain and therefore are pathways into our mode of thinking. From the education perspective, gestures might actually provide insight into the mind of the speaker (Roth, 2001b). Again, it appears that Vygotsky's teachable moment may be a reality evidenced through nonverbal signals.

In short, we derive deeper understanding from speakers who gesture.

REMEMBER

1. Locations evoke memory.
2. Gestures alone can also evoke memory.
3. Use location in the room to separate management from teaching, as well as using location to teach different content.
4. Students taught by a teacher using gestures demonstrated a better memory of content than those students taught by the same teacher not using gestures.

Creating Psychological Safety

Psychological safety is essential for complex learning. This section reveals specific moves presenters can use to make the environment safe for learning.

Establishing safety in classrooms is accomplished through a learning environment that is high in challenge and low in threat—what Caine and Caine (1994) call "relaxed alertness." As presenters and facilitators, our primary responsibility beyond content expertise is the safety of the group—emotional and cognitive safety. Establishing emotional safety sets a norm of participation based not on right answers but on engagement. Participants must be assured that they will not be exploited by their answers or their participation. On the other hand, we want to let the group know that in a cognitively safe environment it is okay to be uncomfortable, challenged, and in a state of cognitive dissonance. As presenters, our challenge is establishing such an environment using paralanguage skills.

Location can be used to enhance cognition and learning. How we use space to take questions from participants and to respond to their questions is another example of the conscious use of location. Presenters are often asked difficult or inappropriate questions. The way the group perceives the question and response determines the level of safety as well as the credibility of the presenters. To illustrate the concept of group safety, I offer a story of how *not* to do it.

A consultant was hired to lead an all-day session for a large group of experienced professional developers in California, most of whom knew each other well but did not know the presenter. The presenter was knowledgeable, professional, and carried with her an air of confidence, or so it seemed at the beginning of the session. She demonstrated good use of the pause; choice of voice, gestures, and other paralanguage skills. There were, however, some inconsistencies within her repertoire. For instance, when she took a question from an individual in the audience, she remained in the teaching location. Her responses included the same voice patterns and gestures as she used when teaching. The primary difference between her teaching and her response to questions was that during the responding phase she maintained high eye contact with the individual who asked the question. This is a pattern that often does not work well throughout the day, and about 4 hours into the session, the system breakdown began.

A question was asked, and she responded from the teaching location. After she responded, within 10 seconds the group began to shuffle paper, shift in their seats, and some even engaged in side talk. This behavior continued for more than 30 minutes, until the next break. After the break, the audience's earlier attentive intensity had dissipated; the presenter lost the group and never recovered.

What happened? How did this situation go awry? Here are a few possibilities:

- *Teacher location contamination* (Grinder, 1993, 2000). The teaching location is where you establish and maintain content and context expertise. When the presenter answered a question and the group was not satisfied, the location became "contaminated" in that the group no longer perceived her as the expert.

- *Breathing*. When the group was not satisfied with the explanation, they stopped breathing deeply for a moment at the end of the explanation. The presenter was not aware of this evidence of dissatisfaction and kept on teaching.
- *Annoyance*. When the group was not satisfied, they became annoyed. When groups are in a state of annoyance, they talk to each other and shut down the presenter. For a detailed explanation of group dynamic stages, see Grinder (2000).

In another example of a lack of group safety, a presenter was working with new teachers, more than 150 in a room. The presentation was centered on state standards, assessment, and supporting science in the K–6 curriculum. In this instance, the speaker managed with the same voice volume and speed as his teaching voice. Thus, when the presenter said, "Quiet, please, look this way," he used the same voice as when he continued, "The standards for science are organized by grade level in the K–6 grade span." This sentence was just as loud, fast, and credible as the management statement. Even worse, this went on all morning. (I could stay no longer.)

The group sat there and seemed to take it (actually they did not, but the presenter was unaware and unskilled at reading the nonverbal feedback from the group, as their comments in the lobby afterward made clear). Several people later admitted that they were not enjoying the session. Others said they did not feel safe asking questions. Safety had not been established, and therefore several participants were silenced and their learning suppressed.

Observing the breathing of a group is one way to monitor for cognitive safety. Eric Jensen (1998) advises that the single most important skill for new teachers to master is reading nonverbal cues from students. As we develop our craft, we must heighten our ability to recognize when a group stops breathing deeply. There are several ways to notice when individuals are breathing shallowly. The shoulders lift, and the upper chest heaves rapidly or freezes in place. Movement becomes jerky, and language lacks fluidity and stumbles. Fillers (*um, uh*) are often present. Shock of any kind will inhibit a group's breathing: a surprise; an off-color comment; a verbal attack on an individual, the group, or the presenter; or a tactless statement.

To detect when the group stops breathing deeply, look slightly over the heads of an audience. You will know that collective shallow breathing is occurring if all the heads suddenly pull back, as if jerked from behind with a string. When you see that a group has stopped breathing deeply, you want to get them doing so again. People must relax by lowering their shoulders and leaning slightly forward. The best starting place is to breathe correctly yourself. Stop what you are saying and pause deeply. You may wish to step away from the spot where the frozen breathing was evoked. Now speak slowly and calmly in a low register. Another way to get a group breathing deeply again is to make them laugh; another is to make them move their bodies. It is impossible to get up, find a new partner, and sit in a new place without richly changing one's breathing patterns.

Sometimes you can just say to an audience, "Breathe!" My favorite technique is to say, "Turn to your neighbor and share where you are in your thinking. You have 90 seconds." What is your favorite line for getting a group to shift (and breathe)?

Developing an Opening Nonverbal Dance

We began this chapter reflecting on the context of nonverbal communication with our verbal abilities. I will close with a suggestion for the next steps and some recommendations for choreographing the first 10 minutes of any presentation or training session you lead.

Remember that our gestures influence how our words are perceived and how the listener derives meaning. Both Bob and I believe that continually adding to our repertoire of skills is a natural and desirable condition of being effective educators. Indeed, effective teachers, presenters, and leaders are those who model precision and clarity of communication in their professional workday (Senge, 1990; Sergiovanni, 1992).

We both also believe that all skills development requires clear intention, knowledge of the structure of the discipline being taught, skills, planning, and practice. Following is a list of questions for consideration, which when answered can provide essential data to guide your opening nonverbal dance.

- Who is going to attend the session?
- Are they attending voluntarily or were they assigned to attend?
- Has anything memorable happened in the room where you are presenting? For instance, a boardroom may have been the location of an earlier strike or a particularly difficult personnel issue.
- What are some of the potential resistance points? For instance, were teachers originally promised the day for classroom preparation, then redirected to your session? Know your group!
- What are their expectations for the day?
- What is their connection with the content you are presenting?
- What behaviors do you want the group to experience in the opening minutes? Laughing? Head nods of agreement? Partner sharing?

You decide the goals and expectations you want, then you choreograph the dance to support the goals you have chosen.

Here is a generic dance step I often use as a template to construct an opening. In the following scenario, let's assume that I am presenting to a group of 50 science teachers on the new district assessment. They are attending because it is a workday at the beginning of the school year. Last year scores went up across the district. They were promised a classroom day, but the district office decided to send me to work with them instead. Figure 4-4 shows how space is used. (See Table 4-2 for the verbal and nonverbal messages.)

Increasing your consciousness and skills in using paralanguage has been the focus of this chapter. This is probably never as important as in the first 5 to 10 minutes of presentation time, and it is so important that it should be planned carefully.

Figure 4-4. Choreographing Space

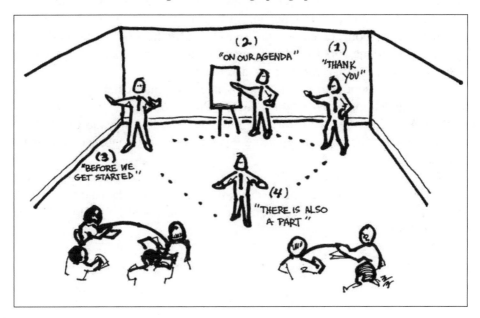

A good friend and colleague, Rodger Bybee, once said of nonverbals, "There is not a lot out there that I have not seen over the past 50 years in education. This, however, is new, useful, and important."

Be kind to yourself, select a skill a week, focus, and reflect. Begin the journey where you find it to be the most useful to you. As you grow and expand your skills, increase your range and enhance your effectiveness. Perhaps our paths will cross and we can share stories on what has worked and what remains as a challenge.

In the next chapter, Bob adds to this basic information about working with special situations.

REMEMBER

1. Psychological safety is essential for complex learning.
2. Aim for learning that is high in complexity but low in threat.
3. When a group is dissatisfied it can become angry.
4. Observe the breathing of a group to monitor for psychological safety.
5. Choreograph the first 10 minutes of a presentation in which you anticipate resistance.
6. Negative energy can be moved out of the room with gestures.
7. Pick a skill a week and experiment.

Summary

In this chapter Kendall Zoller built on the previous information about presentation delivery with a number of nonverbal strategies that enhance memory, create psychological safety, focus groups, and direct energy. The chapter explored how nonverbal communication influences the flow of information in a seminar or classroom. Five specific moves from Michael Grinder's work were presented as a framework for influencing information flow: *choose voice, pause, ABOVE (pause) whisper, freeze body,* and *third point.*

Rapport is essential to learning, and nonverbal signals can maintain rapport with a group and increase or deflect energy. Procedures for doing this were described. Also described were ways to affect memory and ways to use specific locations from which to communicate types of content to enhance participant understanding.

Ways to create conditions for psychological safety were also presented, a condition necessary for learning at levels of high cognitive demand. In general, the chapter has offered a range of paralanguage moves to be explored by the reader at his or her own pace.

Chapter 5

How to Work With Special Situations

Win your audience with ideas from the theatre.

Presentations offer unique challenges and frequently call for approaches that stretch us beyond the usual. The first topic in this chapter views presentations through the lens of the stage and explores the use of sets and props. The next two topics address issues common to presenting and stage work, nervousness and listening, and offer tips for both. A special section on listening follows, then the topics of cultural responsiveness, speaking globally, and working with resistance. The chapter closes with structures and tips for effective co-presenting. In sum, this chapter addresses some approaches to presenting that can make the difference between ordinary and extraordinary. In fact, it takes us full circle, because it provides some final touches that will support you in making presentations transformational, our focus in chapter 1.

Notes From a Safari Journal

Evening. First chance to sit, reflect, leisurely refer to field books, maps, journal entries. We started to leave Ngorongoro Crater about 3:30 after a film fest at a flamingo-filled lakeside. Sue and I dozed in the rocking, bucking 4 x 4 vehicle on the way back to the rim and Sapa Lodge. How we slept it is impossible to know. The experience is indescribable. I look at Sue; she is smiling. I watch a person look out the window at the lodge, smiling, head shaking in almost disbelief. I notice myself grinning. There is no part of this that I do not absorb within me—this night, the silver gray clouds, the backlight with spasms of white light, tiny shifting patches of pale blue blanketing, the shading and illuminating of the greens below in a wide valley or crater.

Presentation as Theater: Using Sets and Props

"All the world's a stage," wrote William Shakespeare in *As You Like It*. A more impressive natural stage than the setting at Ngorongoro Crater can rarely be found, and the parallels between stage work and presenting are many.

"Is it difficult to maintain the accent of the character you are portraying throughout the play?" someone asked. We were backstage, a small group of theater goers interviewing an actor who had just finished a performance. "No," he said, "it's not hard, but that's not the problem with stage accents." The next thing he said startled me and caused me to wonder what similarities might exist between a stage performance and a presentation:

> Audiences will develop self-actualizing hypotheses. If the first few times you speak, they think they can't understand the character's accent, they won't be able to understand it for the rest of the play. For that reason, whenever I'm using an accent on stage, I always deliver my first lines slowly and with highly crafted enunciation. Once they believe they can understand the character, I can speak more rapidly and still be understood.

How similar, I thought, to the early stages of establishing a relationship between a presenter and an audience.

I checked this perception with one of the most effective presenters I know, Michele Garside, superintendent of the Laguna Salada School District near San Francisco. Michele combines state-of-the-art knowledge about professional development, constructivist learning theory, and years on the stage in community theatre. She confirms that the best presenters seem to have a flair for the theatrical. One of the manifestations of this is their careful attention to setting a stage for the presentation or workshop, especially their creative use of audiovisual aids. These aides can quite properly be considered stage "props" and can add luster, interest, and focus to a well-crafted speech or workshop. They can also enhance retention. This section explores the use of some common and not-so-common tools that presenters use for these purposes.

Take Time to Set the Stage

Michele reminded me that the presentation always starts before you do. When your audience enters the presentation room, what they initially see and hear begins their learning experience. The set, the accumulation of onstage accoutrements within which the performance will be conducted, typically includes a screen (depicted as A in Figure 5-1) and two flip charts (B). The screen serves as the central focusing point in the presentation, and the flip charts mark the edge of the stage. The central "performance" will occur within that space. If flip charts cannot be found, portable display walls, chalkboards, or tall potted plants can mark the left and right boundaries of the stage.

The table in the center (C) becomes a location for the overhead projector and a prop table for those overheads, markers, script prompts, and other items the presenter wants close at hand. Overhead projector carts should be used only for transport. They provide an inadequate working space for the speaker.

The table behind the screen (D) is a place to spread out and organize those props that will be used less frequently and those that may be optionally used.

Two high presentation stools (E) serve as alternative locations in which the presenter may be seated and still give the audience full visual access to him or her. For audiences larger than 150 or so, a set of risers on which flip charts can be placed helps the audience to see.

Figure 5-1. Setting the Stage

After arranging the set, skillful presenters check the sight lines, moving to various parts of the room, sitting in audience seats, and making adjustments to ensure that each participant can easily see (and hear) the presenter. Depending on the purposes and instructional design of the "performance," presenters will sometimes arrange the furniture so that audience members can also easily see and interact with each other. A final check ensures that the presenter has clear walk lines, providing ease of movement within the audience.

Being Strategic With Music

What the audience hears as they enter the room is also an important part of the set. Just as lighting and music on a stage develop mood before the play begins, welcoming music sets a tone and invites relaxation. Music affects the emotions, respiratory system, heart rate, brain waves, and overall learning capacity of your audience.

A simple way to think about music use is to play light classical, light jazz, or New Age music as people enter, moving to breaks with a bit more tempo, and generally increasing the liveliness of the music as the day proceeds.

For a more sophisticated use of music, I turned to Michael Dolcemascolo (2003, 2004), friend, colleague, and assistant director of professional development at Onondage-Cortland-Madison Board of Cooperative Education Services (OCM BOCES) in Syracuse. Michael credits Eric Jensen (2000b) for teaching him about presentation music. Michael is a musical master in a workshop and contributed heavily to this information about music.

A word of caution is appropriate, however. Michael is a musical master in the same way that John Dyer (chapter 3) was described as a master humorist. He operates at levels of complexity higher than I can manage, and higher, I imagine, than some of us want to attempt. So select ideas that are useful to you now without thinking that what Michael does is a standard for music use in presentations.

Think of music as a movie director might, suggests Michael. Directors use music to set the mood for a scene as well as to mark transitions between them. Michael asks how did audiences know in the movie *Jaws* that a shark was coming? He answers his own question: Ta dum, ta dum!

Michael thinks in categories of music. Some categories that follow the structure of a presentation are background music, opening, break times, transitions, and closing of a seminar. Others set mood, pump energy in the room, or create a "we can do it" spirit.

To bypass the problem of having to cue up different sets of music, Michael puts music on his iPod that contains just snippets of pieces. You can do the same by recording on a CD or tape a few standard bits of music you would like to use. Then just select the appropriate time to play each one.

Seminar Categories

Welcoming music. This music welcomes people, warms the room, and signals that this will be a pleasant experience. Classical, baroque, or New Age music is appropriate. Pachabel, Josh Grobin, Vivaldi, Mozart, Enya, and Andrea Bocelli are possibilities.

Opening music. This music signals that we are starting. I have seen this used in high school classes in which the teacher starts the music loud, and the students know that they must be in their seats before it ends. For adults, these musical pieces provide a joyous tone to starting and often elicit a smile. Michael starts opening music loud, fades it, and then stops. Speaking begins. Show tunes like "Getting to Know You" or "Oh, What a Beautiful Morning," grab the audience's attention. So do pieces like the theme music from the TV show *Cheers*.

Break music. For breaks and lunchtime, soft jazz like Keiko Matsui, Al Jarreau, Dave Brubeck, Nora Jones, or Diana Krall are good selections. For afternoon breaks consider more lively music like Neuveau Flamenco artists, Jesse Cook, Ottmar Liebert, Gypsy Kings, or the upbeat sound of the Buena Vista Social Club.

Transition music. During the first break, Frank Sinatra's "The Best Is Yet to Come" sends a message you want people to receive. After break, pieces like "Welcome Back Kotter" are fun. Aretha Franklin's "Respect" or "Think" are also good selections.

Closing music. Say good-bye with Roy Rogers and Dale Evan's "Happy Trails to You." Try James Brown's "I Feel Good." (See also celebration music below).

Mood Music

Activities. To set up activities like lineups, try theme music from *Mission Impossible* or *Hawaii Five-O*.

Move to groups. For movement to small groups, use "Hi Ho, Hi Ho, It's Off to Work We Go."

Energy. For high energy try Gloria Estefan's "Get on Your Feet" or Salsa Line Up's, "Hot! Hot! Hot!"

Celebration. Both Eric and Michael support the idea of celebrating accomplishments in a seminar setting. Some of the music Michael might play is Louie Armstrong's, "It's a Wonderful World," Tina Turner's "You're Simply the Best," and Queen's "We Are the Champions."

Most modest-size cassette players will produce adequate volume when enhanced through a sound system. I've recently discovered iPods, the MP3 player made by Apple, on which I can carry hundreds of songs. I connect this to a speaker system and can easily choose music to match the mood and culture of the group. Michael organizes his iPod by categories for workshops.

Music remains one of the world's great connectors. Customize your selection to match the regions, cultures, and ethnicities of your audience.

Using the Set

Earlier, Michele Garside offered ideas for creating the presentation space using theatre concepts of stage and props. Here we explore special ways of using these.

In the theater, actors occupy various stage locations for specific purposes. They sit or stand to add visual interest for the audience, and they may reserve a specific location on the set for certain types of communications, like delivering soliloquies. In *Hamlet*, for example, notice that the director will usually have the actor move to the same place on the stage to represent reflection and inner dialogue. In a similar manner, presenters will sometimes reserve a portion of the set as a place from which to tell stories, another location from which they can change character and deliver data, and perhaps a third from which they become a colleague and engage in informal conversations with the audience. This presentation stance is often played from one of the presentation stools or by sitting, legs dangling, on top of the center prop table (C in Figure 5-1). Many presenters will move to a designated spot on the set to make comments to the audience about processes that they are using. In chapter 4, Kendall Zoller described how to choreograph through specific locations for different presentation functions.

Having set the stage, the presenter also has the option of working off the set to give special emphasis to certain ideas. Examples of paralanguage were presented in chapter 4. Another form of paralanguage is "out there," in which the presenter, moving toward a wall, points beyond the wall and names some negative ideas that people "out there" might have. This eloquent stage move ensures that audience members do not think that you are talking about them when you are discussing counterproductive attitudes or behavior. I use this principle when I move "offstage" to give a counterexample about the directions for an activity. Some other "out there" examples: "In other settings teachers may be viewed as laborers and are told what to do"; or "In some faculties there are deliberate intentions to not get along"; or "No, corporal punishment is not on the table—even though it may occur out there in other places."

Once, watching the *Merchant of Venice,* I was stunned at the emotional impact of an actor gesturing toward the audience. Shylock had moved stage front, and in an accusatorial tone spoke at length of discrimination, all the time gesturing toward the audience. I was flooded with guilt and shame and intrigued that such a simple stage move had such an effect on me.

Select and Place Props With Care

Michele tells me that when a director works with props, great care is taken in the selection and placement of the prop on the stage or in a waiting area. Each prop must enhance the production. Nothing should be onstage or on a prop table that does not have a purpose in being there. In presentations, good presenters intuitively follow this principle by initially removing clutter from the presentation space. Between "scenes" they act as crew; they clean up, rearrange how charts are hung, and straighten furniture.

A *set* is sedentary, whereas a *prop* is movable. Sometimes the same item can serve as both. For example, a chair that is part of the set onstage can be shifted to center stage, turned around, and straddled sideways to illustrate an informal posture in a conversation. It thus becomes a prop. Or, the two presentation stools (E in Figure 5-1) can be placed facing each other to illustrate two persons talking to one another.

Overheads are props, and much has been written about their effective use. Slides or color photos or PowerPoint images can be transferred to an overhead transparency format, bringing color, and therefore interest, to a presentation without the fuss and inflexibility of working with slides. Fewer images of this type are more effective than many images. Too many become a visual handicap, making the presentation disjointed and making people forget the structure of the speech while looking at the pictures. Some presenters recommend no more than seven overheads for a 50-minute talk. Each transparency, even if it contains no more than one picture or half a dozen key words, is usually enough for 5–10 minutes of speaking. (See chapter 6 for Powerpoint information.)

Little has been written about flip-chart markers. In chapter 2, I made recommendations for pen brands and colors. Here is a tip for working with large groups. When the audience is 150 people or more, a large, broad-tipped pen is useful in charting key words as visual organizers for a portion of your talk. For example, in introducing an unfamiliar term, you might *print* (avoid cursive, it's harder to read) three words—*what*, *why*, and *how*—as an advance organizer for your comments. Two brands of pens give fairly good service. Sanford's Magnum 44 Marker™ is good but has the disadvantage of being permanent ink. Sakura's water-based SG7 Extra Broad Marker™ is also good but is limited in color choices.

By far the best flip-chart pen for normal size groups is Charters™ Markers (see chapter 2). A yardstick, correction tape, and white-out correction pen are handy tools to carry in your prop bag for your presession chart making. (See chapter 6 on creating graphic displays.)

To focus visual attention on overheads, the Learning Resource's transparent counters are excellent. Direct the group's eyes by placing these colorful circles on the section of a transparency under review. (They are available at www.learning resources.com/Index.pasp). You get 250 three-quarter-inch circles that come in six colors. They also make a collection of transparent geometric shapes that can be used on overhead projectors.

Signal systems represent another form of presentation prop. I'm partial to a set of chimes made of three metal bars of graduated length mounted on a block of wood. You can find them online at www.equinoxbooksandgifts.com/; they cost about $20. I use them to signal the beginning of a session or the end of an activity, or to call small groups' attention to the front of the room for an announcement or instruction. Other auditory signaling devices include train whistles and bicycle bells. Of course, as the presenter, you are also a prop, and hand claps, your raised hand, and other devices in which you use your own body in a patterned way can also become a "signature" signal for an event. (See chapter 3 on *ABOVE (pause) whisper* as a signal for attention.) A teach timer or meeting minder, which is a clock device that shows time countdowns on an overhead, is available from Stokes Publishing Company, www.stokespublishing.com. For Macintosh PowerPoint users, the Hog Bay Timer will place a countdown digital clock on the screen to inform participants of the remaining time in an activity. This is available at www.hogsbaysoftware.com/.

Hardly any conversation I have about expert presenters is complete without Suzanne Bailey's name coming up. Michele told me that Suzanne would use people cutouts as props. Three-foot-high butcher-paper human figures are distributed. Participants are asked, "Who else needs to be in the room to do this work?" Children, board members, or parents are examples of groups that participants might name. On the cutouts they draw faces, write attributes, and perhaps list the questions that these people would pose if they were present. This activity brings these people into the room and broadens the perspective through which audience members construct their learning.

Appearance
You are the ultimate "prop." You are always your most important audiovisual aid. Your clothes and grooming make a statement to the audience, and within the first few minutes, that statement speaks. Michele advises that if you are given

a choice between dressing up or down, dress up. Whatever teachers wear in the classroom to teach is appropriate there, but in front of a group of adults it may often appear inappropriate. Remember, from the perspective of presentation as theater, you're wearing a costume when you enter the presentation room.

Make sure you look your best. If that involves a trip to the hairdresser or barber, consider it a professional investment. (You can tell that to the IRS.)

Keep jewelry simple. Avoid earrings or bracelets that flash or jingle, because you don't want these to distract from your message.

Dress up. This means suits or sportcoats and (some say) skirts for women. (Others say dress pants are fine for women.) The point is to look well groomed. Wear nice shoes.

Choose a hairstyle that suits you and does not require constant fiddling. There's nothing more annoying or distracting than a presenter who is constantly pushing the hair out of his or her eyes. (Could someone please get this person a bobby pin?)

Preparing the stage beforehand gives you time to visit audience members as they arrive. Doing this can dissolve presenter nervousness, our next topic.

REMEMBER

1. Develop a flair for the theatrical.
2. The presentation always starts before you do. Arrange the "set," the "props," and the ambiance before participants arrive.
3. Music affects the emotions, respiratory system, heart rate, brain waves, and overall learning capacity of your audience.
4. Think of music as a movie director might—to set mood.
5. Collect and categorize music: welcoming, opening, breaks, transitions, closing.
6. A flip chart can be a stage border, a prop, or a focus point.
7. Use the best materials—the audience deserves this.
8. You are the ultimate prop; dress at a level more formal than the group.

Make Nervousness Work for You

You need to be bright to feel nervous. Being bright,
you can take action to gain confidence.

My first reaction to nervousness is frequently to wish it away, hide it, or be self-critical about it. I also know that when I dance with my own nervousness, like the fox, I can use its energy to fuel my attention and performance, and I can ultimately transcend its debilitating effects. The experience of nervousness is universal. Actors experience it, especially when they step onto the stage for the first time. Figure 5-2 lists some of the manifestations of nervousness. Often, being observed by others, or just the prospect of being observed, creates a keyed-up state in which adrenaline increases, the heart beats faster, breathing rate increases, pupils dilate, and response time quickens. Both novices and professional performers experience it, even some of the world's most famous presenters. All this can be a plus when properly utilized. It helps the speaker to meet the demands of speaking, and it has an energizing effect that improves performance.

Notes From a Safari Journal

Several times now we've seen it—perhaps the most nervous creature out here. Juma says it's called a bat-eared fox. Its ears are enormous; they are black-edged and oval, and Juma says the fox uses them to hear insects, which it eats! Very skittish, its head pops up over the tall grass, it looks intently at us, and then whoosh, it's gone. It keeps the fox safe, I guess. Also, Juma says, the fox has to keep moving to get enough food because the insects are not territorial.

Figure 5-2. Signs of Nervousness and Physical Distress

sweating

dry mouth

rapid heartbeat

yawning repeatedly

short breath

inability to speak loudly

tense, tight throat

tense face

tense body

butterflies in stomach

nauseous feeling

weak knees

coldness

itchy or twitchy feeling

high-pitched voice

rapid speech

Sources of Nervousness

According to Turk (2001), there are six major sources of presentation nervousness: (a) audience size, (b) audience importance, (c) speaker familiarity with the audience, (d) difficulty of the subject, (e) vulnerability of the presenter's public persona, and (f) experience of the speaker.

Large audiences often seem more intimidating than small ones. Also, the degree of importance that the speaker assigns to the audience affects nervousness. I once worked with a military man who gave regular briefings to Ronald Reagan when he was president of the United States. The man's rehearsals were lengthy and intense, and his nervousness quotient was understandably very high. The better known the group is to the speaker, the more predictable it is, and the less presenter apprehension there is likely to be. A speaker is likely to experience more nervousness the more difficult the topic is, if this is the first time presenting this content or if the presenter is delivering "bad news."

Being overly concerned with how you will look to others guarantees anxious feelings and reduction of resourcefulness. Whenever one becomes concerned about looking good, smart, or well informed, or not looking clumsy or irrelevant, the butterflies amass, take off, and vengefully fly out of control. Whenever we try to be something we are not, the risk factor goes up and pulls anxiety with it. So think about the audience, not yourself. How can you serve it best? Finally, the most anxiety-producing source of all is lack of experience. Fortunately, it is also the factor we can do the most to correct.

What causes these sensations of distress? The hormone adrenaline is the major player in creating these symptoms. As you know, the purpose of adrenaline is to help us to survive attack.

When the hippopotamus went after me in the Ngorongoro Crater, you can bet I had plenty of adrenaline pumping through my system. In that setting, the adrenaline surge was totally functional. Chemically, it alerts my brain and my body to be prepared for fight or flight. My heart beats faster; muscles tense, preparing me for physical exertion; blood leaves my extremities; a coagulating process occurs in my blood for protection against injury; and, in extreme cases, I can get nauseous or even vomit. Even throwing up has a purpose. In prehistoric days, when humans were still largely hunters and gathers, meat was not always dependable. So when meat was available, they gorged. Since outrunning a saber-tooth tiger is incompatible with the process of digesting food, the food on those occasions was disgorged. That biological and historical information doesn't help us to deal with the jitters in today's speech—or does it? Actually, the realization that the adrenaline puts our mind and body in sync for perceived danger can be useful.

Seven Tips

You can make the state of nervousness your ally by imagining that, like the bat-eared fox, the purpose of its presence is to protect you and support you in doing a job of which you'll feel proud. This is an extension of a principle from the Japanese martial art of aikido. Aikido, literally translated, means "the way of blending energy" (Crum, 1997). From this perspective, all of life, including presentation anxiety, is simply energy with which to dance. Since nervous energy is a mental phenomenon with physiological results, presenters can achieve desired states of calm by employing techniques of mental and/or physical preparation.

Because body and mind are connected, the treatment of one addresses the other. What follows are seven tested techniques for converting nervousness; four of them are physical, and three of them are mental. I invite you to explore these and to develop the personal patterns that are best suited to you.

Breathe

This is the simplest and possibly most effective relaxation technique. Just before you present, take three deep breaths. They should be full and slow, all the way down, filling the lungs. Concentrate on your breathing. Think of nothing else. Just three good deep breaths are enough. They add oxygen to the system, route blood to the neocortex, distract your attention from fear, and help to clear the mind.

Do Progressive Relaxation

Tense and relax your body, part by part. For example, first tense the toes and then relax them. Then tense your feet and relax them; then do the ankles, and so on, all the way up.

Walk

Notice that athletes walk and stretch prior to performance. This warms up not only the muscles but also the psyche. Walking vigorously just prior to your presentation uses adrenaline, gets oxygen into the body, and relaxes the large muscles.

Center Yourself Physically

When you are centered, you become more in touch with who you are and are less dependent on outside approval. The centered state is simple, natural, and powerful. The following is one way of centering yourself (for others, see Crum, 1987). Stand. Allow both arms to drop naturally to your sides. Have your feet spread so that they are appropriately balanced beneath you. Take some long, deep breaths. With each slow exhalation, imagine that you see the tension flowing out of your body from head to toe. Allow your spine to lengthen; mentally reach toward your hair and pull a strand of it up so that your neck is elongated and your spine is comfortably stretched. Now, from this position, sway slightly back and forth for 10 to 15 seconds, gradually decreasing the size of the sway till you reach center. Now imagine that you are pushing both feet into the floor, then release. Your body will let you know when you have that centered feeling from which your presentation can take place.

Experienced presenters use presession nervousness as a signal to take special care in planning. As suggested earlier, the greatest stress producer is lack of experience. The next three strategies help to overcome this.

Overprepare, Overprepare, Overprepare

All "butterfly redirection" starts with planning. Be very clear and particular about your opening. If this is a special occasion and you are feeling some extra nervousness, memorize the first 7 minutes so that you can deliver these lines even if your mental space closes down. Plan to stand still during the opening so people can "measure" you.

Write Notes

Write down what you plan to say. Rewrite it and simplify it. Some may want to mind-map it. Rewrite it again. Continue to rewrite it, organize it, and list it until it is finally in very succinct form, with each idea that is written on the paper automatically triggering in your mind the related ideas that you wish to present on that section.

Mentally Rehearse

Rich mental rehearsal, along with the previous two mental techniques, will redirect 80% of most people's nervousness. Much has been written on the topic of mental rehearsal. We are learning from the athletic community how rich envisioning creates what is known as the Carpenter effect: this causes nerves, muscles, and the entire body to behave as if they have experienced an actual practice. This technique has been successfully employed with athletes in team and individual sports and with peak performers in leadership roles. Fortunately, the technique also works in complex and interactive areas such as teaching, facilitating, and presenting.

There are three keys to good mental imagery: (a) create rich visual, auditory, and kinesthetic internal representations, (b) make adjustments until they feel right, and (c) make the representations from your perspective as well as the audience's perspective.

For example, imagine yourself preparing to present a topic to a group in the near future. Close your eyes. Take three deep breaths. See yourself in the room. Notice the way your body is organized in space. If you are standing, notice your posture. Notice where your feet are on the floor in relationship to your shoulders above them. Notice the placement of your hands and the expression on your face. From the audience's perspective, what would people see on your face? Where would your eyebrows be—raised or lowered? What degree of animation do you have? What would they hear? Notice the pitch and the rhythm of your voice. Listen to the patterns of your speech. Hear what you say. Be aware of the amount of floor space that you are using, your gestures, your walk, how you handle the overheads. Now step into your own body in that picture and sense what it feels like. Make any adjustments that you might need in order to have the feeling be correct. Keep watching the audience and your own performance and continue making adjustments until they are exactly the way you want them.

Mental rehearsal does not take long. It's possible to rerun a rehearsal film, making adjustments several times. Each time you run the film, your body responds as if you had actually been there. What was unfamiliar becomes familiar. What is familiar becomes predictable. What is predictable lacks anxiety-producing elements.

When you are relaxed and confident you can present well. You can even listen better, one of the hidden attributes of a good presenter.

REMEMBER

1. Everyone gets nervous.
2. Nervousness evokes physiological changes in breathing, heart rate, pupil dilation, and response rates.
3. Adrenaline is the culprit for physical changes. It is also the resource for preparing for perceived danger.
4. Because both the mind and body are actors in nervousness, either physical or mental strategies can bring you control
5. Thinking about your appearance or how you are doing increases nervousness.
6. Thinking about the audience can decrease nervousness.
7. Breathing releases fear (see also chapter 4).
8. For high-anxiety situations, memorize the first 7 minutes of your presentation.

Why the Listening Presenter Is Asked Back

Be appreciated because you listen.

Notes From a Safari Journal

We are rolling along at a steady clip. The viewing roof of the Land Rover is raised. It's hot, all windows are open, and we are catching as much wind as we can. Standing, I lower my voice to say something confidential to Sue. Juma, up in the driver's seat, eyes on the road and hands on the wheel, responds. I constantly can't believe how sensitive he is to every sound and how he listens intently to our experiences. Both Sue and I are impressed with how much he is there for us.

Nervousness and listening are two givens in an actor's work. An actor at the Ashland Oregon Shakespearean Festival said to me that a good stage actor has to catch other players on stage. "What is this *catch*?" I asked. He explained that to be authentically responsive to a fellow actor, one has to listen deeply and receive the meaning of the lines being spoken. You can't not listen and have the performance be convincing. In this section, I report how presenters "catch" their audience, deepening relationship and increasing learning.

Who the audience perceives you to be, especially in relationship to it, is a critical factor in establishing a learning environment. I was surprised recently when a participant in a seminar told me that my listening was the most important part of the presentation to her. After all, my job is to present, to deliver communications, isn't it? In fact, I sometimes tease audiences with an old line taught to me by Dick Suchman, the originator of Inquiry Training. "My job is to present, yours is to listen. If you get through before I do, please let me know."

As I reflected on her comment, however, I realized that listening is an important part of what we do when we present. In what follows, I explore why listening is important and how to monitor and improve your presentation listening.

The Benefits of Listening

An optimal learning environment is one in which individuals participate fully in the presentation experience without pretense or artifice. They feel free to be themselves; to know or not know; to have opinions; to admit fatigue, boredom, or lack of understanding; or to say that they are thirsty or have to go to the bathroom. An optimal learning environment is one in which participants feel safe: to form bonds with others, to develop community, to take charge of their learning, to question, to challenge, and to risk the discomfort that sometimes accompanies rich learning by publicly living at the edge of their own competence and knowledge. An ideal learning environment is one in which participants feel recognized and valued (because they are) for their resources, noble intentions, and individuality.

When you present, you do many things to develop such an environment. Of all that you do, perhaps the most unexamined is listening. Honest listening conveys that you are attempting to understand. This is a more potent message than "I understand," because to attempt to understand communicates that you value the participant. Listening shifts the audience's attention from the presenter to the audience member or, better yet, draws attention to the relationship between the two of you. Listening invites the audience to witness a dialogue, an unscripted and unpredictable event, and, therefore, one that is energizing because no one knows how it will end. Finally, listening reveals the presenter; it illuminates the person behind the role and the practiced show.

How to Listen

Here are five principles of presenter listening that are used by premier speakers and presenters. You might use this list as a self-check or ask a friend to watch for these patterns the next time you are presenting.

Stop and Look

Stop whatever you are doing. Stand still. Look fully and attentively at the speaker. Make eye contact. These attending behaviors signal your willingness and desire to hear and understand what the speaker has to say. Empty your mind of the desire to develop responses. Prepare to listen.

Verbally and Nonverbally Attend

All behavior in an interaction has message value, so give your fullest attention to the speaker as he or she proceeds. Allow your body to reflect your understanding, nodding, smiling, or grimacing as appropriate. Listeners unconsciously construct enormous meaning from a speaker's nonverbal behaviors. In fact, one theory about nonverbal signals is that language evolved and is normally used for communicating information about events external to the speakers, whereas the nonverbal code is used to establish and maintain personal relationships.

Also use the verbal skills of reflective listening, providing wait time, and paraphrasing. Nonjudgmentally ask the speaker to clarify terms, phrases, or concepts that are unfamiliar to you. A caution here is that when you are listening, your responses to the speaker should constitute about 10% or less of the verbal interaction between you. Also a caution about paraphrasing: Authentic paraphrasing is the single most powerful communication tool presenters possess. However, done poorly, it increases psychological distance rather than closing it. My friend and colleague Bruce Wellman says that there are four ways to annoy people with paraphrases:

1. *Use too many words*. The best paraphrases are brief.
2. *Paraphrase too often*. It should be used occasionally, not after every sentence. Paraphrase when you want to acknowledge the message, check understanding, summarize, or shift levels of thinking (Costa & Garmston, 2002),
3. *Use the wrong voice*. The approachable, melodic voice described in chapter 4 is the proper voice, not the flat-toned, credible voice.
4. *Use the wrong pronoun*. Well-formed paraphrases start with the pronoun *you*, never *I*, as some of us were improperly taught.

For a full discussion of the paraphrase, see Costa and Garmston (2002) and Garmston and Wellman (1999).

Punctuate Responses

Presenters punctuate to add meaning and clarity to speech. They punctuate when they use unfilled pauses (silence) and filled pauses (*ahs* and *ums*). They punctuate by using nonverbal marks, such as moving to new floor space or using hand signals to separate purposes (now I'm listening, now I'm answering a question), thoughts (some authors take this position, others take that position), relationships (now I'm facilitating your thinking and am expressing no opinion, now I'm offering an opinion), and ideas (here are three ideas, first, second, and third).

Three punctuations are universally useful in listening to audience members: the pause before responding, which gives you time to reflect and simultaneously models thinking behaviors; the movement to a new place in the room to begin your response to the speaker; and the use of the speaker's name. Above all else, I have learned that speaking to people by name generates mutual respect and makes the presentation room a friendlier climate. If I don't know a name, I ask. If I can't pronounce it on the first try, I keep trying, requesting corrections. Everyone's name is difficult for someone to pronounce. I'm most frequently called Bob. However, in Southeast Asia, the closest most people can come to that is Bobpt. It still makes me feel good to be "recognized."

Acknowledge

Because I conduct seminars on presenting, I often get rich feedback from audiences on my own behavior. It never ceases to amaze me how important it is for audience members to get a simple *thank you*, *yes*, or a respectful *uh huh* from the presenter after making a comment.

Segue Gracefully

To exit the interchange with an audience member, you might recognize a question or comment from someone else. You might just return to your presentation stance. A simple acknowledgement, "Thank you," permits an easy segue into your content. You may utilize the speaker's comment to underscore an idea and connect it to your theme. You may choose to seize this as a teaching opportunity and conduct a mini-lecture. You may choose to answer a question inferred from the speaker's comment. To explore other ideas on answering questions, see chapter 3.

Listening Don'ts

As obvious as it may seem, most of the tips on how not to listen are the opposites of the preceding list. I've watched some knowledgeable and well-intentioned presenters, however, quickly lose audience rapport through their listening behaviors. Here are some of the more damaging patterns.

I stress the word *patterns* because these behaviors in isolation are not counterproductive. In fact, at times they may be called for and useful. As patterns of listening, however, they seem to communicate that this is not a dialogue, it is a show, or worse yet, it is an "I get you to talk so I can say what I want to say" ploy.

Don't add. Whatever is said, the presenter usually has something to add. Frequently this begins to appear as if the presenter is attempting to demonstrate his or her own knowledge.

Don't interrupt. Beyond being bad manners, this is perceived as impatience, and most of the time it reveals your incomplete understanding of the person's points. Interrupting is appropriate, however, when you need to check your hearing or understanding, or if you've diagnosed a pattern of verbal diarrhea.

Don't check your notes, overhead, fingernails, or shoelaces. Anything that takes your full, undivided attention away from the speaker communicates a devaluation of what is being said. This includes pointless movements, repetitively shifting your weight from one foot to the other, behaving like a pacing tiger, or unconscious patterns such as pencil twirling. In fact, any movement that is not related to your listening is distracting to an audience. The same is true, of course, when you are speaking.

Don't debate. Repetitive debate suggests several possibilities. First, you may not be listening, and this is what is being communicated to your audience. Second, you do not have regard for the views of others. Third, you are trying too hard to "sell" your position or program. I've learned that whenever I get so impassioned in what I'm presenting that I began to "sell," I've lost my effectiveness. The presenter's job is to invite exploration and expand choices. The "salesperson" in me often awakes "sales resistance" in you. Then we both stop listening.

In a sense, one could describe listening by borrowing a metaphor of Henry Ford's about money. He said that money is extremely simple; it is part of our transportation system. It is a simple and direct method of conveying goods from one person to another. So, too, is listening. If you are truly listening, it is unlikely that you will offend.

REMEMBER

1. An accomplished stage actor "catches" other players on stage.
2. Listening is perceived as unrehearsed and brings you closer to the group.
3. Authentic listening communicates that you are trying to understand; hence you value the person speaking (and by implication the full audience).
4. Stop, look, fully attend, pause, paraphrase, and inquire.
5. Use names.
6. Be courteous.
7. Don't automatically add, interrupt, check notes, or debate.

How to Avoid Unintended Offense

Be alert for mental models different from your own,
to honor those you might unintentionally offend.

I talk to teach, yet when I carelessly offend, I teach what I do not intend.

I am White, American-born, and male. I am, or have been, a teacher, an administrator, and a professor. These accidents of birth and role both open and close me to experiences, viewpoints, and frames of mind. I am usually careful when I make presentations to avoid unintentionally offending others through carelessness in my language or insensitivity to their perspectives.

However, during a painfully memorable presentation in a midsize school district, I learned more about how little I know about my own language of offense. My teachers were four persons of another race and one of my own. In gentle and skillful ways, these people courageously caused me to become aware of how some clever and "innocent" lines were, for most of the audience, furthering unconscious acceptance of stereotypes and, for some of the audience, wounding and breaking the learning momentum as they went inside themselves to engage in internal dialogue and feelings. I had lost the attention of these people.

"No more Indian jokes, huh?" the man smiled, as he gave me a bear hug at the morning break. I had used a line I had learned long ago, and with a delivery polished through testing with many audiences. "You know how generalizations are formed? All Indians walk single file [*pause*]—at least the only one I ever saw did." Nothing in the surface structure of this sentence is derogatory, yet to a member of any ethnic minority group, the remark elicits a *transderivational* search for meaning. This means that we go inside, subconsciously locate memories or meanings related to the remark, and are flooded with feelings. Embedded in the remark are unconscious presuppositions about American Indians and, by relationship, other minority groups.

> The person who is telling the joke is being active in the perpetuation of racial stereotypes. Those who listen—even if they don't laugh—are passively perpetuating them. The only way to actively interrupt the process is to speak up and say, "I don't think jokes like that are funny." (Source unknown)

Presuppositions carry messages below the surface structure of language. Before this book went to press, one reviewer asked me if I presumed the readers of this book were White and male. Something in the way I was expressing myself brought that thought to her. Actually, I had presumed that some—not all—of the readers would be like me; hence my efforts to bring some light to other perspectives. The reviewer's question reminded me that try as I might and regardless of my intentions, I do write from a White male perspective, that being my experience. Some presuppositions in my language must have triggered that idea for the reviewer.

We react to presuppositions emotionally, even though we are not aware of what is stimulating the feeling. Recall the old Vaudeville line "When did you stop beating your wife?" What is presupposed there? I made that comment once in a seminar and evoked a strong response from a participant. Surprised, at first, at this woman's reaction to this "innocent" line, I began to realize the deepest presuppositions in that Vaudeville story (endured by appalling numbers of women who are trapped in relationships of brutality) that women are to be beaten. The line "innocently," and out of conscious awareness, supports that point of view. The fact that the presenter's communication slips beyond conscious awareness is very important, for that is the channel of deepest and uncontested learning (O'Hanlon, 1987).

Nor are occupation or role groups immune to our unintentional verbal battering. Presenters may make disrespectful asides about salespersons or lawyers.

What happens to the teacher in the audience who is married to an attorney? How do you think he or she feels when the lawyer joke is told?

So what? Isn't a joke just a joke? At least three implications of the unintentionally abusive comment come to mind.

First, a slight on any subgroup diminishes us all. If I can laugh at them, by inference I can, and may, laugh at you. Each group—liberal, conservative, gay, teacher, union, Jewish, Christian, Muslim, Hispanic, Asian, Black, White— has a collective history and a language, and each member of each group has a personal history that compellingly contributes to certain well-formed and well-intentioned points of view, values, and perceptions. To be disrespectful of the experience from which other people have derived meaning and behavior is to be egocentrically nearsighted and to devalue who we are and how we learn.

A second implication of such comments is that stereotyping groups—any group—contributes to less understanding, deepens our human and cultural isolation, and inhibits our ability to resolve complex problems in a multifaceted world.

A third implication is of immediate concern to the presenter. Just as four-letter words are guaranteed to offend some audience members, comments that put down one gender, race, or group are guaranteed to break the momentum of attention and learning for those audience members who identify directly or indirectly with the group mentioned.

Some words evoke strong feelings, just as do four-letter words. I once watched Kendall Zoller eliciting comments from an audience. One person used the word *killed* in reference to an event at a school. I could see the breathing stop in the room. Kendall, in responding, spelled the word, which removes some of its evocative power, and then mentioned that because of its tone, he respectfully would not record it on the chart.

I Don't Know What It Is Like to Be What I'm Not

Try as we might, we never really know the experiences of a person of an ethnicity, culture, or gender different from our own. It is offensive to act as if we do. Some time ago, my daughter Wendy shared an article with me about White privilege, which helped to reveal to me things I take for granted as a White person in this culture. One of the ideas I remember from that article is that I am never held up as an "example of my race." Such an idea would never occur to me, but many others have encountered this and understand it for the unconscious racism that it represents.

A Credit to Your Race

Carolyn McKanders, an African-American friend and colleague from Detroit, told me this story.

> I was presenting to an all-white middle school staff in a rural community. At break time a friendly and very excited group of participants approached me. One woman exclaimed, "Carolyn, if we close our eyes, you could be Oprah. We think you sound just like her." I smiled politely, realizing that this was truly

meant to be a compliment and that the person making the comment had no idea that some minorities might consider the comment racist and offensive. They had never interacted with an articulate, personable black female before. The only one they "knew" was on television.

A close friend of Carolyn's provides another example. She is an African-American woman and a computer analyst. She accepted a job at a major retail corporate office, where she was the only member of a racial minority. During her first day on the job she received many stares and some standoffishness. Finally, one woman ventured a closer look and made the remark, "You must be very proud. You're really unique to be here."

In the book *Skin Deep* (Featherstone, 1994), professional women of color report similar experiences.

As a White person, I stand helplessly outside these experiences. I can, to a degree, understand, but I can never know. Feagin and Sikes (1994), after interviewing 200 Black respondents say, "Sympathetic whites may have an intellectual understanding of the consequences of racial discrimination. Profound understanding or empathy, however, involves feeling the pain and comprehending that discrimination is a series of unforgettable life crises."

Nor is the phenomenon of racial or ethnic discrimination limited to Blacks. People of Asian, Hispanic, Indian, Arab, Native American, and others live within, yet also apart from, the majority culture. In the United States people of color have experiences that White (and particularly Nordic) people do not. In *Skin Deep*, professional women of color all wrote that while they appeared (and were) extremely competent in their professional lives, they were plagued by feelings of insecurity related to their color. (Featherstone, 1994)

An insight as to why the findings in *Skin Deep* might be so is offered by Feagin and Sikes (1994). In the White–normed corporate environment, Black women consciously choose their speech, their laughter, their walk, their mode of dress, and their car. They learn to wear a mask. Black employees in corporate America are under constant pressure to adapt, unidirectionally, to the values and ways of the White world.

This pressure to act in ways incongruent to one's identity eventually leads to insecurities about one's true value to the work. If I have to be someone else to be successful, then who I really am must be inadequate—incapable of succeeding.

Men of color also carry these burdens. It is not unusual for a Black male to confess that in every interaction he is aware first of his race. Carolyn tells me that this is a common Black male perspective and is frequently expressed.

The list could go on and on. Here are three revelations that surprised me. The first is from Carolyn. She confesses to me that as a Black woman traveling in this country, she still puts energy into mapping out a safe route for her travel. These experiences are part of the everyday life of African Americans and other minorities and significantly affect their attitude, behavior, and understanding about life. They shape both one's way of living and one's life perspective. All women experience this concern for safety, but it is exacerbated for women of color.

A second surprise to me was that not only do Whites not understand the experience of people of color, but also people from "minority groups" do not understand the experience of other minorities. Another revelation is that men do not understand that many women in this culture, regardless of color, experience themselves as part of a "minority" group, with all the attendant social and political disadvantages.

Finally, the more a minority assimilates to the norms of the dominant culture, the more that minority is at risk of becoming disconnected from its own and other minority identities. This disconnection sometimes gives rise to stereotyping and putdowns of people from the same and different ethnicities.

I have been fortunate to travel to other continents, countries, and cultures. As I witness what is new to me, I unconsciously try to make meaning based on my own experiences and mental models. The French sometimes have a reputation among American travelers of being unfriendly. A friend recently pointed out to me that what might appear as unfriendly to us may represent a French priority of family closeness and attention. In cases like this, understanding can reframe experiences.

So What's a Presenter to Do?

Above all, do not say, "I don't see color." This is insulting. What you're saying is "I don't see you." In the world of social work, people are taught to tactfully acknowledge their ignorance, then ask for information. For example, during an interview with a Native American woman, the examiner noticed that she winced when she was referred to as "Native American." The examiner politely stated, "I'm sorry. I'm not sure how to speak of your nationality. Would you help me with this?" She smiled and said, "Gladly—I am a woman of the Chippewa Nation. I want to be referred to as Chippewa."

Don't assume that a person was born in this country and that therefore you can entertain some generalization about their experiences and culture. In the 1990s the number of Blacks who immigrated from sub-Saharan Africa nearly tripled, and the number of Blacks with origins in the Caribbean grew by more than 60% (Swarns, 2004). By 2000, foreign-born Blacks were 30% of the Black population in New York, 28% in Boston, and about 25% in Montgomery County, Maryland. A similar pattern of increased immigration occurred on the west coast and in the southwestern states for Asians and Hispanics.

Educate yourself. Respect and learn from groups other than your own. Notice and appreciate similarities and differences. Noticing can promote sensitivity toward others (and their experiences).

Recruit a mentor who can help you to learn about another culture. Once when I was working in Israel, a staff member whispered to me, "Don't touch the women who are deeply religious." Horrified, I asked, "Have I been doing that?" "Yes," he replied. "Who are they?" I asked. "Women wearing wigs in the seminar," he told me. I needed to be taught to look.

It is also important not to be intimidated by the limits in our own knowledge base. Several times I have been told, "That's not okay in my culture." On probing a bit, I often find that this is a statement of personal history, not a statement about the broader culture the person represents.

Learn More

Because diversity issues are always present in content and audiences, I am vigilant about creating opportunities for these to surface. No presenter, content, processes, frameworks, or models are neutral. Here is one strategy I learned from Carolyn.

Examine your "suitcase." Participants are given folded paper resembling a suitcase. The presenter informs participants that all of us are "carrying" an invisible suitcase with all of our "stuff" in it. We carry it everywhere we go. It contains all of our life experiences and the resulting knowledge, skills, values, beliefs, assumptions, hopes, fears, biases, and prejudices. The paper suitcase contains written sentence stems germane to the content and audience, such as the following:

My learning style is . . .

My teaching strengths are . . .

Life is . . .

Latino children . . .

African-American families . . .

A fear for me is . . .

A hope of mine is . . .

Participants privately complete the items, adding any additional desired stems and comments. These are not shared. Participants are then invited to reflect on and share with their partners questions such as the following:

What was affirmed for you?

What are you learning about yourself?

What might be some implications for your work, with the content and with this population-community?

To what might you be blind?

What are your strengths?

What are or may be some of your biases?

What additional learning might you seek?

What are you keeping and discarding from your suitcase?

At the time this is being written, Americans live in a heightened awareness about the world around them and representatives of other cultures. Muslim-American men in particular are undergoing close scrutiny and sometimes discrimination. I am conscious of my own automatic reactions as I unconsciously make connections to terrorism and am quick to monitor my thoughts and feelings. Perhaps I am luckier than most. I am still filled with strong positive feelings for the Saudi Arabians I met recently during the Islamic holy month of

Ramadan. What I carry in my heart is the sense of community, laughter, and spirituality that I encountered there. It is important to remember that while a regime may be repressive, individual people need not be.

REMEMBER

1. A slight on any subgroup diminishes us all.
2. Stereotyping any group contributes to less understanding and deepens our human and cultural isolation, making it more difficult to solve complex problems in a multifaceted world.
3. Presenter comments can be unintentionally hurtful, breaking the momentum of attention and learning for audience members.
4. Any group can understand the consequences of racial discrimination. Deep understanding, however, involves feeling the pain and knowing discrimination as a series of unforgettable life crises.
5. Don't say, "I don't see color." This is insulting.
6. Be open, be curious, be learning.

How to Speak Globally, Even to Local Audiences

*You are well received when you forget your culture
and remember your humanness.*

With increasing frequency, educators in North America are presenting to groups with a wide range of linguistic and cultural differences. In these settings, to be understood requires one to understand, respect, and utilize the uniqueness such groups present. Learning to do this involves inner work—knowing and being secure with who you are and having judgment-free curiosity about others. It also requires learning how culture shapes the perceptions and experiences of others. Feelings of self-worth, evaluation systems for oneself and others, and systems of thinking and meaning-making are all indelibly influenced by one's culture (Jacqueline Brown, personal communication, 1999).

Here I share some of my experiences with and reading about designing and presenting to cultures other than my own. Two worthwhile books are *Speaking Globally* (Urech, 2002) and *The Geography of Thought* (Nisbett, 2003). Urech provides tips for 37 countries on names, dress code, time, nonverbal communications, and more. Nisbett asks, Do Asians and Westerners think differently? He answers in the affirmative and explains why.

One thing I learned in examining literature about speaking to international groups is that the foundation of presentation success is what you already know and what is described in this book. The challenges are in knowing your audience and modifying your work to accommodate what is deemed respectful and appropriate to them.

In Syria, I once taught a 6-day seminar with my wife to educators and paraprofessionals in Aleppo. The dominant cultures were those of the Middle East, India, and southern Europe. In the minority were British, American, African, and French cultures. Here are some ideas we tested to enhance learning under these conditions.

Modify Design and Presentation Style

As Sue and I designed the seminar in the abstract, we knew we would need different pacing than if we were presenting to a homogeneous group. Yet when the first persons we met were Assad, Armenag, Hagop, Shanti, Fadwa and Nour, we knew at a more immediate level the unique challenge before us. Both our design and presentation needed to be specialized. We learned the following lessons:

1. *Build trust.* Obviously, this is true for any audience, yet it requires special consciousness when working with diverse groups. Because our charge was to teach Cognitive Coaching[SM]—an application of interpersonal communication skills in which active listening, inquiring about thinking, and self-disclosure are used to improve teaching and student learning—trust was a particularly relevant issue. Just as when we work in the United States with specialized subgroups, we understood that any actions on our part that could be interpreted as confrontational would be seen as a personal challenge and an exercise in power and dominance. This would destroy the trust required to learn the Cognitive Coaching[SM]. skills. In Spanish, for example, the word *confianza* is loosely translated as trust, meaning an honest boldness, an assurance, and a firmness of opinion as well as a relationship that permits a certain secretiveness and privacy. (Griffith, 2000) If *confianza* is not earned and developed among participants and between participants and presenter, trainees will "shut down" and learning will dramatically suffer. To establish and maintain *confianza* requires a slower pace, sometimes taking as much as 20% more time to achieve the training goals.

2. *Explain vocabulary.* When a word does not exist in a language, neither does the concept. We anticipated, defined, and checked participants' understanding of words essential to our content. The term *mediation*, for example, describes a relationship in which the purpose is to support another person in self-directed learning. It is not a relationship in which one person is advising, suggesting, or solving problems for another. Because this concept is fundamental to Cognitive Coaching[SM], we needed to establish language we could use to guide and illuminate training experiences.

3. *Stress the basics.* Distinguish essential from desirable skills and teach the essential. For example, over our 6 days we focused on the essence of one coaching map for planning and a second coaching map for reflecting conversations. We introduced the planning map on day 1. We modeled it, described its essential

elements, and provided practice. On day 2 we offered refinements to the map, modeled again, and provided practice. We asked participants to commit the map to memory. We returned to its practice many times, adding other essential listening, questioning, and responding skills designed to enhance thinking. A high degree of competence in both maps and supporting skills was achieved for almost all participants by the end of the 6 days.

4. *Minimize reading.* Although each participant was provided a Cognitive Coaching[SM] workbook, it became clear that perhaps half of the group was struggling to understand the written materials. Because of this, we used workbook exercises and text only to reinforce concepts that could be verbally presented, demonstrated, and practiced.

5. *Give clear directions.* We rediscovered, in this setting, the importance of having participants understand the intention of exercises, the learning to be gained, and the specific do's and don'ts of practice. This same degree of clarity was required when we structured conversations for small groups. We continued to be surprised when what seemed abundantly clear to us was puzzling or misunderstood by group members. We got better at being clear as the seminar progressed.

6. *Make personal connections.* Participants' responsiveness to us increased the more we were able to make personal connections with individuals. Our asking a music teacher for help in locating Arabic music, getting directions and tips for shopping in Aleppo's famous *souk*, inquiring about national dress, and learning about families, prior work assignments, and local attractions we should see inevitably led to the respondents' greater public participation in the seminar and greater willingess to ask questions and seek assistance.

7. *Honor other languages.* Periodically, we would ask for an Arabic equivalent for an English word or American expression. In some practice activities, we asked a local speaker to give examples in that language. Our hunch is that by working occasionally in other languages, some practices were made more meaningful. Perhaps more important, we presented ourselves as learners, too.

For me, these ideas are grounded in a greater commitment I hold as a professional developer: to make presentations, whenever possible, that not only teach concepts or skills but also offer possibilities for meaningful communications among learners—in this case between the group and ourselves.

Often a measure of success is my own transformation. Sue and I came away from this experience feeling confident that we had learned a great deal about presenting to groups with linguistic and cultural experiences different from our own and, perhaps most important, knowing that we have made a number of new friendships.

A different kind of special situation can challenge presenters, and that is the resistant group. This is our next topic.

REMEMBER

1. The foundation for success in speaking to international groups is what you already know about presenting.
2. You probably need to modify your pace to allow more time for comprehension.
3. You may need to enunciate with greater clarity than usual.
4. Anticipate and plan when to explain vocabulary. If a word does not exist in a language, neither does the concept.
5. Distinguish between what is essential and what is nice to know. Stick to what is essential.
6. Honor other languages, occasionally asking for translation into another language, especially when communicating complex content.
7. As with any other group, make personal connections with group members.

Ways to Redirect Resistance

To overcome resistance, interrupt the system in which it exists.

Suzanne Bailey and I once worked with a group that tested our reactions to their (feigned) resistance. They didn't tell us what they had planned, so our responses to them, and theirs to us, were spontaneous.

There were secretive reminders to be disruptive in the morning session, to whisper, and to be otherwise inattentive when Suzanne and I began to present. Because of our response, many of the behaviors that had been planned were not executed. The disruptive behaviors they did initiate were ineffective in getting us off the track.

The key is that we didn't resist. Because resistance persists within systems of resistance, the intentions of these adults to test their disruptive powers and study our reactions failed to even get off the ground. Incidentally, we were honored by their trust and their gumption to work on such a bold experiment during our 3-day workshop on "Becoming a State-of-the-Art Presenter."

Resistance to change and learning is common. Following are some concepts and strategies drawn from the literature on psychology, hypnosis, group dynamics, and personal experience.

First, let's consider the type of system that resistance needs in order to live. Run water through a hose. Knot the hose, and you have instant resistance. Untie the knot, and the water once again flows through its natural course.

A participant voices a complaint. We counter with logic, knotting the hose. Or we paraphrase, openly listening without defensiveness, without explaining our behavior, and the water flows freely. Resistance can exist only when we resist the resistance. To bypass the resistance, break the system.

Resistance is a healthy reaction that enables people to maintain stability under difficult conditions.

Approaches to Resistance
Fog
Manuel Smith (1975) wrote a classic and seminal book called, *When I Say No I Feel Guilty*. The content was the early foundation for assertiveness training and suggested that everyone has a natural right to feelings and positions without having to defend them. One of the first resistance-countering strategies he offered was the notion of fog. To fog, you rephrase what the attacker says. "That's an ugly shirt," someone says. "You really find this shirt offensive!" you answer. You cannot shoot fog, stab it, or put up a wall against it. It is just there, permeable, and will float around objects unaffected by their presence. The first approach to resistance is based on this notion.

Smith's book, while "old," is still valuable. A recent book on this topic is *How to Say No Without Feeling Guilty: And Say Yes to More Time, and What Matters Most to You* (Breitman, 2000).

Paraphrase
Authentic paraphrases—not statements like "What I hear you saying is . . . ."—communicate to another person or group that you are attempting to understand. Attempting to understand signals that you value the person. To be authentic, a paraphrase should use the voice tone of the original statement, be brief, and use the pronoun *you*. Paraphrases borrow the tonal quality of the speaker and let the speaker know that you understand feelings as well as content. Silence should follow your paraphrase, giving the other person a chance to respond. Usually the person does respond, providing greater. (See Costa and Garmston, 2002, for a treatment of paraphrasing and pacing and leading).

Assume a One-Down Position
I don't pretend to be a better mathematics teacher than you. Although my work has led to an understanding of which cognitive processes separate the high-achieving from the low-achieving student, and although I know many specific ways to teach the low-achieving student some strategies that will increase his or her performance, I cannot begin to know the particular circumstances and students with whom you work. Please bear with me if I offer some things that are inappropriate; adopt those that will work for you and advise me where I might strengthen my knowledge base.

The intent of this type of statement is to shift the focus from the presenter's expertise to the participant's expertise and to eliminate possible power struggles.

Preempt

Another prevention strategy offered by Lipshitz, Friedman, and Omer (1989) involves anticipating a difficulty or an emotional block that participants may have in completing an assignment. The presenter foreshadows this and gives the impression that it is a normal expectation of learning and that it will serve as only a temporary and not a serious barrier. The presenter then offers tips about how to overcome it.

> Some of you may notice that when you begin to use these skills, you get worse before you get better. Your mind may offer compelling arguments to stop the innovation because it's interfering with your effectiveness. This is a very natural part of the process of growth—even your own admonition to quit. This will not last long.

> There are at least two things you can do to prepare for this: (a) be willing to live through a brief period of discomfort, and (b) select just a part of this new teaching technique to practice each day. Overrehearse it until it becomes second nature.

In this statement, the presenter has anticipated and incorporated potential resistance into the instruction. Should resistance emerge, it will feel to the participant like part of the instructions. It seems, therefore, not to be resistance at all but a form of cooperation with the presenter. To do this effectively, the presenter's language must be artfully vague, letting each participant tailor his or her own understanding from the fabric of language given to all.

Anticipate tensions that participants might feel. I will sometimes say, in assigning a reading activity, "Completion of the reading is not the goal. The important task is to engage with ideas in the text important to you. Here are some ways to do this."

Even with all your skills, however, in some audiences there may be 1% or 2% of the people whose major pleasure is to see you fail. Whatever you do, they will be able to find fault. Perhaps you speak too quickly or too slowly. Perhaps your clothes clash with the color scheme of the setting. It's somewhat reassuring to know that whatever you do, you will help these people to reach their goal.

The way to keep grounded, if these people are in your session, is to know that whatever is going on is about them, not you. When you have clear outcomes, know your content well, are clear about your plan, and have rapport with the general audience, you are providing the best opportunities possible for learning. You can do no more.

Having a common approach to resistance is critically important whenever you share the stage with someone. Next we will examine structures and tips for co-presenting.

> ## REMEMBER
>
> 1. Resistance is a healthy reaction that enables people to take care of themselves under difficult conditions.
> 2. Resistance persists only in systems of resistance. Unknot the hose and let the water flow.
> 3. Fogging and paraphrasing are effective strategies for working with resistance.
> 4. Take a one-down position to avoid power struggles.
> 5. Foreshadow concerns and normalize their appearance.
> 6. Anticipate tensions participants may feel.

Brilliantly Co-Present Your First Time Out

Learn the invisible structures of co-presenting
to be effective and appear effortless.

We arrived at 6:00 A.M. in Eureka, a coastal town in northern California. Suzanne Bailey and I had driven all night to reach the setting where we were to conduct a co-presentation—our very first. In fact, we had not worked together at all up to this point, although we knew each other. At the end of the day we were stunned by participant reaction and the smoothness and power of the day.

Driving home from Eureka, we tried to understand what made the day go so well. That was our first understanding of co-presenting and our first attempt to write about it (Bailey & Garmston, 1988).

Co-presenters resemble two paddlers steering a canoe downstream. Both need to agree on a destination and continually monitor the direction to make sure that they're still going where they want to go. Deftly, they correct, correct, correct—paddling one side, then the other. At times, paddles at rest, they may recalculate the goal itself. Is the destination that was agreed upon 10 minutes ago still appropriate?

Co-presenting is an intricate process, and, done well, it's extremely rewarding. Done poorly, it produces calluses and a colossal pain right where the canoeist meets the bottom of the boat. So many people experience more pain than pleasure in co-presenting; why try it at all?

After 2 years of co-presenting, Suzanne and I had begun to understand how to maximize the pleasures and minimize the pains that are inherent in this valuable presentation method. The pleasures can be bountiful for both participants and co-presenters. My experiences since that time with a host of talented co-presenters in the Adaptive Schools and Cognitive Coaching[SM] communities have deepened my appreciation of this form of teaching. Since the first edition of this book, my co-presenters continue to teach me more.

Accentuate the Positive

Co-presenting improves almost any training effort in several ways. It adds to the energy that trainers bring to their presentations. It lets each presenter come to the other's rescue when necessary. Payoffs for session participants include better training designs, increased diversity, and the benefits that come from the behavior that co-presenters model while they train.

Presenting is hard work, so conserving energy is an important factor. Presenters who work by themselves manage many cognitive tasks at the same time; monitoring audience reaction, keeping track of content, and managing time. Co-presenters benefit by conserving personal energy. In co-presenting, neither person is "on" all the time. While one speaks, the other can perform important presentation functions, such as assessing the audience or planning modifications in the lesson. When using PowerPoint, one presenter can be looking ahead and revising for the group. Co-presenters also benefit by drawing energy from each other. Watch any TV news show and notice how the banter between the anchorpersons contributes to their liveliness and energy.

Co-presenters rescue. Presenters tell us that one of their biggest fears is going blank in the middle of a presentation. When one co-presenter goes blank or gets off the track, the partner can come in with necessary corrections.

Participants benefit because they usually get a much better training design. Co-presenters can test ideas with each other and reassess direction and strategy during initial planning and during the presentation. I recall a session in which Suzanne and I had planned a 90-minute presentation on co-presenting for consultants. We thought that we had developed a reasonable design for teaching this topic, but one of us felt uncomfortable with the plan. After we discussed it, we realized that we had based our entire design on some faulty assumptions about what information the consultants needed to know. We identified more appropriate assumptions and reworked the design. The resulting product was much more useful. Recently, Claudette Landry and I spent most of the evening redesigning a day 2 for a group based on our day 1 learning. The results were phenomenal.

Participants also benefit from the diversity, variety, and richness that two presenters bring to a session. They get variety in personality, approach to the topic, and presentation style. They also get audio relief. Presenters bring the sum of their total lives to the training room. Who you are, your values, and your ways of being are more persuasive than anything you say.

In addition, participants get closer monitoring, and from this they get more advocacy for their needs and interests. Two people are available for break-time chats with participants, and both can follow up on individual concerns. Two sets of antennae are alert for participant needs.

Co-presenting rivets group-member attention. Participants focus on both presenters individually, the interaction between them, and the session visuals. In a positive sense, a two-person presentation resembles a circus—so much goes on at any one time that the conscious mind can't take it all in. Co-presenters who are skilled in metaphor, suggestion, and other forms of accelerated learning can use this perceptual overload to accelerate trainee acquisition of skills and knowledge.

Modeling between co-presenters also reinforces the presentation message. Here the canoe metaphor is particularly apt: It communicates a real relationship. The play beneath the play is dramatized in front of participants for their right brains to see, feel, and communicate to their analytical left brains. This may be the most eloquent and persuasive lesson taught, as it is about collaboration in a true team. The more co-presenters operate synchronistically, as in a dance, the more powerful the subliminal message and the more enjoyable and productive the learning experience.

Forms of Co-Presenting

Co-presenting can take five main forms: tag team, speak and comment, speak and chart, perform and comment, and duet. When you use PowerPoint, a sixth form becomes available: speak and track.

Tag Team

In the tag-team style of co-presenting, presenters take turns: One is on while the other is off. Many find this method the best for beginning a co-presenting relationship. It also works well for delivering new material that one or both presenters have not yet internalized.

Working at this level, one co-presenter monitors the audience as an extra set of eyes and ears while the other delivers the material. Those new to professional development will find that tag-team presentations allow them to train at higher levels than they could before. Teams get richer data about audience responses for use in their post-presentation debriefing. Don't, however, allow yourself to get stuck in this form. I know accomplished presenters who use this form most of the time, losing spontaneity, innovation, and energy in the process.

Speak and Comment

The speak-and-comment form of co-presenting puts both presenters on stage at the same time. One makes a statement, and the other adds to it. One leads; the other supports.

The leader is in charge of the content and makes process decisions—when to move on, end discussions, or proceed to the next content area. The supporter does whatever is necessary to achieve the goals of the particular session segment. He or she may add humor if the leader gets too dry, use proximity to stimulate wakefulness in sleepy participants, or move props. This is the beginning, and the easiest, level of "spontaneous broadcasting." Speak and comment lets co-presenters capitalize on their different perspectives and experiences.

Speak and Chart

The speak-and-chart method extends speak and comment. Using speak and chart, the leader presents content and elicits participant comments while the supporter records participant or co-presenter ideas on a flip chart or overhead transparency. The supporter acts as the session's neutral and invisible documenter. Successful speak-and-chart presentations demand the following critical attributes:

- Both must clearly understand who plays which role.
- The leader must monitor the accuracy and speed with which the supporter records. The leader can repeat statements, pause, or say, "Let's give the recorder time to catch up," if necessary.
- The recorder must summarize spoken ideas quickly, without distorting concepts or vocabulary. (It helps to record only what the lead person paraphrases.)

- The recorder remains silent and neutral. The recorder also avoids eye contact with the group, as this causes the group to split attention between the two presenters.

The speak-and-chart method works well because approximately 40% of people report that they best absorb information visually. In contrast, only 20% report auditory processing as their preferred method of learning, and audiences can reach auditory overload very quickly. Thus, visual aids improve participant learning. They also help participants to develop a group memory, to which the participants and the co-presenters can return as needed.

Perform and Comment

Art Costa and I discovered that audiences will sometimes observe what is irrelevant in skills demonstrations unless we help them to focus their efforts at data collection. By assigning observation roles to pairs or trios, we can assist participants not only to see and hear greater details but also to examine interactions and relationships. We call this the perform-and-comment method.

For example, to learn more about the potency of questioning in a Cognitive Coaching[SM] seminar, the performing partner might demonstrate an unrehearsed conference with an audience member. The second partner has instructed members of trios to record their observations on (a) the questions asked by the coach, (b) evidence of teacher thinking as manifested by verbal or nonverbal responses, or (c) the essence of the relationship between coach and colleague.

The second partner has tacit permission to stop the conference at any time, drawing the audience's in-the-moment attention to particularly relevant transactions occurring before them.

Duet

Duet is the epitome of exemplary co-presenting. Jane Ellison and Carolee Hayes do it brilliantly. This form carefully blends several ingredients to produce maximum effect with minimum display of effort. Both presenters are onstage at the same time. They balance the stage: One stands on the right, the other on the left. When one moves to the left to make a point, the other drifts unobtrusively to the right. They choreograph their movements. The speaker avoids blocking the recorder's visuals. Just as in tennis doubles, they play the net: one forward, the other back; one embedded in the audience space, the other on stage. The following are some ways you can recognize co-presenters operating as a duet:

1. They employ brief content chunks. One talks briefly for 30 seconds to 2 minutes, then the other talks briefly. (You may wish to experiment with longer periods.)
2. They may finish sentences for each other. First presenter: "You should know that . . ."; second presenter: ". . . the first consideration is trust."
3. They use physical proximity as a tool. Co-presenter duets do best when they stand 3–7 feet apart.

4. They subtly cue each other with looks, proximity, hand gestures, voice tempo, and intonation. Agree on these beforehand. I once worked with an exceptional presenter who was not picking up on my handoffs to her. We discovered that she was missing my cues because I was giving them kinesthetically and visually, whereas she paid attention to verbal inter-actions. Once we discovered this, I changed my signaling system.

5. They stay focused all the time, each attentive to the other and the audi-ence. A participant once told Suzanne and me that when one of us was speaking, the other looked as if the most interesting presenter in the world were speaking. We model rapt attention to each other's words. It's as if we were hearing the words for the first time.

6. They use a synchronistic style—the mutual telling of a story, exchang-ing speaker roles every other line or so, or sometimes speaking together at the same time.

7. Co-presenters who are attentive to their own development will change who delivers what content as well as their style of content delivery, so that each time is really the first time the words are spoken.

Getting Started

All of these co-presenting methods can produce exciting results, but only if both people work compatibly and understand the basic ground rules that keep co-presentations orderly. That's the first order of business.

Several interpersonal factors contribute to a team's success as co-presenters. The most important is agreement on key issues: beliefs concerning adults as learn-ers, training-philosophy orientation to the topic, strategies for co-planning, and approaches to resolving problems together. Consider the problems that face a team when one partner tries to contribute to sessions by controlling his or her feelings while the other person tries to promote harmony by using and expressing feelings. They're headed for trouble unless they can discuss their communication approaches and arrive at a commonly understood strategy together. Such differences in as-sumptions and style can cause havoc that overrides even the best intentions.

The ability to maintain personal composure plays a tremendous role in co-presenting. No matter how compatible the team, eventually something will threaten, annoy, or embarrass one or both members. We once heard a co-presenter come close to revealing a highly personal and embarrassing bit of in-formation about the partner. It took all the composure the partner could muster to stay unthreatened and consciously attuned to the content they were presenting.

On another occasion, we watched a co-presenter unexpectedly launch into a diatribe on a favorite topic. This wasn't part of the planned agenda and, if contin-ued, would have prevented the partner from delivering a previously agreed-upon portion of content. The partner later reported feeling unequal, useless, and angry at this insensitivity. It took a lot of composure to get through the balance of this training day. This ability to take charge of one's own emotions relates to the next critical criterion in a good partnership, the matter of discipline.

Discipline yourself to stick to the agreed-upon design. Monitor yourself and refrain from telling that favorite story if it adds little to the program. Discipline means forgoing the cute line when it does not serve the purpose. It's being able to see that time is short or that the point has been made, and eliminating portions of well-rehearsed content or activities as necessary.

Cutting things short, even when absolutely necessary, can be very difficult. We've observed that presenters who are exceptionally strong at storing workshop content in auditory loops sometimes have a hard time abbreviating content when time is short. This may be because their content is stored in sequence and must be retrieved in a certain order. Some find it hard to cut material when content is new. Sometimes, presenting the content intact becomes more important to the presenter than the effect of the content on the audience. Nonetheless, co-presenters must be ready to adjust planned content and activities to meet the unique requirements of each setting, and that takes discipline.

Trust in each other is the final ingredient to a successful co-presenting partnership. By this we mean trust in the other person's judgment, trust in the other's ability to manage emotions, trust that he or she intends no harm, and trust that he or she can respond to the unexpected. It also means trust that each will submerge one's own ego and help the other to look good.

Co-presenter trust is more important than it may appear on the surface. It supports collegiality and becomes a metaphor for the honor and respect the co-presenters have for the participants. Audiences probably respond as much to co-presenter trust, mutual respect, and collegiality as they do to the content being presented.

In most cases, co-presenter trust develops over time and is subject to occasional interruptions. People with a natural affinity for each other probably develop that trust fairly rapidly. Ultimately, co-presenters develop trust in each other just as they do in other relationships—from experiences together in which consistency, confidentiality, interest in one another, risk taking, understanding, and honest communication occur.

Taking the Platform

Now the team is established. Both presenters agree on philosophy, strategies, and approaches. They know that they must maintain personal composure and discipline themselves. They also trust each other. Now they're ready to co-present.

This leap into the training room is a big one, though, and it requires some forethought. Making several agreements ahead of time is recommended.

Give Permission

Agree that each presenter has permission to do whatever is necessary to meet session goals and maintain audience rapport and resourcefulness. Rapport exists when the audience remains responsive to you. Audiences are resourceful when they seem energetic, capable, and receptive to the material you present. Both rapport and resourcefulness are essential.

We suggest giving each partner ongoing permission to monitor and intervene even if the interventions are unpredictable. For example, each must know it's okay to tell a joke if the other gets inappropriately serious.

Develop Signals

Develop signals to help each other out. For "your turn," co-presenters use intonation shifts, incomplete sentences, and palms turned up. They use physical proximity or eye contact for "I want to add something." A finger on the wristwatch signals "We are running out of time."

Each team should develop signals that suit its own needs and should agree on how to use them. For example, once one partner signals that time is running out, he or she should leave the other presenter alone. Remember, partners need to trust one another to make the appropriate adjustments.

Change Arrangements

Agree to change prior agreements if necessary. Just because something worked in Atlanta doesn't mean it will work well in Chicago.

There Is No Single Correct Way

Agree that there is no one correct way to present a concept or teach a skill. When we plan an activity either before the workshop begins or in a huddle during the presentation, one of us may say, "I think we need to do this." The other may respond, "Yes, and you know, here's another way we could do it." And so it goes. The best co-presenters intuitively continue this form of brainstorming, going for at least three ideas. Once three are achieved, ideas become generative, and four, five, six, and seven will then flow easily. From that rich collection, the team can easily and mutually select the course most likely to help them reach the desired outcome.

Forge Mutual Understandings

Agree on some explicit understanding to support the co-presenting relationship. Suzanne and I have found several ideas that serve us well. At all times, we agree, our overriding goal is to produce optimal learning. We each have a responsibility to maintain composure and to help the other partner look good. We will do whatever it takes to achieve our desired outcomes, whether that means interrupting each other, running copies, fixing the furniture, planning during breaks, prospecting with participants before the session, or working with audience members at lunchtime to help resolve problems.

Tips for Success

With these agreements in place, most co-presenting teams will be in good shape. A few additional tips will pave the way for quick success.

Planning forms the basis of the presentation. Before they take the stage, excellent co-presenters do the following:

1. Work together to determine presentation goals, time allocations, major information areas, and the processes that will promote the goals
2. Separately take responsibility for fleshing out details for the different information areas
3. Develop a training outline with space for initials down the side to designate alternating responsibility for each segment
4. Identify all logistical considerations—charts to be made, materials to be developed, printing to be done—and assign responsibility

Co-presenters exchange information and ideas that will help the session. We share strategies that have worked in the past, materials we have developed, and knowledge that we think will enrich the other partner's presentation. In addition, we share vignettes, stories, and metaphors that might help to illustrate a training point. I always leave a co-presentation event with more ideas, tools, and information for my work.

Before the presentation, co-presenters should compare their wardrobes to make sure their clothing is compatible. Both members should arrive at the training site early to establish rapport and make sure the room can support the session goals.

Afterward, analyze what worked, what didn't, and why. Good co-presenters apply this information when planning future sessions. They also assess their co-presenting teamwork and commit to refinements.

Finally, they celebrate and pat themselves on the back. Not every session will go perfectly, but co-presenting can be an exciting, effective, and rewarding way to teach. It conveys the instructional content, but it goes deeper, too. The very presence of two people instead of one can be a metaphor for the message. Co-presenting communicates collegiality, collaboration, and peer learning. Co-presenters communicate about being human, allow little mistakes to show, and laugh with the audience.

Now, when I co-present with anyone, we try to signal that we are all learners. That's an important metaphor, no matter what the topic.

REMEMBER

1. Co-presenting improves almost any training effort.
2. Usually much better training designs are produced.
3. Choose from several forms of co-presenting: tag team, speak and comment, speak and chart, perform and comment, or duet.
4. Develop signal systems with your co-presenter.
5. Agree on key topics: outcomes, planning processes, permission to do whatever is necessary to serve the learners, signaling systems, and debriefing patterns after the presentation.

cont.

6. Maintain personal composure at all times. Your partner depends on you being emotionally resourceful, no matter what is happening.
7. Make your partner look good.

Summary

This chapter examined special situations and suggested approaches that can make the difference between ordinary and extraordinary presentations. Viewing presentation as theatre connected presentation work with the world of stage, sets, and props. Just as Shakespearean actors deliver soliloquies from predetermined parts of the stage, the learning-focused presenter uses presentation space in a deliberate fashion. This is congruent with the study of nonverbal communication in chapter 4.

Keeping with the theatre metaphor, music was explored as a movie director might work with it—to set the mood for a scene as well as to mark transitions between scenes. Onstage or giving a presentation, being nervous is natural, and this chapter details several ways to manage untidy flows of adrenaline.

Breaking beyond the world of theatre, thoughts on listening, cultural sensitivity, and unintended offense were offered. Considerations were also offered for working with international groups and working effectively with group resistance. Finally, skills and structures for co-presenting were presented.

CHAPTER 6

To See Is to Retain
Michael Buckley*

*The brain processes 4 billion bits of information
per minute but is conscious of only 2,000.*

The speaker says, "Touch your chin." Most of the audience responds by touching their foreheads. Why? The speaker's hand was on his forehead, and the visual data outweighed the verbal. Visual input plays an important role in learning; a visual preference for processing information is dominant among modality systems. Many studies over many years have addressed the question of what percentage of learners is supported best by visual, auditory, or kinesthetic learning opportunities. Each decade our methods of investigation and information become more sophisticated and precise. Sousa (2003) reports the occurrence of sensory preferences as visual, 46%; kinesthetic-tactile, 35%; and auditory, 19%. It is important to keep in mind that these are *preferences.* Human processes are not limited to one modality and are wired primarily for visual input, which was fundamental to hunting, gathering, and thus surviving.

In this chapter, Michael Buckley reveals secrets to good graphic and chart making. Talent is not a prerequisite, he says. Some have it and some don't (I am one of the don'ts), yet nearly all the techniques involved in making art can be learned. I am a living testimony to this claim. He believes that with a little diligence, practice, and some training, excellence is within the reach of most of us, and competence is available to us all. Anyone who can write or print letters and numbers has all of the requisite motor skills and visual coordination necessary to draw convincing graphic symbols.

For those who don't feel good about their art abilities, Michael suggests that the cards for art were stacked against you early. The contributors might have been the curriculum of early schooling, little or no practice, initial inhibitions, and a lack of awareness about the mental processes involved in drawing. This chapter will show all of us simple ways to create "satisfying" visual symbols.

PowerPoint is a visual medium as well. In the early days of PowerPoint it was frequently misused. Today good examples exist of how to use it as a good teaching tool.

*With the exception of the introductory section and the summary, Michael Buckley is the author of this chapter.

Instruction supported by visuals creates significant differences in learning! Table 6-1 shows the effect size of auditory and visual instruction on elementary students in an integrated science and social studies unit (Nuthall, 1999). The effect size was greater for visual instruction than verbal instruction (.90 vs. .74) immediately after instruction. Dramatic instruction was higher than both (1.12). (Effect size reports how many standard deviations the average score in the group being studied is above the control group. So, assuming a standard deviation of 10, an effect size of 1.0 would indicate that the experimental group scored 34 percentile points above the average score in the control group; Marzano, 2003).

Table 6-1. Effect Sizes for Visual and Auditory Instruction

Modality	Effect Size
Dramatic	1.12
Visual	.90
Auditory (verbal)	.74

In this study, verbal instruction involved telling students about content or having them read it; visual instruction involved using pictures or other forms of visual representation. Dramatic instruction had students engaged in or observing some dramatic representation of the content.

Reviewing this and other research, Marzano (2003) presents a broad view:

When students are first exposed to content, learning should ideally involve the use of stories or other forms of dramatization along with the use of visual representations of information. In subsequent exposures, learning experiences should involve discussion and (ideally) tasks that require students to make and defend judgments.

Create Graphics With Ease and Confidence

By Michael Buckley

Walking into the room just before the presentation began, we saw a few people seated and talking quietly. Taped to two walls were large sheets of chart paper with drawings and words on them. Some of the sheets had colorful images, others were nearly all text. On a stand in the center of the room just past the entry doors was a chart with only a single word surrounded by a lassolike rope of color. Placed on each chair was a handout, its cover visible. It listed the topic, speaker, and conference and had a small line drawing of simple figures in a group. My companion turned to me and exclaimed that we should do something like this for our workshop. I looked around at the result of what appeared to have been long hours of tedious work. "Why bother?" I wondered.

The answer to that has at least two parts. First, it's not such a bother. Many of the most engaging and memorable charts we saw were made in a matter of minutes by people who would hardly consider themselves artists. By learning a few simple fundamentals that work in multiple formats, they opened up a world of possibilities for creating learning-supportive graphic display. Secondly, with so much of the brain involved in processing visual information, and visual symbols being instrumental in many sign systems, it seems natural to assume that graphics are an important communication tool. It is increasingly clear that visuals bolster learning, understanding, and communication. Certainly the graphics in that room *looked* better than most, and they drew our attention effectively. More than that, as evidenced by current research in learning, these graphics likely *worked* better than most, increasing the scaffolding of the cognitive hooks that occur in a resource-rich environment.

In this section we'll consider some questions about designing visuals, suggested answers to those questions, and tips and advice for increased effectiveness. Techniques for drawing convincing and effective images (without having to know "how to draw") will be explored. We'll see several ways to enhance charts by using graphics that don't involve drawing anything. A simple colored underline, a headline printed in a bold style, color, or size; a box or frame, simple colored "bullets," or a wide swath of pastel chalk can elevate an adequate chart to the level of a powerful and effective tool. When you choose to draw, you won't need to draw anything more complex than the letters of the alphabet. Even straight lines are within everyone's grasp, especially if you use chart paper with pale blue grid lines. In fact, many of these symbols work best when they're not precisely drawn, as you might imagine after looking at Figure 6-1. In fact, we'll see that most effective symbols have just a few simple parts. Several of the concepts presented here are principles that you can employ without changing the way you write or draw on a chart. As you apply even just a few of the tips in this section, you'll soon be making memorable, more effective charts.

In a cave in Lascoux, France, there are some strikingly detailed and spatially accurate depictions of animals, people, and geometric patterns. Many appear to be narrative in intent. Inside the pyramids of Egypt, hieroglyphics are marked on and into the rock, recording significant concepts and historical details. In the Pacific northwest of North America, large cedar poles covered with carvings are used to tell stories, like narrative poems. Since earliest times, our communication, and the possibility of extending the duration of that communication, has depended on visual cues. Indeed, Juma, Bob's guide in Africa, consistently saw details, shapes, colors, and movement not discernible to Bob.

Visual processing in the brain, rather than being a supplement to cognition, is a form of cognition. It's been suggested by observation and study that students learn at higher cognitive levels with art and music woven into instruction than without them. Using multiple and complementary sign systems, we increase the opportunities to bridge modalities, enhance recall, and construct meaning. Manipulating signs that are conventionally used to represent something else in a social setting develops higher order, more complex, and therefore intelligent thinking, and it fosters logical memory, selective attention, decision making, and language comprehension.

Figure 6-1. Suggestionism

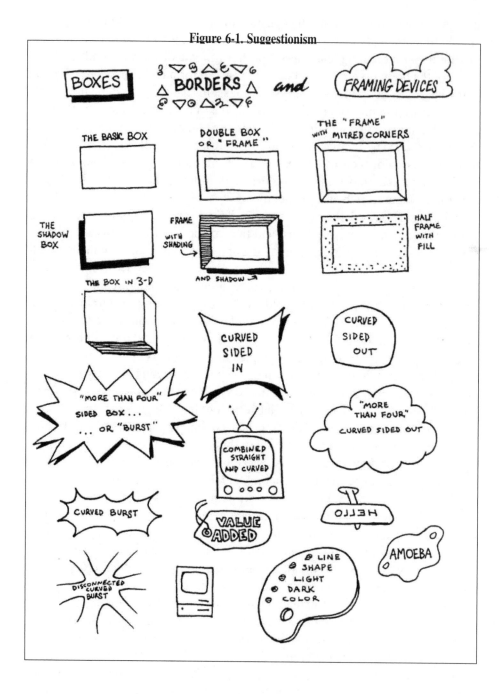

What are graphic symbols? They may be as simple as *A, B, C*. It's liberating to recall that graphic symbols used on flip charts, like most symbols, are a sort of visual shorthand, intended to call to mind a concept or thing, not be an exact replica. Most of the symbols we encounter and use daily are built of modular units or elements, assembled in a particular way to signal a concept. All of the letters of our alphabet can be made with combinations and variations of straight and curved lines. Such abbreviated markings standing in to represent complex ideas are typical of sign systems in their simplification of components. Cartoons, road signs, letters, numbers, and dollar signs are all simplified signs as signal, and all use similar visual elements: lines combined to make shapes. The richness of a symbol system, from DNA sequencing to languages, is rarely a function of the number or complexity of elements, but rather a result of the combinations and relationships of those elements.

Considering Design

Great art communicates before it is understood."
—T. S. Eliot.

It's unlikely that you'd randomly place letters or numbers on your charts simply because you like the shape, or merely to decorate and "jazz-up" your overheads. So too, graphics are not selected just to help a chart look good. Consider what task you intend the graphic or symbol to perform. Use a graphic to create a mood or an atmosphere for a session or presentation. By using colorful, loosely made symbols or cartoonlike images, you can suggest a light-hearted and relaxed mood. Presenting very neat, spare, and orderly charts using just one or two colors might create a more serious or reserved setting. The choice of images also influences the perceived atmosphere. Balloons and clown faces might not be the best choice on charts dealing with test scores or budgets. A graphic can be used to clarify or reinforce a verbal or written statement or question. A metaphorical drawing, like a star or a heart image, can open the range of meaning to encourage creative thinking. Lines, boxes, circles, bullets, and other graphics can link items that are related or separate chunks of information that are discrete. These same few tools can be used to create structural sketches, showing the architecture and relationships of organizations or dynamic processes.

Graphics are used to do the following:

- Remind of key concepts
- Foreshadow specific points
- Provide emphasis or draw attention
- Organize visual content

Commonly, charts are used in conjunction with other information formats, including handouts, overheads, and verbal input. You might think of the charts as a way to keep multiple overheads visible simultaneously and for extended periods of time, or as a kind of index to the presentation or the handout, or as a reminder of something said during the session. Remember, however, that as a different format from handouts, overheads, and vocalization, charts are most effective when they exploit their own format attributes rather than duplicate those of other media. Editing, condensing, simplifying, and reducing the material are key aims when choosing content for charts. By keeping content spare, good use is made of the chart's size and impact. Trimming unnecessary information is challenging, but careful editing improves the clarity and delivery of charted information. By keeping graphics simple and using the minimum of marks, you make the task easier. The clock example in Figure 6-2 shows how just a few small marks can effectively convey as much meaning as more detailed drawings.

Figure 6-2. Simplicity

Not Just Taking Up Space

Here are some guidelines when considering the space available on a flip chart. You might think of the chart as visual "real estate"—a certain amount of space to develop. There's room on a chart for many symbols, or "structures." You could fill up the entire sheet with information written in small letters, closely fit. Examples of this kind of data density are the phone book, classified newspaper ads, and legal notices. A chart, however, is less frequently used as a repository for large amounts of data, like reference material, than it is to transfer information to groups of people as part of a multiple format presentation. As with towns and cities, it's helpful to have some space without buildings. Sometimes the more desirable real estate has more open space than average. The function that this "real estate" will be assigned is a primary consideration in the design. For example, headlines or category titles work best at the top, in larger letters. Lists and agendas depend on orderly design to be effective. The very bottom quarter of a chart is difficult to see from a few rows back, so avoid using that space if possible. Don't cram everything into one chart. If you've edited and reduced as much as you can, and it would all fit tightly onto one sheet, use two. Divide as evenly as practical between the two, so it doesn't look like a chart plus a leftover, appearing unplanned or less significant. It might seem wasteful to use the second sheet, but the real waste would be one page that can't be read. White space is useful, not empty—the eye moves as it reads, and it follows certain flow patterns; that movement can be influenced by graphic design. We all know how incomprehensible even simple text can be if it's not easy to read and people's attention is therefore diverted from comprehension to deciphering. Keep the connections and separations between the chunks of information visible and clear. List positive aspects, for example, on one side of the page, and negative attributes on the other side. Use white space to separate groups of information or as a pause or breath in the reading of the chart.

An effective strategy for making accurate assessments of charts, including the text and graphics on them, is delightfully simple: Just walk away! Viewing a flip chart from the same distance as the intended audience would see it provides a reliable and wide-ranging yardstick for measuring several aspects of your charts. How far away will the last row of participants be, and will your lettering be large and clear enough to read from that distance? Like faces, chart graphics can appear at their best when viewed from a slight distance, rather than with the often unforgiving and critical scrutiny of close-up inspection. An exercise we use in our graphics workshops is helpful when considering graphics or how much text to use on a chart and how large to make it.

Try the following: In a space that allows you to be the equivalent of 8–10 rows away from your chart paper, set up a chart pad or a sheet of chart paper on a stand or taped to a wall. Take a letter-size sheet of paper and walk away from the chart about as far as seven or eight rows might be, and hold the sheet of paper at arm's length between your eyes and the chart paper. You should be unable to see all four edges of the chart paper beyond the edges of the paper you're holding. Fold the paper in half, hold it at arm's length again, and continue this process until the paper in your hand takes up about as much space in your field of vision as the chart paper does. You'll see that, to the persons in the back rows, the size of your chart may be equal to the space a postcard held at arm's length would occupy in their field of view. I suggest that you make small, "thumbnail" sketches of the charts at about this size. You'll immediately know what will fit without overcrowding or illegibility. This can be helpful when choosing the information you'll put on them.

Who is the audience? What are they familiar with? Consider their environment—home, work, and cultural. I've had some difficulty getting people in Hawaii to recognize the letter *B* from the logo of the Boston Red Sox, but in Cambridge, Massachusetts, not a person missed the reference. Symbols familiar in one work setting might not be meaningful in another—or worse, they might have entirely different meanings! Try to absorb some of the local or collegial symbols before the workshop, like cactus in Arizona, pine trees in Maine, or report cards for teachers. You'll likely be familiar enough with your audience to come up with some symbols, or ask someone from the group prior to the session.

Developing Fluency

There you are, at a chart stand in front of a room full of colleagues, printing on a chart pad. You know very well that you have difficulty making the letters of the headlines the same size across the page, yet you move ahead without hesitation and write the word AGENDA across the top of the page, level and even from start to finish. Have you found the power of mind over matter? Or did you print "*AGENDA*" beforehand lightly in pencil on the sheet? Perhaps you've been able to use the pale blue guidelines on the paper to keep reasonably aligned. Maybe you've had some practice and have a capacity that has grown from that practice. Whatever strategy you employ, making the charts should *not* be your primary focus during a presentation. By appearing to create your charts effortlessly, you can keep attention on your message. This apparent ease can come from planning and practice.

Lettering and Color

Perhaps the single most influential aspect contributing to legibility is contrast, the difference in lightness and darkness between the "ground" (paper) and the text (Figure 6-3). Many of us wonder, "What color should I use to write this?" Black ink contrasts very well with white or light-colored paper, but you would use a white or light-colored chalk for a blackboard. This extreme example suggests that generally, dark colors, including dark browns, greens, and blues, would work best for text on chart paper. We'll see later that other guidelines help to make choosing and using color easier and less random. Deciding whether to useupper case (capital letters) or mixed-case (capital and small letters) text involves several variables. For all but very short lines of text, mixed-case printing is the easiest to read, since the words themselves each have distinctive shapes, or "footprints," and can be recognized without mentally spelling and assembling the letters. All capitals, where each letter form resembles a rectangle or circle, takes longer to decipher, as we may need to recognize and combine each letter. For charts prepared ahead of time, running text (such as sentences) should be in mixed case. Headlines and column titles are commonly made with larger lettering, and all capitals can give a separation from the running text of sentences or phrases. On charts made during the presentation, another consideration is how you normally print. If you are so focused on making your printing in a style you're not familiar and comfortable with, you risk attention drift, both yours and the participants. Try to use only one or two styles of text on each sheet, unless you're mimicking a ransom note.

Figure 6-3. Lettering Styles

When choosing colors, especially for text, consider using similar colors for related items, making the connections and groupings more apparent and consistent. Colors can be used as accent, to connect or link items, or to separate parts. In addition to enhancing the visibility, different colors tend to generate different physical responses. Red is a color that stimulates or excites optical and neural responses, whereas greens and blues are more visually soothing.

Try the following: Print the same word in different colors and styles. On a sheet of chart paper draw three lines in pencil, as shown by the dotted lines in Figure 6-4. Use each of the small rectangles to write the same word, but use a different color for each word, or vary the text as all capital letters, script (like handwriting), printed, or simply different sizes. Be sure to walk away from the chart and see what works for legibility. You should see that, as a generalization, small, thin, light-colored (e.g., yellow, orange, pale green, or pale blue) letters and script letters are more troublesome to read at a distance than large, dark-colored (black, brown, purple, dark blue, or dark green) letters, thick letters, or printed letters.

Figure 6-4. Legibility

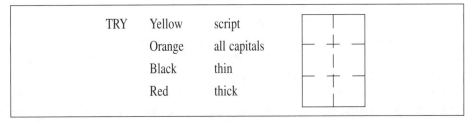

TRY	Yellow	script
	Orange	all capitals
	Black	thin
	Red	thick

Red as a text color can be difficult to read from a distance, or if the text is small. Color deficiency, often called color blindness, is a dimming of the perception of certain colors, most frequently red and green. It occurs in about 8%–12% of males of European descent and in 1% of females. Be aware of this possibility when choosing color to sort, categorize, or discriminate among items. If you are using pale or light colors, like yellow, try a wide lettering style or the wide side of a chisel-tipped marker to print a word. Then go back and outline the edges or the center of the letters, with thin, dark lines, like

The Process of "Unnaming"

Our perceptions of the world are shaped by the way we focus our attention. When computing numbers, we think perhaps of amounts or quantities, but when we teach how to write numbers, we concentrate on the shapes of the marks. This cognitive shift can be deliberately made. Most of us are familiar with the optical illusion of the "vase-face" (Figure 6-5), a shape that can be perceived alternately as a pair of facing profiles or the silhouette of a goblet with a perceptual shift. When we intentionally see, or perceive, one image instead of the other, we are shifting not only negative and positive spaces, but also foreground and back-ground.

Figure 6-5. Vase Face

This deliberate concentration of attention to perceive marks in a particular way is the basis for recognizing visual elements independent of the assembled representation. If we can forget what the image depicts, and actually "unname" the image to see its parts as discrete pieces of a construction, it's possible to visually isolate the parts and survey their relationships, or syntax. After that rec-ognition can come the replication, or drawing, of the elements to reconstruct the image, followed by the ability to reassemble the basic units to create other differ-ent symbols. We might use language to describe to ourselves the organization of elements, as in "That line is halfway up the circle, with a line that is thicker crossing it near the left side of the circle," or we might picture something that the shape reminds us of, like a doughnut or a bagel for the letter *O*. We've all gone through this process as we learned first to print, then to write.

Try the following: Look at Figure 6-6 and draw an *E* using a thin stroke, as in the left column. Imagine that it is a skeleton on which the "flesh" or "body" of the block style graphic will rest. Draw all the way around this frame a line that matches the *E* shape and turns it into a block letter. Think of the line that you're going to draw around the frame as a container that nearly always extends the same distance away from the skeleton. The star image and some others do not follow this pattern, but many do. In the second column from the left, the outline, or block, shape is shown, and in the top column the skeleton of the *1* is shown in dotted lines. If it's helpful, you could pencil in the skeletons of the other shapes. The drawings in the third column can be described as being a shadow, or offset, of the shape, matching it as if it were a black cutout underneath. It is set off, shifted down and to the right, much like a cartoon character would burst through a wall, leaving a hole that matched its silhouette. In the fourth column, a line connects the corners of this shadow to the shape itself, to give the impression of a three-dimensional object.

Figure 6-6. Block Letters

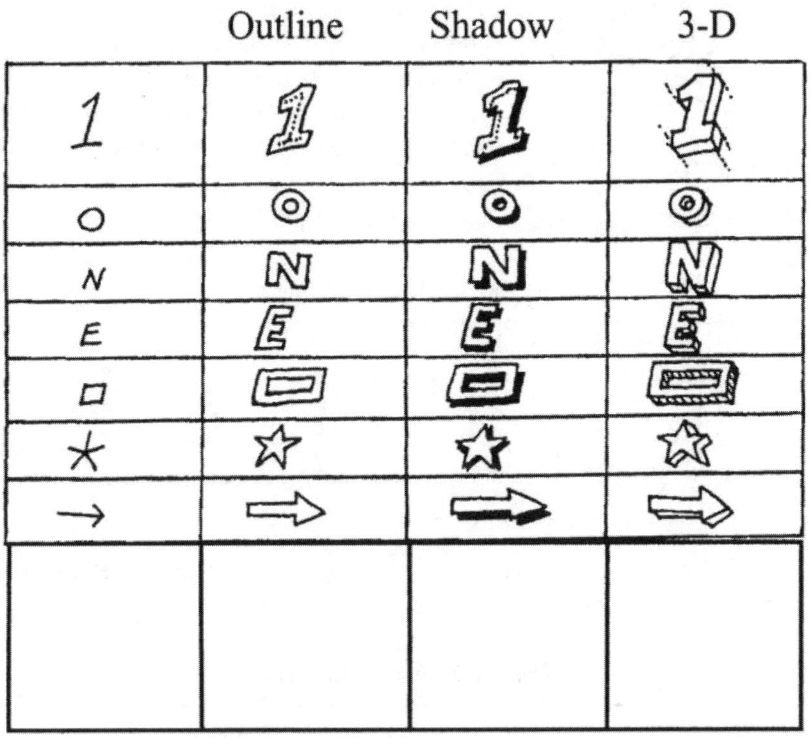

	Outline	Shadow	3-D
1	*1*	*1*	*1*
O	◎	◉	◎
N	N	N	N
E	E	E	E
□	▭	▭	▭
★	☆	☆	☆
→	⇨	⇨	⇨

The basic block letter is also the starting point for many of the decorative type styles shown in Figure 6-3. These styles are best used as headlines or in short lines of text. Once you've practiced these letters a few times, you'll be able to draw the shape of the block letter without having to follow a guide. Like driving a regular route, it can almost be done without thinking, relying on muscle memory. Some letters will be more difficult to do at first, especially those with curves like *S* and *B*, in which the inside radius is smaller, or *M*, *N*, *W*, and *X*, which have wedgelike shapes intersecting with letter stems. By using a large version of an alphabet, you can practice or trace the letters to familiarize yourself with the shapes enough to draw them easily, without using any template.

A simple way to make your lettering more visible when using chisel, or slanted, tip markers is to rotate the tip of the marker to produce thicker, wider marks (Figure 6-7). Some people discover it as they work. Until you do, it may not be something you know or have heard.

Figure 6-7. Chisel Marker

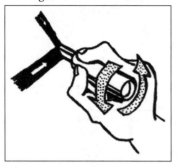

Draw a box, a square, or a rectangle using the pointed tip of the marker. Don't worry about how straight the lines are. Make the box about as big as a CD jewel case, then, with the wide part of the marker, draw a wide line on the outside of the bottom and right-side lines, as shown in Figure 6-8. If you start the wide lines somewhat short of the outer ends, you'll end up with a box that appears to pop out a little from the page. Or just use the thick lines like shadows to suggest the box without actually drawing one. I sometimes think of this as the "sleeping *L*" shape.

Figure 6-8. "Sleeping L" Shape

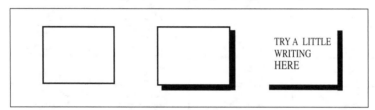

In the following exercise (Figure 6-9), you will see that the relationship of the elements can be central to the perceived meaning.

Figure 6-9. Shapes and Faces

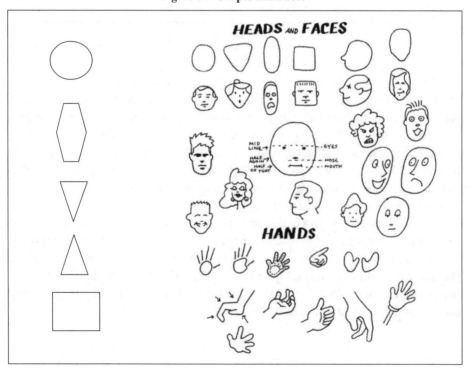

Take any of the shapes in the figure (or make up your own). Put marks in the places you might find features, and see how quickly a face can be called to mind with a minimum of detail. There are patterns for placement of facial features that are common to most people, with the eyes about a third of the way down the head, as shown in the illustration of heads and faces, but these are not critical for facial symbols, as you might guess from the drawings.

Figure 6-10 shows shapes that are good, simple symbols for facial features.

Figure 6-10. The Blockheads

You can also choose nearly any shape to contain the facial features or to be the head. Try it. It may seem silly, but the results of only a short time of this kind of experimenting can yield dramatic results for your visual presentations. Seeing an image or a drawing is a little like hearing or reading a word. Just as we see the word as a whole and not separated into letters, we don't always consciously recognize and assemble the individual elements of a picture in order to derive its meaning. Often the shape, or "footprint," of a word is immediately recognized. This similarity is also instructive for creating the symbols, as drawing a face soon evolves from the first steps of making different lines and shapes according to a predefined tutorial to being able to instinctively transcribe an image by its constituent parts.

Before the Show

After outlining your presentation, select the material you intend to use for charts, remembering that not all the content is suitable for use on a chart pad. You could think of the material you'll use as supportive, as a reminder, or to apply emphasis. Plan ahead as much as possible, using an outline or private agenda to map out which graphics will be used and when. Plot, create, or sketch your charts prior to the session. This way, at the presentation, you can focus your attention on the group, rather than "Which color should I use?" or "I hope the people in the back can read this!" Planning will give you that freedom. Using pencil, lightly outline the charts you can plan ahead; even if it's just a headline, a pencil guide makes it so much easier to concentrate on your presentation, and drawing in the graphics you're going to use is a valuable time-saving practice. It's unlikely that anyone you're presenting to will even be able to see the pencilmarks, and you will have the spacing and size already marked out. Use smaller thumbnail sketches to plot your charts first. As Bob described earlier, have some charts already prepared to post on the wall or on a chart stand as soon as you enter the room, before participants arrive; even if it is just to have the time-consuming questions about which workshop this is not interfere with your preparations. Charts can be premade, on pages in an unused chart pad, keeping several pages between them to use during the presentation, or as separate chart pages inserted into a chart pad prior to the session, taped at the top, again several pages apart. A small piece of masking tape at the edge of the premade chart can serve as both a label and a handle for quick and seamless flipping to the desired chart.

Some Basic Visual Display Formats

Figure 6-11 shows several visual display formats. A poster contains one concept and is meant to quickly catch attention; it is a bold, quick read, with high impact.

Figure 6-11. Visual Display Formats

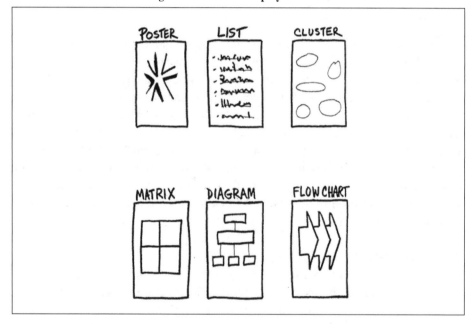

A list can imply a hierarchy, even without numbering. In a cluster, information is placed into separate areas. It encourages the viewers' engagement with and connection of the data. A matrix may take longer time to absorb, depending on the content. A diagram shows the relationships of the parts to the whole and offers an overview of the systems and structures. A flowchart is useful for showing action or change over time, or a process or protocol. The direction of flow should be determined by the content.

It can be a real challenge to be confronted with the question "How can I come up with the right images for my charts?" Yet we are surrounded by raw material. If you spend some time looking carefully at cartoons, greeting cards, signs, advertisements (especially in the yellow page phone books), newspapers, and magazines, you should begin to see the great variety of symbols. Take some time to look analytically at how they are put together.

There are also plenty of resources for free clip-art images; the online possibilities are astronomical. These images can be starting points for making your own images, or if they are in the public domain, they are yours to use. Start a file folder or scrapbook of images you find useful or appealing. If you practice making one or two for just a week, you'll have symbols ready to use. The image doesn't have to be a literal representation of the concept. Consider drawing the effect or result of what you want to illustrate; for example, heat can be suggested by beads of perspiration, wind by the bending of trees or just a couple of lines.

Comics are a great resource, and we're all familiar with cartoon shorthand, like a word, a thought balloon, or motion lines. If you don't draw people comfortably, but you'd like to show someone speaking, just a balloon with the words would do the job. Combine symbols not ordinarily joined, like that same word balloon attached to an inanimate object. This could provide an interesting exercise in metaphorical thinking.

There are also certain symbols that have become common referents, like the heart shape as a stand-in for the word *love*. Make and keep an assortment of symbols. Spend 10 minutes or so a week, or more if you can, just doodling. You may be surprised at the results. They don't have to involve any thought, direction, intention or specified outcome, and they can be done in any size, on paper that you already have around you, with pens, pencils, or even lipstick. You'll end up with a little library that may yield useful graphic icons when you need them.

So now you say, "Look, I *really* can't draw" or " I *really* don't have the time to practice" or "I *really* don't want to try." Then just walk away—and trace! That's right, trace. "Isn't tracing illegal, or at least some sort of cheating?" you might ask. That depends. Tracing other people's signatures is commonly seen as criminal, at least in intent, and there does seem to be some moral component to many people's view of tracing, but even the Old Masters used tracing. A caution here, though: I recommend that the tracing of published images be kept strictly to personal practice only. Copyright, the legal right to use or reproduce an image or symbol, is a complex and binding legal concept best left to professionals, and I make no claim to any legal expertise.

Be careful about using or copying known trademarks or logos, although, generally speaking, use on a chart for a single event is unlikely to be the target of copyright enforcement. There are, however, plenty of images that are copyright-free, or in the public domain (like the heart image referred to earlier), and I've worked with a company called MiraVia to produce ChartArt, images specifically for use on charts in presentations (Buckley, 2002). These are letter-size images that slip beneath the chart paper to be traced, and the company is also developing art for computer-based presentation technology like PowerPoint.

Remember to use care regarding offensive or negative stereotypes or characters. If you develop your own favorite image or symbol, you might take it to a copy shop and have copies made on firm stock, like a card stock, and also enlarge and reduce the size of the image to suit your needs. You can take these with you where needed and trace through a sheet of chart paper.

Born to Look

Some of the earliest recorded markings made by humans were drawings, and many written alphabets were originally pictures. We continue to communicate visually, and we invest much in images and their presentation. We know, from recent science, that much of the brain is involved in processing visual data, and most of us rely vitally on this processing for the lives we lead. Yet we often do so unconsciously, with a certain sense of entitlement and an expectation of reliability. There is more to seeing than just looking, and knowing about seeing can give us a richer view of the world around us and an awareness of our capacity to unlock some of the power and immediacy of visual communication. Many of us have long believed that creating any artwork requires a "gift" or a talent and that, if we are without such inborn skill, we're unable to make art. Indeed, there are those who possess extraordinary aptitudes for particular mediums, yet it is still possible for any one of us to harness some of the great power of visuals to reach each other deeply.

Figure 6-12 shows some easy but creative ways to draw stick figures. You don't have to be a great artist to draw the human figure.

Figure 6-13 shows different layouts you can use. Each serves a different purpose, as described. Remember: In visual imagery, less is more.

REMEMBER

1. Visual processing in the brain is a form of cognition.
2. It can be liberating to recall that graphics on flip charts are just symbols meant to recall certain things, not replicas of the thing itself.
3. You might think of charts as a way to keep multiple transparencies in view at once.
4. White space is useful, not empty. The white space provides a route for the eye as it moves.
5. Walk away from your chart to view it, from where the audience will be.
6. Unname an image to see its discrete parts and their relationship to one another.
7. Make your charts before the presentation and free your presession time to be with group members.

Figure 6-12. Stick Figures

Figure 6-13. Layouts

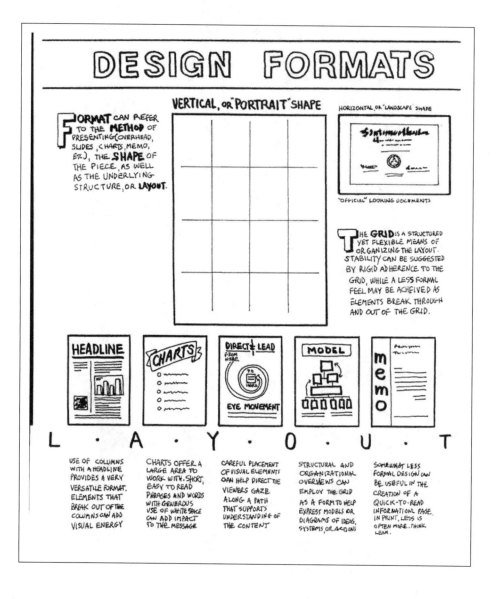

PowerPoint Tips and Traps

Be sharp without being slick.

I was in a 200-year-old French farmhouse when I made my first solo with PowerPoint. Strange it should be this setting, where in the early morning the radio was tuned to a shortwave broadcast of BBC; where in the early 1940s French resistance fighters guided downed RAF and American aviators through and over the Pyrenees Mountains into Spain, often through winter snows and dodging German soldiers. It was a strange place for me to come face to face with what I had been avoiding, a multiday workshop supported not by charts, pens, and transparencies but by a collection of script and images I could carry in my laptop.

PowerPoint commands 90% of the market share on presentation software. Yet eye rolling is not uncommon when experienced presenters respond to the suggestion that they might like to start using PowerPoint. This is because it has been misused, overused, and abused. It has essentially been treated as an infor-mation-dispensing machine, especially in its early history. Because I had suf-fered through so many poor PowerPoint presentations in the past, I too had a healthy wariness about using it. However, one day at a conference in Beijing, I watched Jay McTighe during a presentation on "Understanding by Design." He used it not only effectively but brilliantly as an extension of good instructional principles. Since then I have observed others use it artfully, most notably Jane Ellison and Carolee Hayes, co-directors of the Center for Cognitive Coaching. Their mindset seems to be to let the speaker do the talking, the group do the processing, and the technology do the pointing—in moderation.

Pitfalls

"Get to the Point, Lieutenant," read one newspaper headline, telling the story of how a senior officer in the U.S. Army, tired of endless charts, graphics, and fly-in words whooshing their way onto the screen, called for a halt to it all. Rather than distilling the essence of what should be communicated, young offic-ers, eager to make an impression on superiors, were filling their reports with unnecessary bells, whistles, and details.

These officers were diverting the audience from the message. Images should be used to make a presentation more interesting, to show things in different ways, to add emphasis—in short, to support the enhancement of learning. PowerPoint images can be so pleasing, however, that there is a risk in overdoing the visuals.

Six Common Errors

There are six things you should definitely *not* do. These are as follows:

1. *Don't use lots of slides.* Slides should not be a memory device to store your presentation notes. This may be comfortable for you, but it is bor-ing for the group. One private-sector man used to use a slide per minute for a 3-hour presentation! He now uses only one, with six images that he

can display independently as he works. His consultancy fee has tripled, and he reports feeling liberated. (This hasn't happened for me, but I am waiting!)

2. *Don't use all capital letters.* Contrary to what some books on graphics recommend, sentence script is easier to read. In normal sentences words appear with ascenders and descenders, which makes for easier letter discrimination. In the previous section, Michael Buckley suggested that you use what you are most comfortable with, script or capitals for in-the-moment recording. That's for charts. Sentence script works best in text, with the exception of titles.

3. *Don't use too many words, complete paragraphs, complicated figures, and detailed charts.* A benefactor once said to Mozart that a selection had "too many notes." (It made for a great line in the movie *Amadeus*, but I'm still trying to figure out what it means!) In speech and electronically we overwhelm receivers when we use more words than necessary. Experts vary in guidance on words per line, but the most common figure mentioned is seven. Simplify figures and charts to show the essence of concepts, not the details.

4. *Don't use only bullets.* Numbers command more attention (i.e., how many ideas are there in this section?).

5. *Don't use too many colors, fonts sizes, and types.* Less is more. Restraint is elegant.

6. *Don't search for your cursor on the screen while the audience waits.* My group in France finally suggested that I buy a laser pointer so I would stop pointing to the computer screen (which only I could see).

Each pitfall interferes with the learners' interaction with content. As I have noted elsewhere, the content you bring is less important than the audience's interaction with the content. With no interaction, there is no learning, just auditory and visual forms of information passing from one place in the room to another.

12 Keys to Potent PowerPoint Presentations

Increasingly, people are using PowerPoint effectively. I asked Jim Riedel, one of the pioneers of good use and a friend and colleague of long standing, for some tips. He suggested many of the following, to which I have elaborated. As a basic guideline, about one slide every 5 minutes is a good starting place.

1. Keep it simple! A few powerful words make the point. Too many words will never be read. A general rule is one concept per slide, no more than six to eight lines per slide and six words per line. Less is more.

2. Shhh! Let the learners do the reading. The words you use should not be read to your participants; let them read the words for themselves. You should speak about major points from trigger words on the slides.

3. Make your slides clear, consistent, and readable (Figure 6-14).

Figure 6-14. Slide Format

Slide Format Tip

Use a common format
- *titles - 36 to 44 pt.*
- *titles - flush left*
- *text - 24 pts or larger*

Common format and background. The slide title should appear in the top sixth of the screen, set in a 36- to 44-point font size. Since people tend to read in a Z pattern—that is, from the top left of the screen to the lower right, place the title flush left. Boldface but don't capitalize each letter; this is a principle, not a rule, however. I sometimes find that caps in the title help to set off the content in the sentence script below.

Legible font. Boldface is easier to read than thin lines. Arial and Helvetica are two good font choices. They are sans serif (a typeface without flourishes on their tips), they are simple, and the letters don't run into one another. Comic Sans is another favorite of mine. I like it because it seems friendly and informal. No font size should be smaller than 24 points unless it is a footnote Use *uniform sizes* on each slide and throughout the presentation wherever possible.

Consistent color scheme with restraint. Use no more than three colors per slide. Yellow on a black background is a good combination. Hot colors like yellow, orange, and red are good for the foreground. The cooler colors of blue, green, and purple are better for background. Strive for contrast. Pair a hot with a cool.

Check grammar and spelling. You lose credibility if your writing is full of such errors.

Check sequence. Have you changed your notes since you developed your slides?

4. Leave space around the words on the slide. It is much easier to read the slide if it isn't crowded or cramped. The lower right is usually the place with the least words and is a useful zone in which to place an image or a logo. This is consistent with what Michael Buckley advises about "white space" on charts.

5.   Face your participants. Don't turn around and read from the screen. Talk about your slides; look at your computer screen, as you talk to your participants. This is the very first mistake I made in the farmhouse in France. It was the best choice of seating, I thought, because of the small room into which we were crowded. I soon sensed, however (and a participant told me), that my having eye contact with the group was more useful than having them watch my back. Duh!

6.   Make sure not to overdo animations and sound effects. Too much motion and sound distracts from your message, and no one will pay attention to the real message. Don't use animations unless they help to communicate a point. For example, I avoid whoosh sounds as letters appear on the screen.

7.   Graphics and clip art enhance your content. Use them to *strengthen* your message; otherwise they, rather than your message, become the focus. Be cautious about too much cutesy clip art. I try to use images from my camera as much as possible when they help to illustrate a concept. Of course, those who work with me know that pictures of my grandchildren usually find a place on the screen, whether I am using transparencies or PowerPoint, but of course, they are always there to make a point. (This is sometimes as simple and important as a speaker connection with the audience.)

8.   That said, do use a high image-to-text ratio. We construct more meaning from images than words. The most effective political campaigns demonstrate this principle. Rich images with limited text have memorable impact.

9.   Know your equipment and make sure to have a contingency plan. Check your equipment before you start. Be prepared to shift gears if necessary. Ask for help if you have trouble; there's usually someone in the group who knows the technology.

10. Number your slides. It makes it much easier to reference materials for your participants and yourself.

11. Beware of too much slickness. Friend and colleague Bill Baker used to warn about appearing so slick and polished that folks might take the session as a sales presentation in which people are expected to buy something.

12. Anticipate content that audience members might feel compelled to have in their notes. Some keynote speakers make a hard copy of slides available with a column in which to write personal notes. Another option in workshop settings in which a number of slides may be directions for activities, is to place quotes and necessary data in the margins of your handouts.

Big bosses in industry (and normal-size ones, too!) have graphics departments make their slides. This is a luxury most of us don't have. To develop an eye for design, what works and what doesn't, see Michael Buckley's section in this chapter on creating presentation graphics.

At the farmhouse in France, several people were present whom I had known in Africa when Sue and I had safaried there. One evening we were treated to a slide show on Tanzania, in which the power of the images was breathtaking. One after another, pictures zoomed in or out, framing a single animal (a leopard), bird (a flamingo), or flower (an orchid) with stunning beauty. We sat, silent and breathless as these images communicated a world of beauty and experience many of us had come to love. Jon Hill, an international teacher now serving in Korea, is the source of these images that illustrate elegance and expertise at visual communications. You can learn about what he does and see how he does it at www.Safari.shots.com.

REMEMBER

1. You are the message.
2. Simple is more effective.
3. PowerPoint should support, not suppress, interaction.
4. Use prep time for content, not slides.
5. Find and emulate models of excellence.

Summary

In this chapter we were reminded that talent is not a prerequisite for making effective presentation charts. Rather, what is essential is an understanding of a few principles, a moderate number of motor skills, and a willingness to learn a few tips.

Instruction that is supported visually does create difference in learning. Graphics are typically used to organize ideas, foreshadow certain points, provide emphasis, remind of key ideas or certain points, and provide emphasis.

Michael provided many tips about lettering. One of the simple yet big ideas is to write in mixed case because it is so much easier to read than all caps. Alternating pen colors for different ideas also makes the ideas more recognizable.

Purposes and model formats were provided for posters, lists, clusters, matrixes, diagrams, and flow charts. The work on PowerPoint is in some ways an extension of the ideas on charting. Practical do's and don'ts were provided. Two major differences exist between charts and PowerPoint. With PowerPoint, audiences know that an image will disappear from a screen. Because of this, they experience an unconscious muscular tension that is not present when they are viewing charts. Charts have the added advantage of serving as devices for group memory.

A second difference is that with PowerPoint, you don't have to worry about your artistic talent. This can be good or bad. It's bad because the temptation is great to include much premade clip art, which in excess takes away from the presenter's message.

With both charting and PowerPoint the mantra is to keep it simple and let the visual work be far less important than your audience's interaction with ideas.

Why Cats Have Clean Paws— Myths About External Feedback

Serendipity is a regular kind of cat. He does what cats do. He purrs, sleeps, "hunts" in the tall grass near our house, jumps into my lap and cuddles with me whenever I am seated for any length of time. He also has clean paws. He always has, and I imagine he always will. Dippity, or Dip for short, is a self-directed paw cleaner. He just can't stop himself. No amount of feedback or praise from me for cleaning his paws, and no amount of scolding for the opposite behavior, is likely to change this.

To compare adult learners to my cat may be stretching things a bit. However, learning for humans is natural as paw cleaning is for cats. I propose that we recognize, trust, and facilitate the natural processes of learning in our professional development activities.

I cannot resist a final and powerful thought as this second edition comes to an end. I will explore some myths about feedback, define self-directed learning, and suggest ways that staff developers can capitalize on and enrich these natural processes of human development.

In this context I define *feedback* as observations from others about one's performance, particularly when the information is judgmentally tainted ("You made a good synthesis when . . .") or accompanied with advice ("Next time you might consider . . .").

Myths About Feedback

Myth: Feedback Causes People to See Themselves More Accurately

Findings from studies of 9- and 10-year-old students and of workers at DuPont and Colgate-Palmolive suggest that externally introduced feedback seems to interfere with learning to manage oneself (Sanford, 1995).

How accurate are children when they describe their own behavior? At the beginning of the study with students, most children could not report accurately on personal behaviors. They would vehemently defend the rightness of their self-observations even when faced with indisputable evidence such as film and recordings. The study formed two groups.

Group 1 worked with instructors who used video and audio recordings to improve the students' accuracy of observation. These students came to depend on the recorded material before making their own declaration.

Group 2 worked with instructors who never gave any feedback. They continually asked each student to self-reflect on how well his or her behavior matched the stated procedure. Group 2 instructors did not correct student perceptions or provide outside evidence. In the beginning the students' accuracy was very low. After a few weeks, the students' reflections became increasingly accurate, and more accurate than students in group 1.

Myth: Feedback Improves Team Effectiveness

Similar results were found with adults. At DuPont and Colgate-Palmolive, members of teams listened to feedback from peers, supervisors, and/or subordinates on how to be better workers. The purpose of these sessions was to increase the understanding of one's impact on others and improve the effectiveness of working together. The exact opposite occurred. Feedback processes were found to undermine these goals and produce nonproductive side effects. DuPont and Colgate-Palmolive are now committed to practices that help people to build their capability for self-reflection and self-assessment. Examples of these were offered in chapter 1.

Sanford (1995) concludes that external feedback actually reduces the capacity for accurate self-reflection. Continuing feedback reinforces the expectation that others will and should tell us how we are doing, and it reduces our capacity to be self-reflective and self-accountable.

Joyce and Showers (1988) made a similar observation about peer coaching. Many educators "believe that the essence of the coaching transaction is in the offering of advice to the partner who is observed. It is not" (p. 94). They go on to say that each partner learns by watching another teach or by demonstrating one's own teaching. Costa and Garmston (2000) describe how mentor teachers use Cognitive Coaching[SM] to develop the teacher's capacity for accurate self-assessment.

What Is Self-Directed Learning?

Just as my cat must clean his paws, certain habits inform the mental practices of a self-directed learner. Self-directed learners routinely do the following:

Self-manage. They approach tasks with clarity about outcomes, a strategic plan, an anticipation of success indicators, and a thoughtful exploration of creative alternatives.

Self-monitor. They establish strategies for paying attention in-the-moment as to whether their plan is working. These metacognitive skills also inform the decision-making process about altering the plan.

Self-modify. They reflect on, evaluate, analyze, and construct meaning from the experience. They apply what they learn to future activities, tasks, and problem situations (Costa & Garmston, 2002).

"Teaching" Self-Management

Self-directed learning requires accurate information about performance. Because the most motivating information is self-generated, professional development activities should include this as a deliberate goal in staff development activities. For example, teachers can increase the accuracy of their recollections of what occurred in a lesson or transpired in a parent conference. Professional processes can either dampen or enhance this skill. Mentoring, coaching, and supervisory practices in which observers report their observations build dependence on input from others and actually rob the teacher of working the internal muscles on which day-to-day stability is required. To build capacity for self-reflection, engage teachers in thinking out loud about the following:

- Their general assessment and feelings about the lesson
- Their recall of specific data to support these assessments
- Their recollection of perceptions as sources of teaching decisions

Like the successful instructors in study group 2, the coach does not "correct" the teacher's recollections but paraphrases, then probes for more specificity. "What happened when you did X?" "What were you thinking then?" "What did you hear students saying?" "What did you see students doing?" "Which students, specifically?" "Did you get what you wanted with that strategy?" On occasion, observer data may be appropriate to report, but only *after* the teacher has recalled as much as possible. If the observer has scripted teacher language, counted on-task student behaviors, or gathered other data of such detail that a person's mind could not record and hold it, then reporting such data to the teacher is, of course, appropriate. Even in these cases, however, mentors can support the development of teacher recall by first asking what the teacher remembers about these areas.

For any behavior being learned in a workshop, there are corresponding metacognitive skills. Focusing on these hastens and sharpens the behavioral learning and at the same time develops further capacity in self-management. Generic to any behavior are self-monitoring questions related to clarifying intention: knowing when to use a behavior, how much of it, and in what form; knowing when to use another behavior instead; and how to know one's choice is sound. Each of these can serve as topics for self-reflective processing questions in seminars.

Summary

DuPont and Colgate-Palmolive were interested in developing workers' capacity to work more effectively together. External feedback about members' behaviors interfered with this goal. We are learning to ask members in educational groups two self-reflective questions, provide think time, and then give opportunities for sharing. "What were some of the decisions you made about when and how to participate? What were some effects of those decisions on you and on others?" In an atmosphere in which self-reflection is valued and these questions are repeated over time, the metacognitive skills of self-observation are enhanced, and team effectiveness increases dramatically (Garmston & Wellman, 1999).

If teaching is indeed a profession in which knowledge workers use information to make independent decisions in a wide variety of complex and unique settings, then self-directed learning is an essential attribute for educators. Given the importance of accurate self-reflection, I believe that a charge for us as professional developers is to eliminate systems and processes that foster dependency on external sources of correction and judgment while we increase each person's ability to act in accordance with aims they have set for themselves and increase each person's capacity to be self-reflective.

With such goals, the learner keeps on practicing even after the staff developer's services are past. Like the cat with perennially clean paws, we will have educators who persevere in self-reflection and self-improvement.

APPENDIX A

Five States of Mind

(The following is adapted from Cognitive Coaching: A Foundation for Renaissance Schools *by Arthur L. Costa and Robert J Garmston.)*

The internal resources for responding productively to life's decisions may be found in five mind states that may be thought of as catalysts, energy sources, or passions that fuel human behaviors. They are forces that human beings access as they strive for increasingly authentic, congruent, ethical behavior. They are the tools of disciplined choice making that guide the human actions needed to resolve the tensions listed above. They are the primary vehicles in the lifelong journey toward integration. These basic human forces drive, influence, motivate, and inspire our intellectual capacities, high performance, and productive human thought and action.

These five states of mind are directly related to processes of transformation (see chapter 1) and fuel the affective or cognitive processes of educational decision making for all the players in the system. Costa and Garmston (2002) categorize and define them as follows.

Efficacy

Humans strive for control, mastery of situations, and to have their efforts make a difference. To this end they are continual, lifelong learners. Efficacious people have an internal locus of control. They pose problems, search for problems to solve, engage in causal thinking, and produce new knowledge. They are optimistic and resourceful, self-actualizing and self-modifying. They are able to operationalize concepts and translate them into deliberate actions. They establish feedback spirals as a means of continual learning.

Flexibility

Because humans can perceive from multiple perspectives, they can adapt and expand their repertoire of response patterns. Flexible thinkers are empathic. They are open and comfortable with ambiguity. They create and seek novel approaches and have a well-developed sense of humor. They have the capacity to change their minds as they receive additional data. They envision a range of consequences, engage in multiple and simultaneous outcomes and activities, draw upon a repertoire of problem-solving strategies, and practice style flexibility, knowing when it is appropriate to be broad and global in their thinking and when a situation requires detailed precision.

Craftsmanship

Humans yearn to become clearer, more elegant, precise, congruent, and integrated. Craftspersons seek perfection, precision, mastery, and pride in their artistry. They seek refinement and specificity in language and communications. They generate and hold clear visions and goals. They strive for exactness of critical thought processes, making thorough and rational decisions about actions to be taken. They are constantly testing, honing, and revising strategies to reach goals.

Consciousness

Humans uniquely strive to monitor and reflect on their own thoughts and actions. Conscious thinkers metacogitate. They articulate and monitor their own values, intentions, thoughts, behaviors, and effect on others and the environment. They are aware of their own and others' progress toward goals. They generate, hold, and apply internal criteria for their decisions. They practice mental rehearsal and the editing of mental pictures in the process of seeking improved performance.

Interdependence

Humans need reciprocity, belonging, and connectedness and are inclined to become one with the larger system and community of which they are a part. Interdependent people have a sense of community—"we-ness" as much as "me-ness." They value consensus and are able to hold their own beliefs and actions in abeyance in order to lend their energies and resources to the achievement of group goals. They are altruistic, contributing to a common good, seeking collegiality, and drawing on the resources of others. They regard conflict as valuable, trusting their abilities to manage differences in productive ways. They continue to learn based upon feedback from others and from their conscious attending to the effects of their own actions on others. They seek engagement in holonomous part-whole relationships, knowing that all of us together are more effective than any one of us alone.

Sample Client Materials
List for Multiday
Workshop

Please provide the following:

<u>For each participant</u>:
1. Name tag with first name printed at about the equivalent of 72-point type:

Sample:

Bob

2. Six 3 x 5 index cards (colored or white, lined or unlined).
3. Book title:_____
4. Learning guide or handout:_____
Order from:_____
_____ .

<u>For each group of six participants</u>:
1. Two packs of 3 x 3 self-stick notes
2. One pack of 3 x 5 index cards
3. One baggie (with a small hole punched to release air) containing one set of water-based, chisel point markers with one each of the following colors: red, black, yellow, brown, blue, dark green (Mr. Sketch is a good brand), one roll of masking tape. Note: These specific colors are important.
4. One Easel flip chart with chart paper (27 x 34) (or equivalent in wall space) (Chartpak E60 & Oravisual A502 are both good brands of easels, Pierce Business Products also makes a good easel, "The Presenter," (800) 372-7577. Avoid flip charts without solid backs!)

Presenter's materials:
1. Four easel flip charts as described above (do not need to be in addition to charts for participants)
2. Easel pads (ideal but not essential are the pads with 1-inch grids)
3. Two presenter stools (prefer with high backs)
4. Two cordless lavaliere microphones
5. CD player (ideally connected into the house sound system)
6. Overhead projector and screen or liquid crystal display (LCD) projector and screen
7. Six to 12 blank transparencies

APPENDIX C

How Instruments Personalize and Motivate

A surefire way to support adults in accelerating their learning and helping them to retain large amounts of new material is to begin instruction with an exercise that activates and engages prior learning. For example, at the very start of a session, each participant could record on 3 x 5 cards ideas for making mathematics compelling. The 3 x 5 cards become a simple "instrument." Participants seated at tables share and organize their ideas by categories, then "shop" for the data at other tables to add to their information base. This example illustrates an exercise that engages the learner, not only with his or her own mental activity but also with other learners. Such experiences tend to generate both information and the motivation to learn more. They also accelerate the retention of new information because they aid the learner in bringing information to the working memory and categorizing it. In the classroom, such activities also level the playing field—students learn from one another—and bring misconceptions about a topic to the surface.

Like other presenters, I've been using learning instruments—surveys, self-assessments, journals—on an intuitive basis for some time. Here are some things I am learning.

Using Learning Instruments

Instrumentation is a technique to facilitate learning through gathering data in a systematic or structured way. Not surprisingly, the first issue for the presenter who uses instruments is purpose. Several classes of learning purposes exist to which instruments make a useful contribution. These include using instruments to assess a group prior to instruction; warm up a group at the beginning of a session; activate and engage prior learning; support concept attainment; aid introspective self-assessment; generate data for diagnosis of a group; take an inventory of knowledge, strategies, and skills; and summarize and integrate learning. Following are some factors and considerations that apply most broadly to all these purposes.

Setting the Stage

Learners get the most value from an instrument when they know why it is being used, how it relates to the larger learning agenda and their jobs, its limitations (e.g., "This is a brief instrument to sample your reactions at this point in time—it is to be used only to begin a conversation"), and how it will be processed or scored and interpreted. For most instruments, enough time needs to be provided for 95% of the participants to complete the written work. To wait for the slowest processor in the room to finish contributes to restless energy and a loss of momentum. Because learning instruments have the common purpose of bringing up data for consideration and conversation, it is rare that everyone would need to complete the written task to achieve this. Ensure respectful silence in the room so that those who would be distracted by talking have the benefit of a quiet atmosphere.

Selecting the Instruments

Many types of learning instruments can be devised by you and are relatively easy to administer. Here are a few that combine simplicity with potency.

Personal Inventories

Ask participants to list or mind-map personal attributes, such as strategies for redirecting classroom behavior, items they consider when reflecting about a lesson, ways they establish rapport, strengths they bring to a topic, or what they wish to learn in this seminar. These inventories activate prior knowledge and can serve as a source of data for conversations in trios or quartets in which the group looks for patterns, or as data for "cross inventories" with a partner in which each person adds to the repertoire of strategies or information. From Suzanne Bailey I learned the "data dump." Each person is asked, for instance, to list the topics considered when planning a lesson, then "dump" the data with a colleague, sharing and extending the knowledge each has on the topic.

Self-Report Inventories

These instruments are more structured and are usually researched and located by presenters rather than constructed. These tools produce information about leadership style, cognitive style, educational philosophy, and other personal attributes. They are frequently in the format of forced choice, rating scales, yes-no, or multiple choice. Scoring, interpretation, and conversations in which participants construct personal meaning are essential activities to follow the use of these instruments.

Conceptual Jump-Starts

These instruments are simple in format yet complex in construction because they require the presenter to locate the simplest possible question that will evoke the richest possible conceptual reflection. Conceptual jump-start instruments are often best administered to trios or quartets.

Here are some jump-start examples. "Compare inquiry with interrogation. What is the same? What is different? What are your conclusions?" "Compare supervision with evaluation. In what ways are they the same and different? What do you infer?"

Here is another type of example. Ask individuals to write a response to the following: "What is the most effective question you have ever been asked (i.e., that produced the most change in your life)? What was it about it or the circumstances in which it was asked that made it so effective?" Based on this data, ask trios to develop a list of criteria for life-changing questions.

Processing Findings

The instruments you use are only as good as the quality of data processing provided. Personal inventories should be followed with conversations with colleagues in which insights are articulated and bridges are built between the personal data and the learning task of the group. Usually a minimum of 10 minutes is needed for this. Longer periods for processing are required—anywhere from 20 to 45 minutes—for more complex instruments designed as self-report, feedback devices, or conceptual jump-starts. It's often useful to ask a group to search for patterns in its responses. What were the major things that were learned? What have we learned about ourselves as a learning community?

APPENDIX D

Room Arrangement

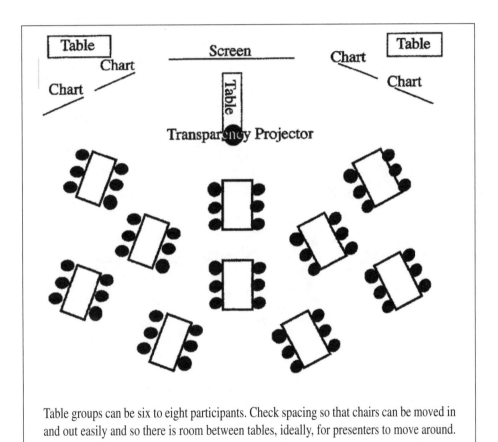

Table groups can be six to eight participants. Check spacing so that chairs can be moved in and out easily and so there is room between tables, ideally, for presenters to move around.

Courtesy of Laura Lipton, MiraVia, LLC.

Appendix E

Guidelines for Preparing a Written Report

Speakers often precede a presentation with a written report. Here are some tips for creating reports that effectively carry your message. These guidelines offer considerations for making reports to policy boards. For less formal reports, pick and choose what will be appropriate for the group you are working with. Harvey Hunt, senior education policy associate, Center for the Future of Teaching and Learning, assisted me with this information.

Five Essentials

1. Know your audience—their responsibilities, perspectives, relationship to your topic, and circumstances in which they will read your report.
2. Know your outcomes: Do you want to inform, influence, request funds? Do you want the group to tell others, vote, or take other action?
3. Know the image you wish to project.
4. Know if this report must be consistent in format or style with other reports.
5. Know the agenda time allotted to discuss your report.

What to Include

1. *Executive summary.* The executive summary is critical. Place it first. Some members of your audience will read only the executive summary. Make it succinct and complete.
2. *Table of contents.* Because you may edit your first draft several times, double- and triple-check that your table of contents is well-organized and still correctly numbered after all the changes you make. Also, strive to squeeze it all onto a single page.
3. *Agency description.* Include a brief statement about your agency—its mission, scope, and results. Use figures to document the effects your agency is having on children and parents in your country as well as in other countries. Make a transition statement to lead readers into the next section, a description of this project.

4. *Project description.* Describe this initiative or project in jargon-free language. What are its aims? Why is it important? Who will be or is being served? What is the specific nature of the service? How does it improve people's lives? How does it supplement but not replace existing services from other sources?

5. *Market analysis.* Research influences many decision makers. Provide figures from unimpeachable sources on population characteristics, projections, related government regulations, and other constraining or enabling factors. You may describe how similar services or programs have made a difference in the past.

6. *Operations plan.* Provide details of your operation, but limit the detail to what is necessary to clearly describe how you propose to execute your plan. Often a budget shown in broad categories is sufficient—staffing, facilities, materials, and other requirements. In your executive summary you gave vague assurances of what you would be doing. If the group needs to know and approve the plan and the budget, you will need to report these in more detail.

7. *Appendixes.* Put into the appendixes all those necessary extra bits, such as managers' résumés, promotional materials, photos, and independent assessments. Emphasis is on the word *necessary*; clutter in a bulging set of appendixes is as bad as verbosity elsewhere in the plan.

Writing the Report

Write the summary first. The summary is a compact version of the big plan. Remind yourself that your audience may read only the executive summary and then ask you questions about the program.

Of the many parts of a written plan, by far and away the most important is the executive summary. The summary must be highly readable and convey passion and purpose. Stick to the hard facts and limit yourself, however difficult this may be, to the length of a concise résumé—no more than a couple of pages. Avoid exaggerated optimism.

Clearly state what is being requested of the group reading the report. Select a format for the report and be internally consistent.

Your readers are often busy people. Use two criteria to format your report—functionality and attractiveness. Use tables, charts, bullets, and other graphics to make information easy to understand. Be consistent in page layout and font size and type. Choose a format, quantities of artwork, and forms that will convey the image you wish to present.

Start writing far in advance of the deadline. Give yourself time for second, third, and even fourth drafts. The more tightly honed your report, the greater its effectiveness. Starting early also allows you space to deal with the unexpected and still make your deadline in good time.

Keep your report as short as possible, stick to essential facts and keep the report focused.

Proofread the executive summary carefully. Any typos in the executive summary will detract from credibility for this report and you. Of course, proofread the entire report, but especially the executive summary.

References

Allen, S., & Wollman, J. (1987). *How to be funny: Discovering the comic you.* New York: McGraw-Hill.

Annenberg/CPB Math and Science Project (2004). *Private Universe: What Are Your Ideas?* Available online at http:www.learner.org/teacherslab/pup/about.htm.

Bailey S., & Garmston, R. (1988). Paddling together: A co-presenting primer. *Training and Development Journal, 42(1),* 52–57.

Bandura, A. (2001). Social cognitive theory: An agentic perspective. *Annual Review of Psychology, 52(1),* 2–26.

Bloom, B., Englehart, M., Furst, E., Hill, W., & Krathwohl, D. (1956). *Taxonomy of educational objectives: The classification of educational goals.* Handbook 1: Cognitive domain. New York: Longmans, Green.

Breitman, P. (2000). *How to say no without feeling guilty: And say yes to more time, and what matters most to you.* New York: Broadway Books.

Brekelmans, M., Wubbles, T., & Creton, H. (1990). A study of student perceptions of physics teacher behavior. *Journal of Research in Science Teaching, 27(4),* 335–350.

Bridges, W. (1980). *Transitions: Making sense of life's changes.* New York: Addison-Wesley.

Bridges, W. (1991). *Managing transitions: Making the most of change.* New York: Addison-Wesley.

Bryk, M., & Schneider, B. (2000). *Trust in schools: A core resource for improvement.* New York: Sage Foundation.

Buckley, M. (2002). *Traceable chart art for flip charts and overhead transparencies.* Sherman, CT: MiraVia.

Caine, R. N., & Caine, G. (1994). *Making connections: Teaching and the human brain.* Boston: Pearson Learning.

Campbell, N., Reece, J., & Lawrence, G. M. (1999). *Biology* (5th ed.). Menlo Park, CA: Benjamin/Cummings.

Costa, A. (Ed.). (1991a). The search for intelligent life. In *Developing Minds: A Resource Book for Teaching Thinking,* (Vol. 1). Alexandria, VA: Association for Supervision and Curriculum Development.

Costa, A. (1991B). *Some thoughts on transfer*. Unpublished paper.

Costa, A., & Garmston, R. (2000). Peer assistance and review: Potentials and pitfalls. *The PAR Reader*. Santa Cruz, CA: University of California New Teacher Center.

Costa, A., & Garmston, R. (2002). *Cognitive Coaching: A foundation for renaissance schools*. (2nd ed.). Norwood, MA: Christopher-Gordon.

Cross, E., & Franz, E. A. (2003). Gestures help words become memorable. *Science News, 163*(16), 255.

Crum, T. (1987). *The magic of conflict: Turning a life of work into a work of art*. New York: Simon & Schuster.

Crum, T. (1997). *Journey to center: Lessons in unifying body, mind and spirit*. New York: Fireside.

Decialdini, R. (1984). *The new psychology of modern persuasion*. New York: Simon & Schuster.

Dilts, R. B. (1994). *Effective presentation skills*. Capitola, CA: Meta.

Dolcemascolo, M. (2003). *Presentation "notes."* Highland Park, CO: Center for Cognitive Coaching.

Dolcemascolo, M. (2004). Private correspondence with the author and co-presentation of these principles at a 4-day workshop in Buffalo, New York.

Doyle, M., & Straus, D. (1993). *How to make meetings work: The new interaction method*. New York: Jove.

Drakulic, S. (1993). *How we survived communism and even laughed*. New York: Norton.

Eitington, J. (1984). *The winning trainer*. Houston, TX: Gulf.

Enderlin-Lampe, S. (2002). Empowerment: Teacher perceptions, aspirations and efficacy. *Journal of Instructional Psychology, 29*(2), 139–147.

Ewing, I. (1994). *The best presentation skills*. Singapore, Malaysia: Ewing Communications.

Feagin, J., & Sikes, M. (1994). *Living with racism: The Black middle class experience*. Boston: Beacon Press.

Featherstone, E. (1994). *Skin deep: Women writing on color, culture and identity*. Berkeley, CA: Ten Speed Press.

Friend, T. (2002). What's so funny?: A Scientific attempt to discover why we laugh. *The New Yorker*, November 11, 83.

Fullan, M. (1993). *Change forces: Probing the depths of educational reform*. Bristol, PA: Falmer Press.

Fullan, M. (2001). *Leading in a culture of change*. San Francisco: Jossey-Bass.

Garmston, R. (in press). Anticipating change: designing a transition meeting. *Journal of Staff Development*.

Garmston, R., & Wellman, B. (1992). *How to make presentations that teach and transform*. Alexandria, VA: Association for Supervision and Curriculum Development.

Garmston, R., & Wellman, B. (1999). *The adaptive school: A sourcebook for developing collaborative groups*. Norwood, MA: Christopher-Gordon.

Goldin-Meadow, S. (2002). *Hearing gestures: How our hands help us think.* Unpublished manuscript.

Goldin-Meadow, S., Kim, S., & Singer, M. (1999). What the teacher's hands tell the student's mind about math. *Journal of Educational Psychology, 91*(4), 720–730.

Goldin-Meadow, S., Wein, D., & Chang, C. (1992). Assessing knowledge through gesture: Using children's hands to read their minds. *Cognition and Instruction, 9*(3), 201–219.

Griffith, A. (2000, Spring).Overcoming cultural and language barriers in facilitation and training. *Facilitation News,* 5(2).

Grinder, M. (1993). *Envoy: Your personal guide to classroom management* (2nd ed.). Battle Ground, WA: Grinder & Associates.

Grinder, M. (1997). *The science of nonverbal communication.* Battle Ground, MA: Grinder & Associates.

Grinder, M. (2000). *Influencing the dynamics for a healthy classroom: Beyond Envoy.* Battle Ground, WA: Grinder & Associates.

Guzzetti, B., Snyder, T., & Glass, G. (2003). Promoting conceptual change in science: A comparative meta-analysis of instructional interventions from reading and science. *Reading Research Quarterly, 28*(2), 117–155.

Humes, J. (2002). *Speak like Churchill, stand like Lincoln: 21 powerful secrets of history's greatest speakers.* Roseville, CA: Prima.

Jensen, E. (1998). *Teaching with the brain in mind* (Vol. 1). Alexandria, VA: Association for Supervision and Curriculum Development.

Jensen, E. (2000a). *Brain based learning.* San Diego, CA: Brain Store.

Jensen, E. (2000b). *Music with the brain in mind.* San Diego, CA: Brain Store.

Johnson, D., & Johnson, R. (1994). Constructive conflict in the schools. *Journal of Social Issues, 50*(1), 117–137.

Joyce, B., & Showers, B. (1988). *Student achievement through staff development.* New York: Longman.

Kelly, S. D., & Barr, D. J. (1999). Offering a hand to pragmatic understanding: The role of speech and gesture in comprehension and memory. *Journal of Memory and Language, 40,* 577–592.

Kofman, F., & Senge, P. (1993, Autumn). Communities of commitment: The heart of learning organizations. O*rganizational Dynamics,* 5–23.

Leonard, G. (1991). *Mastery: The key to success and long-term fulfillment.* New York: Dutton.

Lipshitz, R., Friedman, V., & Omer, H. (1989*).* Overcoming resistance to training: A non-confrontive approach*. Training and Development Journal, 43*(12), 46–50.

Lipton, L., & Wellman, B. (2003). *Pathways to understanding: Patterns and practices in the learning focused classroom* (3rd ed.). Sherman, CT: MiraVia.

Louis, K. S., Marks, H. M., & Kruse, S. (1996). Teacher's professional community in restructuring schools. *American Educational Journal, 33*(4), 757–798.

Marzano, R. (2003). *What works in schools: Translating research into action.* Alexandria, VA: Association for Supervision and Curriculum Development.

Marzano, R., Pickering, D., & Pollack, J. (2001). *Classroom instruction that works: Research based strategies for increasing student achievement.* Alexandria, VA: Association for Supervision and Curriculum Development.

Massell, D. (2000, September). The district role in building capacity. *Consortium for Policy Research in Education, Graduate School of Education Pennsylvania State University, 32,* 1–8.

McNeill, D. (1992). *Hand and mind: What gestures reveal about thought.* Chicago: University Press.

Miller, P. (1981). *What research says to the teacher.* Washington DC: National Education Association.

Morgan, N. (2003). *Working the room: How to move people to action through audience-centered speaking.* Cambridge, MA: Harvard Business School Press.

Nickerson, S. (1995). Breaking the language barrier. *Training and Development Journal, 49*(2), 45–48.

Nisbett, R. (2003). *The geography of thought: How Asians and Westerners think differently and why.* New York: Simon & Schuster.

Noonan, P. (1990). *What I saw at the revolution: A political life in the Reagan era.* New York: Random House.

Nuthall, G. (1999). The way students learn: Acquiring knowledge from an integrated social studies unit. *Elementary School Journal, 99*(4), 303–341.

O'Hanlon, W. H. (1987). *Taproots: Underlying principles of Milton Erickson's therapy and hypnosis.* New York: Norton.

Perkins, D. (1995). *Outsmarting I.Q.: The emerging science of learnable intelligence.* New York: Simon & Schuster.

Perkins, D., & Salomon, G. (1991). In A. Costa (Ed.), *Developing minds: A resource book for teaching thinking.* Alexandria, VA: Association for Supervision and Curriculum Development.

Pritchard, R. J., & Marshall, J. (2002). *Student writing achievement and attitudes toward school in healthy and unhealthy districts.* Athens, GA: Department of Curriculum and Instruction, University of West Georgia.

Rosenholtz, S. J. (1989). *Teachers' workplace: The social organization of schools.* New York: Longman.

Roth, W. M. (2001a). From Activity to Gestures and Scientific Language. *The Journal of Research in Science Teaching, 38*(1), 103–136.

Roth, W. M. (2001b). Gestures: Their role in teaching and learning. *Review of Educational Research, 71*(3), 365–392.

Rowe, M. B. (1986). Wait time: Slowing down may be a way of speeding up! *Journal of Teacher Education, 37,* 43–50.

Sanford, C. (1995). *Myths of organizational effectiveness at work.* Battle Ground, WA: Springhill.

Saphier, J., & Gower, R. (1987). *The skillful teacher: Building your teaching skills.* Carlisle, MA: Research for Better Teaching.

Scheps, M. H., & Saldler, P. M. (Prod.). (1992). *Project Star: A Private Universe* [Video]. Cambridge, MA: Harvard Smithsonian Center for Astro Physics.

Schlosser, E. (2002). *Fast food nation: The dark side of the all-American meal.* New York: Houghton Mifflin.

Senge, P. M. (1990). *The fifth discipline.* New York: Doubleday.

Sergiovanni, T. (1992). *Moral leadership.* San Francisco: Jossey-Bass.

Sinetar, M. (1991). *Developing a 21st century mind.* New York: Villard Books.

Smith, M. (1975). *When I say no I feel guilty.* New York: Dial Press.

Sousa, D. A. (2003). *The leadership brain: How to lead today's schools.* Thousand Oaks, CA: Corwin Press.

Sprinthall, N., & Thies-Sprinthall, L. (1983). The teacher as an adult learner: A cognitive development view. In G. Griffin (Ed.), *Staff development* (82nd Yearbook of the National Society for the Study of Education, Part 2). Chicago: University of Chicago Press.

Swarns, R. (2004). African American becomes a term for debate. New York: *The New York Times,* August 29, pp. 1, 14.

True, H. (1995). *The power of humor: Speaking secrets of the masters.* Harrisburg, PA: Executive Books.

Turk, C. (2001). *Effective Speaking: Communicating in speech.* New York: Spon Press.

Urech, E. (2002). *Speaking globally: Effective presentations across international borders.* Rollinsford, NH: Boon Network International.

Weintraub, D. (2004). *A conversation with the governor: "There's still a lot to learn."* Sacramento Bee, May 30, p. E3.

Weisman, R. (1995). *Intercultural communication theory.* Thousand Oaks, CA: Sage.

Wheatley, M. J. (1992). *Leadership and the new science.* San Francisco: Berrett-Koehler.

Whitmore, J. (1994). *Coaching for performance: A practical guide for growing your own skills.* London: Brealey.

Wohlmuth, E. (1983). *The overnight guide to public speaking.* Philadelphia: Running Press.

Wright, P., Horn, S., & Sanders, W. (1997). Teacher and classroom context effects on student achievement: Implications for teacher evaluation. *Journal of Personnel Evaluation in Education, 11,* 57–67.

Zander, R. S., & Zander, B. (2000). *The art of possibility: Transforming professional and personal life.* Cambridge, MA: Harvard Business School Press.

Robert J. Garmston, Ed.D

Bob Garmston is professor emeritus, School of Education, at California State University, Sacramento, and director of Facilitation Associates, an educational consulting firm specializing in leadership, learning, and organizational development. With Dr. Art Costa, he is co-developer of Cognitive Coachingsм. He is also co-developer and co-director of the Center For Adaptive Schools with Bruce Wellman, an initiative developing collaborative groups within schools intent on strengthening student achievement.

Bob is an award-winning author of books and articles, authoring more than 100 publications on educational leadership, learning, coaching, and staff development. Formerly a principal in an international school in Saudi Arabia, he has been a teacher, principal, acting superintendent, and curriculum director in the United States. Since the mid-1990s he has been a frequent presenter at international school conferences in many regions of the world. He has held leadership posts in professional organizations, including the California and international Association for Supervision and Curriculum Development. (ASCD) He lives in Sacramento, California, near his five children and four (bright and cute) grandchildren. He may be contacted at Fabob@aol.com.

Michael Buckley

Michael Buckley has served as both illustrator and author in this book. His illustrations appear throughout the book and his writing appears in chapter 6. Michael has worked in New England as an illustrator, a graphic designer, and a fine artist since 1980. His graphic work has appeared in numerous publications, on labels and logos, and on posters and T-shirts. His drawings and paintings are exhibited and collected locally, nationally, and internationally. He currently resides near New York City, where he teaches, paints, draws, presents workshops, and occasionally collaborates on special projects such as this one. He may be contacted at MicBuck@aol.com.

Kendall Zoller

Kendall Zoller is an independent consultant specializing in facilitation and presentation training for educators. He is past director of the Center for Mathematics and Science Education at California State University, Sacramento. He is project director for multiple grant projects, including the National Science Foundation and the California Science Project. He is a doctoral candidate in the Joint Doctoral Program for Educational Leadership. Kendall's current research examines the TIMSS-R study by looking at teachers' nonverbal patterns from eight participating countries.

Kendall provides trainings on facilitation and presentation skills as well as science and leadership. He is also a past fellow and current mentor to the National Academy for Science and Mathematics Education Leadership, where he provides trainings to support new fellows advancing in science and mathematics leadership across the country. With Bob Garmston he is currently designing a training program for instructors at police academies in California. He can be reached at kzoller@csus.edu.

Index